FOURTH EDITION

EARNED VALUE

Project Management

QUENTIN W. FLEMING
and JOEL M. KOPPELMAN

Project Management Institute®
Newtown Square, PA

Earned Value Project Management—Fourth Edition
ISBN: 978-1-935589-08-2

Library of Congress Cataloging-in-Publication Data

Fleming, Quentin W.
  Earned value project management / Quentin W. Fleming and Joel M. Koppelman. -- 4th ed.
     p. cm.
  Includes index.
  ISBN 978-1-935589-08-2 (alk. paper)
  1. Cost control. 2. Program budgeting. 3. Production control. 4. Project management.
  I. Koppelman, Joel M. II. Title.
  HD47.3.F59 2010
  658.15--dc22

                              2010032160

Published by: Project Management Institute, Inc.
                14 Campus Boulevard
                Newtown Square, Pennsylvania 19073-3299 USA.
                Phone: +610-356-4600
                Fax: +610-356-4647
                E-mail: customercare@pmi.org
                Internet: www.PMI.org

PMI Publications welcomes corrections and comments on its books. Please feel free to send comments on typographical, formatting, or other errors. Simply make a copy of the relevant page of the book,
mark the error, and send it to: Book Editor, PMI Publications, 14 Campus Boulevard, Newtown Square,
PA 19073-3299 USA.

To inquire about discounts for resale or educational purposes, please contact the PMI Book Service
Center.

                PMI Book Service Center
                P.O. Box 932683, Atlanta, GA 31193-2683 USA
                Phone: 1-866-276-4764 (within the U.S. or Canada) or +1-770-280-4129 (globally)
                Fax: +1-770-280-4113
                E-mail: info@bookorders.pmi.org

The paper used in this book complies with the Permanent Paper Standard issued by the National
Information Standards Organization (Z39.48—1984).

10   9   8   7   6   5   4   3   2

CONTENTS

LIST OF FIGURES

INTRODUCTION

AS WE APPROACH THE HALF-CENTURY POINT of modern earned value management (EVM) we find it interesting to note that there are really two perceptions of the concept. Both are valid. But one is better suited to the management of major projects, and the other appropriate for use on all projects. We cover both in this book, but do have a bias in favor of simple, broad-based EVM for use on all projects.

Ask anyone who has ever worked with earned value as a part of the United States Government to describe the concept and they are apt to say: "Earned value is any management system compliant with ANSI-EIA Standard 748."[1] True. This is a valid definition. Any management control system which satisfies the 32 criteria as specified in the ANSI-EIA Standard 748 (ANSI-EIA 748) will represent a full and robust earned value system. This approach is appropriate for all highly complex projects of significant size and duration. But with all due respect, the 32 criteria are likely to be too prescriptive for the typical project. Thus, for the most part, this fully compliant approach has been limited to major projects. The Appendix to this book describes the 32 ANSI-EIA 748 criteria one by one, together with our interpretation of what is required to fully comply with all criteria.

The second perception of earned value is employing the concept based on implementing a few fundamental principles, using project management best practices. This approach can employ the earned value technique to all projects, of any size and duration, in any industry. Some organizations have elected to call this second approach "Earned Value-Lite."

Most important: This second approach is consistent with the description of earned value coverage contained in the Project Management Institute's *A Guide to the Project Management Body of Knowledge (PMBOK® Guide)* — Fourth Edition.[2] This is the recommended approach of the authors. And should any organization feel the need to expand the concept to include all the requirements of a full ANSI-EIA 748 earned value system compliance, they can do so easily.

As with our earlier editions, we intend to continue to build on the fine earned value work done by the United States Government, particularly the Department of Defense (DoD). The DoD has taken this industrial engineering concept and made it into a respected management science. Their fine work has been adopted by management scholars around the world.

The one area where we want to take a strong new position is in the notion that earned value performance data can be used "exclusively" to forecast and control the completion date of a project, commonly called project time management. This concept goes by several names, and probably most frequently by the title "Earned Schedule."

Our position is that EVM schedule variances are an important first indicator that the project is falling behind its baseline schedule plan. But for various reasons to be covered in this update, EVM schedule variances cannot be used by themselves to forecast the completion date of a project. To forecast the completion date of a project, EVM schedule data must be used in conjunction with other scheduling techniques— particularly critical path scheduling— to provide a reliable way to manage the completion of a project. Earned value scheduling data by itself has a questionable time predictive capability.

QUENTIN W. FLEMING
Tustin, California 92780

JOEL M. KOPPELMAN
Bala Cynwyd, Pennsylvania 19004

---

1 American National Standards Institute/Electronic Institute Alliance. (1998, May 19) ANSI/EIA-748-1998, Earned Value Management Systems. Arlington, VA.
2 ANSI/PMI 99-001-2008.

1

IF EARNED VALUE IS SO HOT . . .

WHY ISN'T IT USED ON ALL PROJECTS?

A FEW YEARS BACK, the authors submitted an article on earned value to the *Harvard Business Review* (*HBR*) for possible publication. To their delight, the journal reacted favorably and the article was published a few weeks later.[3] But before accepting the article for publication the *HBR* editors put the authors through a due diligence process never before or since experienced by them. The screening began with a phone call from the senior editor, whose opening question set the tone for their review. His question: *"If earned value is so hot . . . why isn't it used on all projects?"* A valid question, and right to the point.

This simple request started a discussion between the authors. Why is it that earned value is not employed on all projects? It certainly should be, but it clearly is not. Their conclusions centered on three likely reasons for this condition. We should start our discussion of earned value management by understanding the resistance to the concept over the years.

Reason #1: Because too often . . . earned value gurus speak in a foreign tongue.
When the earned value concept was first introduced in the American factories by Frederick W. Taylor and his industrial engineers, they used clear, unambiguous terms to describe the three dimensions of the new concept. They called their baseline plan, simply, the "planned standards." The resulting measured performance was called the "earned standards." And the actual costs to compare against the earned standards were called the "actual hours." What could be easier to understand? No special training or translation was required, and that was a century ago.

Then the concept lay dormant until the early 1960s, when the industrial engineers chose to start the measurement of performance on the Minuteman missile

---

3   Quentin W. Fleming and Joel M. Koppelman, (2003, September). What's your project's real price tag? *Harvard Business Review*, pages 20 to 22

development project. Only this time the approach got a little complicated with the terminology being introduced. The baseline plan was then referred to as the "Planned Value of Work Scheduled," or "PVWS" for short. The measured earnings were called the "Planned Value of Work Accomplished," or "PVWA." And the actual costs of accomplishing the work were called "Actual Costs of Work Performed," or "ACWP." In status meetings the presenters would often use the terms PVWS, PVWA, and ACWP, and the audience would gently doze off and think about other more pressing issues.

By 1967, when the Department of Defense (DoD) issued their initial policy on earned value management, the three dimensions of earned value were standardized with a new set of acronyms. The plan was now referred to as the "Budgeted Costs of Work Scheduled," or "BCWS" for short. The earned value was now called the "Budgeted Costs of Work Performed," or "BCWP." Actual costs were called the "Actual Costs of Work Performed," or "ACWP." In status review meetings the presenters would often go to another shortened version and talk about their "S" and "P" and "A," and again the audience would drift off to dreamland.

But today there is hope for a common simple language which everyone can quickly grasp. Special orientation should not be required for anyone to understand the status of any project employing earned value. Since 1996, the Project Management Institute (PMI) has issued a landmark document which has become in essence the de facto standard for project management in the world today. It is called *A Guide to the Project Management Body of Knowledge*, or the *PMBOK® Guide*, as it is more commonly known.[4] Earned value management has an important place in this evolving document. Starting with the second edition of the *PMBOK® Guide*, released in 2000, the three dimensions of the concept have been called simply: the "Planned Value," the "Earned Value," and the "Actual Costs." We have thus come full circle and essentially match the original terminology used by Frederick W. Taylor a century ago.

However, there are still the holdouts. Some love those incomprehensible terms like BCWS, BCWP, and ACWP. Fortunately, with the passage of time, their numbers are quickly decreasing.

Reason #2: Because originally the earned value technique was made overly prescriptive for broad-based use on all projects.

A little history and an outline of the evolution of the concept is in order. Modern earned value management was introduced by the United States Air Force on the Minuteman missile project in the early 1960s. Fact: the Minuteman was not your typical project. Rather, it was a mega-dollar, multiple-year, state-of-the-art, highly

---

4   Project Management Institute. (2008). *A Guide to the Project Management Body of Knowledge*(*PMBOK® Guide*) — Fourth Edition. (ANSI/PMI 99-2008). Newtown Square, PA.

complex endeavor. These giant projects are not in the majority.

The Air Force, with the objective of preserving the concept as a continuing project management technique, set out to define the requirements for their new management system. They conceived what was then called the Cost/Schedule Control Systems Criteria, or C/SCSC.[5] The C/SCSC was essentially a project management system consisting of 35 precise criteria which had to be met by anyone using the concept. Later DoD implementation documents contained over a hundred and fifty checklist questions which required compliance by projects. This documentation resulted in a heavy requirement for the typical project manager to satisfy. While the United States and other governments mandated C/SCSC on major projects, the broad-based acceptance on non-government work was minimal. It wasn't that project managers deliberately resisted the concept. Rather, the C/SCSC and related implementation questions were simply too much for employment on most projects.

Later, through a joint effort between the DoD and private industry, the C/SCSC was rewritten and replaced by ANSI-EIA Standard 748 (ANSI-EIA 748) in 1996. However, there were still 32 precise criteria/guidelines to satisfy. The ANSI-EIA 748 is likely perfect for a Minuteman-type project, with all its complexities But it is likely far too prescriptive for most typical projects, in the opinion of the authors.

Then in 1996 PMI issued their *PMBOK® Guide.* In the four editions of this document earned value as a project management technique has taken an important place as a project management good practice. Earned value, as described in the *PMBOK® Guide,* is based on a few fundamental requirements, like, you must define the project, plan and schedule the project, add resources, etc. Thus, the *PMBOK® Guide* represents the minimal earned value standard applicable to any project. And the ANSI-EIA 748 is still the appropriate requirement for larger, more complex projects. The two are compatible.

Reason #3: Because, frankly, sometimes management doesn't really want to know the full truth about what their projects might cost and how long they will take to finish.

Important point: The authors are not suggesting that project managers and their executive managements are deceitful and would intentionally withhold the full truth. That is not our position. However, the one basic characteristic common to all project managers is "optimism." They think they can complete their projects as planned . . . no matter how challenging, no matter what the odds.

Thus, when a project management technique like earned value comes along, which states that, at the 20% point of completion, the actual results can be fore-

---

5   The C/SCSC was in use from 1967 until superseded by ANSI-Standard 748 in 1996.

casted within a plus or minus confidence band, many project managers become alarmed at the prospect. Their concern: An adverse forecast could become a "self-fulfilling prophecy." They are repelled by the forecasts, and openly resist using the technique.

In fact, the project actual results at 20% represent nothing more than an "early warning" signal, a report card, that tells the project and executive management what will happen if they continue on their present performance course. Ignoring the facts does not make bad news get better. Earned value simply allows the project managers to take advantage of their actual results, and change their course if they do not like the projected final results. Corrective actions, taken early, can change to final result.

IN SUMMARY

The modern earned value concept was re-introduced by the United States Air Force in the 1960s, about the same timeframe when the founders of PMI were formulating plans for creating this new professional society to advance the art and science of project management. Since that time, PMI has documented, released, and revised their *PMBOK® Guide* for the project community and has set the standard for excellence. Imbedded within this important document is a sort of system description for fundamental earned value management which can be applied to projects of any size or complexity, in any industry.

One can only wonder what impact there might have been on the broader acceptance of earned value and the other project management techniques if the community had only had the benefit of the *PMBOK® Guide* to set the minimum standards for project excellence.

Would the authors have received that phone call from the editor of the *HBR* which started, *"If earned value is so hot . . . why isn't it used on all projects?"*

2

EARNED VALUE PROJECT MANAGEMENT: AN INTRODUCTION

EARNED VALUE PROJECT MANAGEMENT is a valuable tool to be used in the management of projects. In its most basic form, earned value represents nothing more than following fundamental project management, managing a project with a resource-loaded schedule. Here, the authors will introduce the concept in a storybook form. This is not a true story . . . but it could be.

Once upon a time there was a young man who wanted to be a project manager. Don't ask us why.

In school, the young man took the most challenging of the technical subjects, and he also liked to manage things to a successful conclusion. He graduated with a master's degree in a technical discipline and immediately went to work for a small but fast growing hi-tech company. This company was a leader in developing new products for their niche of the market. They had just gone public, and their Initial Public Offering of the stock was a huge financial success. On day one, he knew he had joined the right company. All he wanted was his chance at bat. He wanted to manage his own project.

But then weeks went by. Months went by. Months! And he had yet to receive an assignment of any consequence. He was becoming discouraged. He considered updating his resume to start looking around again. If his present employer did not recognize his talents, perhaps others would. He did not have time to waste. This young man was in a hurry.

Then one day, as he was walking down the hall, the Chief Executive came up to him. She inquired as to how he was getting along. Then she asked: *How would you like an important assignment to manage a new company development project for us?* The young man could hardly get out his enthusiastic acceptance. Then the CEO said: *OK, if you're interested, call my secretary and get on my calendar for tomorrow.* As she was walking away, she commented to him: *This is an extremely important project for our company, and I think you could manage it nicely; see you then.*

5

The young man got little sleep that night. Imagine, his chance to actually manage a project, to be a project manager. He was in the Chief Executive's office a full 30 minutes before she arrived. When they met, she started out by saying, *This is one of the most important potential new products we have in the pipeline, but it needs some innovative thinking, and that's why I think you would be the right person to take this on. I need fresh ideas incorporated into this product.*

She outlined her thoughts for the new product, and it was exactly the type of work he had prepared himself to do. She asked him to pull together a half dozen cross-functional people from within the company and to prepare a project management plan for her review and approval. *If you have any problem getting people released, use my name to break them loose,* she said. *I don't want stonewalling by anyone; this new product is important to our future growth.*

Then she closed the meeting by saying: *Time to market is most critical on this project; I know our competition is working on similar products, and I want to be first into the marketplace.* The young man got the message, and it was better than he had ever hoped. On his way out, she also mentioned another issue: *I would also like you to use a technique I have heard about but can't seem to get started here . . . earned value management. Have you ever heard of it? Yes of course. We studied earned value in college and I think it would work well on this project,* was his reply. *Good. I look forward to seeing your project plan,* was her closing remark.

The young man circulated within the company and got the commitment of the right people to do the project planning job. This was a young startup company, so the impenetrable "stone walls" so pervasive in older more established companies had not yet set in. All he had to do was mention that the big-boss was behind this assignment and he got his people. He didn't even have to describe the details of the assignment; they all knew it had a high priority.

Planning for Earned Value Project Management

The newly formed team met at the project manager's apartment to prevent interruptions and phone calls. *It shouldn't take us very long to put a plan down on paper,* was his opening remark. They spent the next few hours conceptualizing and defining the project. The project manager, after he captured their ideas, would prepare the final plan for review and approval of the team, then submittal to the CEO. The project manager wanted everyone to buy into the project plan. They all knew exactly what was required in order to employ earned value performance measurement. It was simply classic project management, "Project Management 101."

First, they had to define what constituted the project, 100 percent of their assumed project scope. For this they created a Work Breakdown Structure (WBS). Next they decomposed the project scope into measurable tasks, each with an estimated value, and then assigned responsibility for the actual performance of each task to a functional manager within the company. For this they developed a WBS Dictionary to record their thoughts. They decided that their project needed 10 units to develop and test, and that each unit would require about the same level of resources to accomplish.

Next, they would take the work conceptualized from the WBS diagram and dictionary, and then prepare a detailed plan and schedule for all of the major critical tasks. After a few iterations they had their Project Master Schedule (PMS), fully supported by critical path methodology. They did a forward and backward schedule pass to give them assurances that their schedule was in fact achievable. The project would take 18 months to perform from start to completion.

Lastly, they estimated the resources which were required to produce these 10 units and constituted the total project. Each article would cost them $150,000 to produce; thus, the total project would require $1.5 million to complete. They charted their requirements as illustrated in Figure 2.1, which they termed their Project Management Plan. This display would contain the three critical components of any earned value baseline plan: a WBS, a Project Master Schedule, and a Performance Display graph. Each element was supported by detailed breakouts. This process is sometimes called detailed "bottom-up planning." The team had done their job, and it was now time for the project manager to take their plan to the CEO for her approval.

Management's Approval

The project manager made a copy of their Project Management Plan and gave it to the CEO's secretary so she could review it prior to their approval meeting. When he was at last able to meet with the CEO, it was obvious that she had thoroughly read the entire plan. Every page was marked up, tabbed, and color-coded. He hoped she liked what she had read.

Figure 2.1 *Project Management Plan*

The CEO opened the meeting on a positive note: *I want you to know, this is the finest project management plan I have seen as head of this company. I plan to use it as a model for approval of all our future projects.* The project manager was off to a good start. She liked it!

Then the CEO went on: *However, you must not have heard parts of my requirements. Time to market is most critical on this project, and you have developed a casual, business as usual schedule of 18 months . . . .That is completely unacceptable. I need this project completed in not more that 12 months. Can you handle that?* The young man took a deep breath and replied: *Of course we can.* Realistically, he had no clue as to how he would accomplish this, but the message from on high was becoming pretty clear.

Also, you have taken this simple job and gold-plated it at an estimated cost of $1.5 million . . . . That also is unacceptable! The boss was relentless: *The very most I could allocate for this project would be $1.0 million. We are not a big company; I have other commitments. Can you handle that?* The young project manager was beginning to understand why she had become a CEO at such an early age. She was one tough person to deal with. Without hesitation, the young man accepted the budget dictate.

The CEO realized that she had come down pretty hard on the young man, so she wanted to provide some consoling words before he left: *Again, I want to emphasize that this is the best project plan I have ever seen in this company, and it will be our role model for others to follow.* Her words were some comfort, although the project manager was now starting to worry about what he would say to the other members of his team. Their buy-in was important to him.

As he was about to leave the office, the chief executive said: *I am very pleased that you are going to employ earned value measurement on this project. I would like to review your performance each quarter, at say every three months into your 12-month, one million dollar project!* The thought racing through the young man's mind was, *She never lets up. What do I now tell the other team members?*

WELCOME TO THE WORLD OF PROJECT MANAGEMENT

Now, let us stand back from this discussion and try to understand what has taken place here. A project team got together and developed a thorough, comprehensive project plan, with considerable supporting data and schedule metrics so that they could measure their earned value performance from start to completion. In particular, they had scoped 100 percent of the total assumed project before they would begin to perform, and they created a detailed plan which allowed for the measurement of project performance.

Their supporting bottom-up detail indicated that they needed a full 18 months to complete the project, but the big boss directed them to do it in 12 months. They estimated the costs to do the project at $1.5 million, and the big boss quickly cut it down to $1.0 million. What do we call this environment that the young project manager had just experienced for the first time in his professional career? We call it: *REAL LIFE PROJECT MANAGEMENT!*

Rarely do we ever get the total time we feel we need to reasonably do the job. Projects are always in competition with other projects to do something first. And the authorized budgets are rarely what we estimate we need to complete any job. We are frequently given what is commonly termed a "management challenge," and we go out and do our best. It matters not if these management challenges are arbitrary, unreasonable, unattainable, unrealistic, or just plain stupid. We as project managers must find a way to get it done. Welcome to the wonderful world of project management!

THE FIRST QUARTERLY PROJECT STATUS REVIEW

Three months went by quickly. It was time for the team to present its performance results to the chief executive and her management committee. This would be an awesome new experience for the young project team, but the thing that was working in their favor was the fact that they were performing against a detailed plan, and they knew exactly what they had to do from the go-ahead to completion.

A brief summary indicated the following results: Three of the ten units had been scheduled for completion at the three-month point, but only two were accomplished; thus, they were slightly behind their planned schedule. They had forecasted expenditures of $300,000 and had committed $300,000, so they were right on with their funding profile. Any optimistic person could easily paint a positive picture of this project: "We are right on our cost spending plan, a little behind schedule; we are doing well," would be the positive spin put on these results by most practitioners.

However, the chief executive had specifically asked that earned value project management be employed on this project. That requirement adds a slightly different orientation to project performance data. Earned value project management requires a detailed bottom-up performance plan, and a "three-dimensional" measurement against the baseline plan. Earned value also requires a periodic forecast of the final expected results, based on actual performance.

In order to employ earned value, there must be a plan in place that will allow for continuous measurement of actual performance results. This may sound complicated, but it is not. Earned value simply requires a focus on the completed physical or intellectual work, together with management's authorized budget for the completed work. This we call the "earned value."

In order to employ the earned value concept, a project must measure three dimensions of performance. The first dimension is called the Planned Value. (Note:

The United States Department of Defense [DoD] has been calling this the Budgeted Costs for Work Scheduled [BCWS] for some three decades, but we choose to call it by the term Planned Value).

To determine the Planned Value, the project must ascertain: (1) how much physical or intellectual work has been scheduled to be completed as of a point of measurement, and (2) management's authorized budget for this authorized work. The Planned Value is simply a direct fallout of those detailed tasks specified on the PMS. (Important point: Earned value requires a baseline PMS, or, stated another way, without a PMS one cannot employ earned value).

In this case, the PMS had specified three units to be completed as of the first quarter, and each unit had a budgeted value of $100,000. Thus, they can determine that the Planned Value for the first three months of the project was $300,000. (Note: The fact that the team's original estimate for each unit was $150,000 is only interesting. Management authorized $100,000 per unit, and management doesn't want to hear about other issues . . . period! Best the team forget about their original $150,000 estimate).

Next they will need to measure the second dimension, called their Earned Value for the same reporting period. To measure Earned Value, they will need to determine: (3) how much of the authorized work they actually accomplished and (4) the amount of management's original budget for the accomplished work. (Note: Do not bother with the actual costs at this point, since actual costs have nothing to do with creating earned value). Their actual performance results: They completed two units, each with a value of $100,000, for a total earned value of $200,000.

The third dimension they need to determine is, Actual Costs, or how much money was spent converting the planned value into earned value during the measurement period. They look at the cost ledger and find that they have incurred actual costs of $300,000.

The three dimensions of earned value project management are now set for the first quarter, expressed in monetary terms, and a performance pattern has emerged for this project:

- The Planned Value was $300,000;
- The Earned Value was $200,000; and
- The Actual Costs were $300,000.

They now need to analyze their performance results to determine if there have been any schedule or cost variances, which earned value project management looks at in a slightly different form from that of traditional project management.

With earned value, a "schedule variance" is defined as the difference between the completed Earned Value less the Planned Value. In this case they planned to accomplish $300,000 of work but only did $200,000, thus they are behind their planned baseline schedule by $100,000. Not so bad, until they realize that they only accomplished 67 cents for each dollar they had planned to accomplish!

Lastly, they need to know if there was a "cost variance." An earned value cost variance is determined by taking the earned value work accomplished, and subtracting the actual costs spent or incurred. They spent $300,000 in actual costs to accomplish only $200,000 in earned value! Not so good when they realize that for each dollar they spent they got only 67 cents of value earned. Thus, this project is behind their planned baseline schedule and overrunning the costs. The negative schedule variance is serious. But the negative cost variance may be non-recoverable!

The team summarizes the results of their earned value performance for presentation to the management committee. Not exactly a pretty sight, but one of extreme importance in the portrayal of the true status of project performance. This project at the end of the first quarter is performing only 67 percent of its planned schedule, and 67 percent of cost performance. Stated another way, it is overrunning its costs by 50 percent. At only the 20 percent completion point, by monitoring these three dimensions of earned value data, the project is forecasting a significant final overrun of costs!

The project has already spent $300,000 to complete only $200,000 of work, so they are experiencing a negative $100,000 overrun of costs. And if the project continues at its present "cost efficiency" rate of earning only 67 cents for each dollar spent, it will need a 50 percent increase in budget will be needed to complete the work ($1,000,000 divided by .67 equals nearly $1,500,000). Also, if the team tries to get back on the 12 month schedule it will likely have to add additional resources and overtime to do the same authorized work, so the projected costs could equate to about a 100 percent overrun. (Note: There are scientific studies which reinforce these three forecasting methods.)[6]

Most executives do not like to hear bad news. But this chief executive knows well that bad news does not get better with time; it only gets worse. At issue: Bad news known at the 20 percent point in a project's life cycle gives management an opportunity to take corrective actions and possibly change the final projected results. Conversely, bad news which is ignored until perhaps the 80 percent completion point severely limits management's opportunities to make the necessary changes to recover performance. Earned value gives management an important "early warning" signal.

Those were exactly the kind of performance results the chief executive wanted to see on this most critical project. She wanted the true status, good, bad, or ugly. She

---

6   All of the concepts and terms used herein are consistent with the earned value coverage in the Project Management Institute's *PMBOK® Guide* — Fourth Edition, section 7.3.2.1, released by PMI in December 2008.

also knew that she had to take immediate action in order to make additional funds available for this most important project. She made a note to herself to cancel two other projects of lesser importance, to free up funds for this project. This project was important to her company, and it had to be funded to completion.

The CEO now declared: *Thank you for this presentation; it has been most informative. I now know that I was perhaps a little too restrictive in my initial budget authorization to you. I will now authorize you a revised budget amount of $1,500,000 to complete this project.* The response from the young project manager was, *Thank you.* He knew that the team needed at least that amount to complete the project.

However, the chief executive continued, not letting anyone off the hook just yet, *I want you to catch up on the late schedule position and complete this project with all the technical features in another nine months. Can you do that?* The project manager's reply was, *Yes, we can, but that will require an accelerated schedule, and that will likely cost us the full $2,000,000 as we have presented to you. .*

Okay, I will authorize this project a total budget of $1,500,000, but ask that you complete it within the 12 month schedule, were the CEO's directions. *However, as we both well know, to recover this late schedule will likely cost us some additional money, so I will put another half a million dollars in my management reserve in case we need it. But it is not your money yet, and we want you back on schedule. Am I making myself clear?* said the CEO. *Absolutely clear,* said the young project manager, *and we promise to do the best we can for the authorized budget..*

But getting back on schedule is your main performance objective, and the budget goal is simply my challenge to you, understand? The schedule comes first, was the chief executive's final comment. *Understood,* said the young project manager, who was getting to fully appreciate the delicate role he was playing.

The Final Results

Standing back from this story, what was emerging was that this project was likely underbudgeted (at $1,000,000) from the beginning. But based on what was authorized and what the project team was experiencing, the likely final forecast of budget needs was in the statistical range of between a half million and one full million over the initial budget. Both the project manager and the CEO clearly understood that fact. But the CEO was not ready to relax her management challenge to this team. She released an additional half a million dollars to the project, but also asked that they get back on schedule. Getting back on schedule would cost additional resources, and likely require the full million to achieve. But she was not yet ready to authorize the full amount.

This chief executive knew the benefits of employing earned value. She believed in the accuracy of data that was being presented by the project team and the final projections of required costs. At the 20 percent completion point the team was predicting an overrun of between 50 to 100 percent, and she was convinced that this would ultimately be the case. In order to fund the completion of this critical company project, she took immediate steps to cancel two other internal company projects of lesser importance. She knew what she had to do in order to free up funds for this high priority project. Other executives who do not employ earned value or do not rely on the performance data often find themselves overcommitted in their project portfolios, sometimes experiencing catastrophic results.

The final results were in: This project was completed with all the required technical features, on time and within the 12 month schedule. But the final actual costs reached $2,000,000. The new product worked exactly as required, and the additional funds to complete the project were made available by the CEO when she cancelled two other projects of lesser importance.

Life was good at this company. The young project manager's professional career was off to a great start. He performed exactly as desired by senior management. Earned value allowed this company to balance the technical requirements against cost and schedule considerations.

Project Postmortem: The Value of Earned Value Management

Issue: Will the use of earned value on projects prevent cost overruns? Answer: Never. Overruns are typically caused by three factors, or some combination of these three factors:

(1) Too little budget authorized by management to do the job;
(2) Poor technical performance from the project team; and
(3) Scope creep.

If management authorizes an inadequate budget, the project team performs poorly, or new work is constantly added because the project scope was never properly defined in the first place, earned value will not prevent cost growth. Earned value cannot perform a miracle.

What earned value will do is provide an "early warning signal" to the project manager, to senior management, and to the customer. It will indicate that the project will likely require so much money to complete, unless actions are taken to change future events. Sometimes project scope will need to be reduced. Sometimes risks will need to be taken. Sometimes additional funds will need to be made available to complete the project.

Earned value project management can help deliver better performance on any project.

3

EARNED VALUE PROJECT MANAGEMENT:

AN OVERVIEW

Earned value is for projects . . . . It is not for continuous business operations.

MOST PRACTITIONERS OF EARNED VALUE refer to it as "Earned Value Management" or simply EVM. In 1996, when we wrote our initial book on the subject, we intentionally inserted the word "Project" into the book's title. This was done to emphasize an important point which is not always understood: Earned value as a technique is effective in the management of projects. But, put another way, EVM has very limited utility in the management of continuous business "operations." What's the significance of this point? We suggest that you employ earned value on your projects, but not on your continuing operations.

The Third Edition of the *PMBOK® Guide* inserted important language which distinguishes between an organization's "projects" and their continuous business "operations."[7] A project is a one-time only endeavor which has unique work to accomplish and also has specific deliverables. You must finish all the deliverables in order to finish the project. Project measurement should therefore transcend all arbitrary fiscal periods. Projects are measured from their start to their finish. An example might be a one-time project to establish a new help desk. Until the project is done, the help desk is not operational. Once the help desk is operational, the project is over and the work becomes a continuous business operation. You measure performance differently.

By contrast, a business operation represents continuous work; it does not end, it goes on from one fiscal year through the next fiscal year(s). Guard services, the company cafeteria, and accounting support are typical examples of continuous business

---

7   Project Management Institute. (2004). *A Guide to the Project Management Body of Knowledge (PMBOK® Guide) —* Third Edition, Section 1.2.2.

operations. Work done in overhead pools is typically continuous operations. The newest *PMBOK® Guide* makes the following important distinction: "Projects are different because the project concludes when its specific objectives have been attained, while operations adopt a new set of objectives and the work continues."[8] Bottom line: Earned value is recommended to help better manage your projects. However, earned value is *not* recommended for continuous business operations.

A simple industrial engineering concept got sidetracked.

The concept of earned value has been around for over a hundred years, or perhaps for only four decades, depending on how one counts the beginning. Over the years it has been gone by numerous titles, including factory industrial standards, the value of the work, earned value management, performance measurement, the Planned Value of Work Accomplished (PVWA), the Budgeted Costs of Work Performed (BCWP), the Cost/Schedule Control Systems Criteria (C/SCSC), the Cost Schedule Planning Control Specification (C/SPCS), simply the criteria, PERT/Costs, and numerous other more unsavory titles.

Whatever term might be used, the central focus of earned value has been consistent over the years: the accurate measurement of the physical work performed against a baseline plan. Most important, it can provide a reliable prediction of the final costs and schedule requirements for a given project. Earned value is based on an integrated management approach which provides the best indicator of true cost performance, available with no other project management technique. Earned value requires that the project's scope be fully defined, and then a bottom-up baseline plan be put in place which integrates the defined scope, with the authorized resources, placed into a specific timeframe for performance.

In terms of the proponents or opponents of the concept, there appears to be little middle ground. Some individuals feel the technique provides a valuable tool, holding considerable potential, which should be employed in the management of all projects. Others are adamantly opposed to earned value, perhaps based on some prior bad experience with it. This group will argue that the effort required to employ earned value far exceeds any utility gained from using the technique. To this camp we respectfully suggest that they give earned value a try in its simplified form, employing only the basics, without all the bureaucratic bells and whistles. They may just find a valuable new tool to help them better manage their projects.

We find ourselves generally in the first camp; we do like earned value. But we also have some definite reservations based on past experience. It is our feeling that the earned value concept holds considerable promise for broad-based project management applications, but only when employed in a simple, more

---

8   Ibid.

user-friendly model than has been typically mandated by government agencies in the past. Our reasoning: The requirements to oversee the performance of major new systems being acquired for government agencies on cost reimbursable type contracts are vastly different from the more typical needs of most project managers today.

Most project managers commit to performing their projects on a fixed-cost basis, within a finite authorization of company resources. Project management tools must be simple and easy to use, or they will be ignored. Likewise, earned value must be made simple, or it will be ignored.

For almost thirty years, earned value was a part of what was called the Cost/ Schedule Control Systems Criteria (C/SCSC). What started out originally as a simple concept used on the factory floor evolved into a sort of exclusive association which required its members to be specifically trained in the use of a cumbersome new vocabulary. Most project managers are interested only in completing their projects according to the approved plan and have neither the time nor the inclination to master a new vernacular. Often, management rightfully rejected the concept in total rather than adopting it in its rigid form. What a shame. For by rejecting this conceptually simple but effective cost management technique project managers have missed an opportunity to employ a powerful tool that can complement their other management tools, in particular, scheduling using the critical path method (CPM).

Please note that it is not the purpose of this book to in any way demean what was originally the C/SCSC. As used by the United States Government and other governments in the acquisition of their "major systems" (where all the risk of cost growth was on them because they elected to employ a cost reimbursable or incentive type contract) C/SCSC was the perfect vehicle. C/SCSC was demonstrated to be beneficial as a government required mandate for some three decades.

However, major systems acquisitions by governments likely constitute only a small percentage of the projects of the world. We speculated earlier that something less than 1 percent of the projects in the world fall into the category of "major projects." The overall dollars may be significant on major projects, but the total numbers of such projects are nevertheless quite small. But how about the other 99 percent of the projects in the world? With these projects all risks of cost growth are not necessarily on the owners or the buyers, but rather on the project managers, because they have made fixed-cost commitments to their companies. All of the risks of cost growth rest squarely with them. Could these project managers not benefit from a cost management technique that helps them to achieve what they have personally committed to perform? We believe there is considerable potential in the universal employment of a simplified and user-friendly earned value approach in the management of all projects.

It is now time to take this simple factory management technique called earned value and employ it as it was originally intended by the industrial engineers over a century ago: to compare baseline "planned standards" with the "earned standards," to measure the schedule performance, and, most importantly, to relate these same "earned standards" against the "actual costs" incurred, in order to precisely measure the true cost performance of projects. This we call three-dimensional performance measurement, or earned value project management.

THE EARNED VALUE CONCEPT IN A NUTSHELL[9]

There is nothing inherently difficult about the earned value concept. It does not require special training to grasp the fundamentals. In fact, many people use some form of earned value in their daily routines and are not even aware they are employing the concept.

For example, most construction type projects will include someone responsible for performing work that they call "cost engineering," which in other industries may be called project controls, management controls, etc. Anytime a construction cost engineer takes the time, prior to paying a supplier's invoice, to verify that the physical work was actually accomplished, that cost engineer is in effect utilizing a simple form of earned value. He or she is focusing on the critical relationship between the actual costs being expended, versus the physical work actually performed. Construction cost engineers focus on the true project performance: *What we are getting . . . for what we are spending.* That is earned value project management in a nutshell.

The earned value concept requires that a baseline plan, called the planned value, be created, typically specified with use of the project scheduling system. Then performance is measured against the planned value, also with use of the scheduling system. The physical earned value performed is then related to the actual costs spent to accomplish the physical work, providing a measure of the project's true cost performance. It may help if one thinks of earned value as representing a resource-loaded scheduling approach.

Earned value provides the project manager with a type of "early warning" buzzer that sounds when faced with impending problems, allowing him or her to take the necessary corrective actions should the cost of the project be higher than the value of what the project is physically accomplishing. Such warning signals become available to management as early as 20 percent into a new project, in ample time to take corrective measures to alter unfavorable outcomes.

---

9   Note: The materials contained in this chapter are consistent with the coverage of earned value contained in the Fourth Edition of the *PMBOK® Guide,* specifically section 7.3.2.

Traditional project cost management

Probably the best way to understand the earned value concept is to discuss a specific example. We will use the model from the introductory story in Chapter 2 of the young project manager implementing his one million dollar internal development project.

To illustrate the concept here, we will contrast the earned value method against the more traditional approach toward the management of project costs. Under the traditional cost and funding management approach, a new spending plan will be formulated by (or more likely for) the project manager for review and approval by senior management.

Figure 3.1 shows an assumed project cost expenditure spend plan. It time phases the $1,000,000 project budget by quarter over a scheduled one-year time period. The projected expenditures for the first quarter indicate that $300,000 would be required for the first quarter. The CEO reviewed the plan and gave her approval for this new internally funded project. Management would expect the project manager to stay within the limits of the $1,000,000 total commitment, by each quarter, and to continuously monitor the performance during the life of the 12 month project.

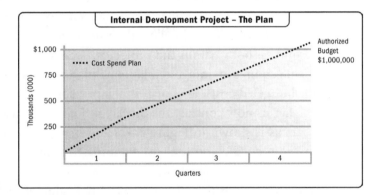

Figure 3.1 *A typical project cost expenditure projection*

Using a traditional cost management approach, at the end of the first quarter the project manager would display the cost performance for the benefit of management, as is now illustrated in Figure 3.2. The approved spend plan called for an expenditure of $300,000 for the first quarter and actual results thus far show an expenditure of exactly $300,000. One could conclude without further review that the project was performing exactly to its financial plan: $300,000 planned and $300,000 spent. Perfect cost performance. Life is good. A fairly typical, but unfortunately potentially deceptive, approach to understanding project cost performance.

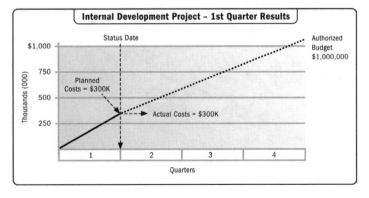

Figure 3.2 *Traditional cost management: Plan versus actual costs*

In fact, looking at the data as displayed in Figure 3.2, nobody could really determine the project's true cost performance results. To determine the project's true cost performance, one would need to compare the physical schedule results in the same format as the cost displays. But if the project's financial support people developed their cost displays using one approach, perhaps breaking out the costs by function, and the scheduling people developed their displays using another approach, perhaps reflecting Work Breakdown Structure (WBS) work tasks, the two critical displays of cost and schedule would not relate to each other. It is impossible to relate the true cost and schedule status when these two key functional groups develop their respective plans using different assumptions. However, and this is an important point, it is a fairly common practice for organizations to have this type of disconnect in their planning. Finance will often reflect project costs by functional organization, and scheduling will often reflect their schedules by work breakdown. The two do not match!

An interesting observation: Most of the projects in the world today would likely display their cost status for management using a chart similar to that reflected in Figure 3.2. Further, most of the schedule displays being used by projects today will not directly correlate to the cost displays provided by the finance people. Thus, most of the projects today likely are *not* working to an "integrated" management approach, which would allow the project to equate the defined scope to authorized resources, both within the project master schedule. Earned value project management requires an integrated baseline plan which relates the defined scope of work to the budgeted costs, as shown in the project schedule.

Let us now contrast the display in Figure 3.2 with an earned value performance chart as is shown in Figure 3.3. Here the total budget of $1,000,000 will be made up from detailed bottom-up planning that allows for performance to be measured throughout the life of the project. There are ten milestones to be accomplished, and each milestone will have a weighted value of $100,000. Each time a milestone is completed the project will earn $100,000.

The amount forecasted to be accomplished at the end of the first quarter is now labeled the "planned value." Performance through the first quarter called for an accomplishment of three milestones, for a budgeted value of $300,000 of work scheduled. The planned value consists of two elements: (1) the work scheduled, plus (2) the budget for the work scheduled.

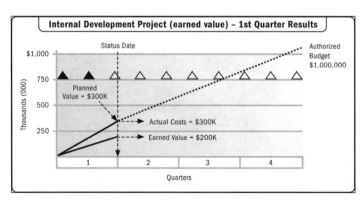

Figure 3.3 *Earned value project management: Three-dimensional*

The new three-dimensional project performance measurement which earned value provides is introduced in Figure 3.3. This display reflects actual physical earned value of only two milestones completed, representing an earned value of $200,000, against the planned value of $300,000. The "earned value" also consists of two elements: (1) the scheduled work which was completed and (2) the original budget for the completed work.

We can immediately see that the project is running behind the work it set out to do during the first quarter. It had planned to accomplish $300,000 in work, but had accomplished only $200,000. Therefore, the project can be said to be running a negative $100,000 schedule variance. An earned value schedule variance is defined as the earned value ($200,000) less the planned value ($300,000) which equals the schedule variance (-$100,000).

Also shown in Figure 3.3 are the cost actuals of $300,000, an amount greater than the earned value of physical work performed of $200,000. Thus it can be inferred that this project has spent $300,000 in actual costs to achieve only $200,000 worth of earned value. An earned value cost variance is defined as the earned value accomplished ($200,000) less the actual costs ($300,000) which equals the cost variance (-$100,000).

We can also call this actual condition what it is: an "overrun" of costs. This project can be said to be running a negative $100,000 cost variance. The delicate relationships reflected with these actual cost and schedule performance relationships can now be used to predict the final costs and schedule results of the project.

Important point: This project is in trouble. But one could not have discerned that condition using a traditional cost management approach. It is only when earned value brings in the three dimensions of performance that we can tell that the project is experiencing problems. Such issues need to be addressed immediately by the project manager in order to avoid adverse cost overruns and schedule slippages.

Traditional cost management versus earned value project management

There is an important and fundamental distinction to be made between the data available for management using the traditional cost control approach as compared to the three-dimensional data available when a project employs earned value. These critical differences are summarized in Figure 3.4 and focus on the variances to the baseline plans.

Using the displays of planned expenditures versus actual expenditures, a project's true cost performance cannot be adequately determined. With a plan versus actual costs comparison there is no way to ascertain how much of the physical work has been accomplished. Such displays merely represent the relationship of what was planned to be spent to the funds actually spent. Cost performance as displayed at the top of Figure 3.4 indicates perfect results against the original spending plan. The project spent its allowance. The utility of such displays only has significance as a reflection of whether a project has stayed within the funds authorized by management.

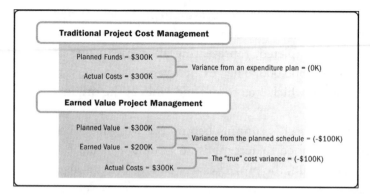

Figure 3.4 *The fundamental differences*

Such displays reflect funding performance, not true cost performance. Yet, most projects today typically represent their cost performance using similar graphic displays.

By contrast, as shown at the bottom of Figure 3.4, the earned value project displays three dimensions of data: the planned value of the physical work authorized, the earned value of the physical work accomplished, and the actual costs incurred to accomplish the earned value. Thus, under an earned value approach, the two critical variances may be ascertained. The first is the difference between the planned value of the work scheduled and the earned value achieved. As reflected in this chart, the project is experiencing a negative schedule variance of minus $100,000 from its planned work. Stated another way, one-third of the work the project set out to do was not accomplished in the timeframe being measured. The team is clearly behind its planned project schedule. Such variances, when used in conjunction with other proven scheduling techniques, particularly the critical path method (CPM), provide invaluable insights into the true schedule status of the project.

Of greater concern, however, is the relationship of the value of the work done, the earned value, to the funds expended to accomplish the work. A total of $300,000 was expended to accomplish only $200,000 worth of work. Thus the project has experienced a cost overrun of minus $100,000 for the work performed to date. This negative cost trend is of critical importance to the project, for experience has indicated that such overruns of costs do not correct themselves over time. In fact, cost overruns tend to get worse. The actual cost and schedule performance results can also be used independently or jointly to forecast the final results of the project with amazing accuracy.

Earned value cost and schedule performance indices: The SPI and CPI

Employing the earned value concept allows the project management team to monitor its own performance against a detailed time-phased plan. Exceptions to the plan provide a wealth of reliable information, primarily centered on the cost and schedule efficiency metrics. Two accurate performance indices become available to the project, as early as the 20 percent point of completion. Such relationships are illustrated in Figure 3.5.

Here the three primary sets of data shown earlier in Figure 3.3 have been converted into a thermometer style management display which reflects the three dimensions of project performance at a given point in time. Dimension one: How much project work was scheduled to be accomplished? Answer: The planned value was $300,000, or 30 percent. Dimension two: How much work was actually performed? Answer: The earned value was $200,000, or 20 percent. Dimension three: How much money was spent to achieve the earned value? Answer: $300,000, or 30 percent, was spent.

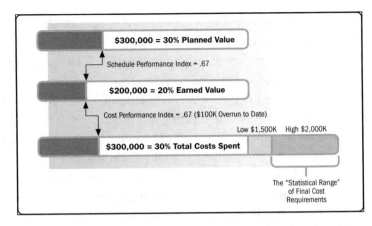

Figure 3.5 *Projecting final costs . . . based on actual performance*

In this analysis, we are indebted to those in U.S. Government who have worked with the C/SCSC concept over the past thirty plus years and to the body of knowledge they have accumulated. These individuals have scientifically demonstrated the utility of these two relationships in assessing the performance of hundreds of projects, large and small, of various contract types, in various project phases, etc. They have developed powerful empirical data.

The first issue to be determined with these actual results: How long will it take to complete all of the authorized work? The CEO authorized a one-year duration, but will that happen? Using earned value metrics, we must determine what schedule efficiency factor has been achieved for this project after the first quarter results. The project plan called for performance of $300,000 in work after the first quarter; however, only $200,000 in physical earned value was actually done. The project is the equivalent of minus $100,000 behind in planned work after the first quarter. At this rate of performance, it will likely take longer than one year to complete the project, unless additional resources are immediately added (bringing in more people, using extensive overtime, etc.).

The amount of the earned value ($200,000) may be divided by the value of the planned work ($300,000), resulting in a planned schedule performance efficiency factor of only .67. Stated another way, for every dollar of physical work planned to be accomplished, only $.67 was done. Therefore this project is said to have achieved a Schedule Performance Index (SPI) efficiency factor of .67. The SPI can be a valuable tool for use in conjunction with a critical path method (CPM) to forecast the expected completion date for the project. The SPI also has utility when used in conjunction with the Cost Performance Index (CPI) to forecast the total required funds to complete the project.

The second issue to be determined: How much money will be required to complete all of the authorized work? The CEO authorized a fixed amount of $1,000,000 to complete the project, but will this be enough? To assess the required funds we must determine the cost efficiency factor after the first quarter. By comparing the amount of physical earned value accomplished to the dollars actually spent to accomplish the earned value, one can determine the cost performance efficiency for a project. When we divide the earned value of $200,000 by the actual dollars of $300,000, we can determine the CPI for the project. Stated another way, for every project dollar that was spent, only $.67 in physical work was accomplished. Therefore, this project is said to have achieved a CPI of only $.67.

The CPI is a powerful tool to use to predict the final costs needed to finish a job. The CPI can be used by itself, or in conjunction with the SPI, to continuously forecast a statistical range of estimated final costs to complete the project. The SPI and CPI metrics can also be used to compare the performance of a single project to all other projects in an organization. Earned value metrics thus prove useful in the management of a portfolio of projects, because they provide accurate and reliable measurements of actual project performance.

Using the CPI and SPI to statistically forecast a range of final project results

Once a project has established a CPI and SPI pattern based on actual performance through a given measurement period, what is the benefit in knowing these two factors? Answer: Both the cost and schedule performance indices can be used to statistically forecast the final required funds needed to complete the project. Independent statistical forecasts can be a sort of "sanity check" on the trend and final direction of the project. They can be compared against the team optimism that often prevails on projects: "Stay out of our way and let us do our thing." Such forecasts can be developed with the CPI alone, or with the CPI used in conjunction with the SPI.

Assume that, in spite of the negative cost and schedule performance results achieved in the initial first quarter of the project, the project manager is still estimating the final costs to be $1,000,000, the amount originally budgeted by the CEO. Would this be a reasonable forecast? Probably not, unless there were an extenuating circumstance which needed to be considered, like a reduction in risks.

A detailed bottom-up estimate for the completion of all the remaining tasks is always the more desirable forecasting method. But detailed bottom-up estimates take time to prepare, and actually interfere with performing project work. An earned value statistical forecast can provide an effortless and reliable estimate of final cost requirements.

The project has already incurred an overrun of $100,000, having spent $300,000 to do $200,000 worth of work. The $100,000 overrun is typically non-recoverable. Any differences between the project manager's forecast and these statistical estimates should be reconciled with senior management. Thus, a best-case forecast would likely be $1,100,000.

However, using earned value data, one can take the total budgeted funds of $1,000,000, divide that amount by the cumulative CPI factor of .67 and quickly statistically forecast that about $1,500,000 would be needed to complete the project. This forecasting technique has been demonstrated to represent a reliable indicator of the "minimum" total required project costs, which many feel is the very best the project may experience.

Another respected method for forecasting final costs relies on calculating the CPI (.67) times the SPI (.67) and using the resulting product (.4489) to statistically forecast the maximum funds likely required to complete the job. This method incorporates the cost overrun to date with a behind-schedule condition to produce a more severe statistical forecast. The estimated amount is now something close to $2,000,000 and is considered by many to represent a "high-end" statistical method.

Thus, we can quickly create a statistical final cost projection of between $1,500,000 to $2,000,000 needed to complete the project and compare that with the "official" forecast provided by the project manager.

Each of these statistical formulas, used to forecast final cost and schedule results, will be covered in greater detail later in this book.

IN SUMMARY

While the modern earned value concept was officially introduced to industry some four decades ago, most of the applications thus far have been largely restricted to the acquisitions of major new systems by agencies of the United States and other governments. For some reason, the technique has not been universally embraced by the countless project managers in the private sector who similarly strive to perform their work and fulfill their fiscal commitments to senior management.

It is the belief of the authors that the resistance to the universal adoption of the earned value concept is not the fault of the technique itself, but rather that of the implementation requirements, the terminology employed, and the countless rules and interpretations that have been perceived by many project managers to be overly restrictive. We must find a way to simplify the earned value concept and reduce it to its bare essentials if it is to be adopted as a broad-based project management tool for universal applications in all industries. We must find a proper balance between the utility of the earned value technique and the effort required to implement it.

That can easily be achieved by getting back to the three-dimensional basics which were used in the industrial factories over a century ago: Simply relate the planned standards to the earned standards and to the actual costs for accomplishing the work, i.e., the earned value method. This book seeks to describe a simple form of earned value for use in the management of all projects.

4

The Genesis and Evolution
of Earned Value

Earned Value is a concept—the concept that an estimated value can be placed on all work to be performed, and once that work is accomplished that same value can be considered to be "earned."

—A. Ernest Fitzgerald
February 28, 1965[10]

Origin of Earned Value Management

IN ALL LIKELIHOOD, most of us became aware of earned value management when it was a key component of what was then called the Cost/Schedule Control Systems Criteria, or simply the C/SCSC. The C/SCSC consisted of 35 standards of compliance (criteria) which were required from management control systems within private industry to assure consistency in reporting of performance in major United States Government acquisition projects. The criteria were imposed by governmental agencies whenever they underwrote the risks of cost growth— that is, whenever they employed either a cost reimbursable or incentive type contract for a new developmental project.

The criteria were first released by the U.S. Department of Defense (DoD) in December 1967, and were consistently used as their approved method of cost management in the procurement of major new systems. Since that time, other U.S. Governmental agencies and several foreign governments have adopted identical or slightly modified performance measurement criteria for application in private

---

10 Letter from Fitzgerald to Lt. Col. E. J. Mason, United States Air Force (February 28, 1965), transmitting *Earned Value Summary Guide.*

industry. Canada, for example, adopted the same criteria but added an additional criterion specifically requiring critical path method (CPM) scheduling on their major projects. The C/SCSC were silent on the requirement for CPM, but did emphasize the importance of having a reliable scheduling system.

While the C/SCSC did include the concept of earned value management, the C/SCSC had broader applications than simply employing earned value; contractor oversight, for example. We owe it to ourselves to understand the fundamental differences. Reason: The opportunities for broad-based earned value management exist . . . but only if the fundamentals can be extracted from within the C/SCSC. Earned value, as it was employed within the C/SCSC, was far too demanding and too inflexible for universal project management applications, in the opinion of the authors.

The earned value concept was originally conceived by the industrial engineers working in factories in the United States in the early years—such scientific management practitioners as Frederick W. Taylor (the father of scientific management), Frank and Lillian Gilbreth, Henry Lawrence Gantt, and others. One former United States Air Force general who was involved in the modern implementation of earned value over forty years ago commented:

> ***The earned value concept came to us right off the factory floor, from the industrial engineers who were comparing their planned standards with the earned standards and actual costs. We simply applied this same concept to our one-time only, non-recurring developmental tasks.***[11]

The favorable experience with earned value management as employed initially on the Minuteman missile program eventually led to the issuance of C/SCSC as a formal management doctrine in 1967.

These 35 formal management control system standards have led to the development of some rather sophisticated approaches to the monitoring of project performance. It has also provided a means to accurately predict the project's final cost and time requirements based on a project's own performance record as of any given point in time. As early as 20 percent through a new project, the earned value performance results can be used to predict the final required costs within a finite range of values. Early at the start of a new project, the actual cost efficiency factor (called the earned value Cost Performance Index, or CPI) has been shown to stabilize, providing data that can be used to predict the final required costs for any given project.

If they were still with us today, the original scientific managers—Taylor, the Gilbreths, and Gantt—would all be pleased with the body of scientific knowledge that has been carefully accumulated over the past four decades. In fact, certain

---

11 Lt. General Hans Driessnack, USAF retired (personal interview, July 3, 1993).

professional management societies have incorporated some of these same findings into their professional repositories of information. Of particular significance to those of us working in the profession would likely be the Project Management Institute's universally read, landmark document, the *PMBOK® Guide*. Earned value is described in Chapter 7, which covers Project Cost Management.

EVOLUTION OF THE EARNED VALUE CONCEPT

The earned value concept was conceived over a hundred years ago, sometime in the latter part of the nineteenth century. For purposes of this discussion, we have somewhat arbitrarily divided the evolution of earned value into distinct phases so that we may address each stage separately. However, as with any such forced classification, there are overlaps in these divisions.

Phase 0—The factory floor: In the late 1800s

For many years, the industrial engineers working in factories in the United States in the late 1800s did what most corporate executives fail to do even today: They employed a "three-dimensional" approach to assess the performance efficiency for work done in the factory. The industrial engineers measured performance against a baseline called "planned standards" and then measured the "earned standards" achieved against the "actual expenses" incurred to accurately measure the performance in their factories.

The result of this approach is earned value management in its most fundamental form. Perhaps of most significance, the industrial engineers have defined a "cost variance" as representing the difference between the actual costs spent, as compared to the earned standards achieved.[12] This basic definition of what constitutes a cost variance is perhaps the litmus test for determining whether or not one is utilizing some form of earned value.

Phase 1—PERT/Cost: 1962 to 1965

The management technique of PERT (Program Evaluation Review Technique) was first introduced to industry as a network scheduling and risk management device by the United States Navy in 1958.[13] PERT's original approach was twofold: to simulate the development planning of a new project in the form of a logic flow diagram, and to assess the statistical probability of actually achieving the plan.

---

12 Bruno A. Moski, Jr. (1951). Cost control fundamentals. In *Plant Executive's Deskbook* (p. 25). New York: McGraw-Hill Publishing Company.

13 Special Projects Office, Bureau of Ordnance, (Washington, DC: Department of the Navy, 1958). *Project PERT*.

As first introduced, PERT placed a strong emphasis on statistical probability, which constituted one of the early difficulties. In the late 1950s, neither computers nor computer software programs were available to adequately implement the concept. Nevertheless, PERT as a tool caught the imagination of both management practitioners and academics.

PERT as a scheduling technique was never as successful as the Critical Path Method (CPM), which came along at about the same time, but in another industry (construction). Two men working with these early concepts described the events at the time:

> *In 1956, E. I. DuPont de Nemours undertook a thorough investigation of the extent to which a computer might be used to improve the planning and scheduling, rescheduling and progress reporting of the company's engineering programs. A DuPont engineer, Morgan R. Walker, and a Remington-Rand computer expert, James E. Kelley, Jr., worked on the problem, and in late 1957 ran a pilot test of a system using a unique arrow-diagram or network method which came to be known as the Critical Path Method.* [14]

Then around 1962, the advocates of PERT as a scheduling tool chose to take another bold step to expand the concept. Their thinking: If one could accurately simulate the logic of a project taking the form of a network diagram, why not add resources into the network and manage both time and costs? The result was the introduction of "PERT/Cost" in 1962. An accurate description of the environment at the time would be that the addition of cost resources into these logic networks merely exacerbated the PERT advocates' problem, since neither the computer hardware nor the computer software programs were available to properly support simple network scheduling.

Neither the original PERT (which then went by the term PERT/Time) nor PERT/Cost survived by the mid-1960s. Today, the term "PERT" does live on, but only as a generic title to describe any network scheduling method. In fact, most of the networks today that are called PERT are actually precedence diagram method (PDM) networks, not true PERT networks.

The important thing that did survive from the short-lived PERT/Cost experience was the earned value concept. The implementation of PERT/Cost in industry at the time required eleven reporting formats from the contractors. One of these formats included a "Cost of Work Report." Its format contained what was then called the "value of work performed" measured against the actual costs:

---

14 Russell D. Archibald and Richard L. Villoria. (1967). *Network-Based Management Systems (PERT/CPM)* (pp. 12-13). New York: John Wiley & Sons, Inc.

A comparison of the actual costs accumulated to date and the contract esti-
mate for the work performed to date will show whether the work is being
performed at a cost which is greater or less than planned.[15]

Earned value as a project management tool was thus initially introduced to
modern industry in 1962. As a part of PERT/Cost, however, it would not last long.
PERT/Cost had a lifespan of perhaps three years, but it did leave an exciting legacy:
the use of earned value data to monitor the true cost performance during the life of
any project.

By the mid-1960s, both PERT/Time and PERT/Cost had all but vanished from
the scene. Industry executives and private companies did not take kindly to being
told what management techniques they must employ and how they must manage
their projects, no matter how beneficial such ideas may have been. The DoD project
managers realized they had to take a more sensitive approach toward private industry; they did just that with the introduction of the C/SCSC criteria approach.

Phase 2—C/SCSC: 1967 to 1996

The United States Air Force (USAF) took the lead to set standards that would allow
it to oversee industry performance, without specifically telling industry what to do.
In 1965, the USAF formed a team called the Cost Schedule Planning and Control
Specification (CSPCS) group. Meetings were held by some of the very same people
who had been involved in the earlier implementation of PERT/Time and PERT/Cost.
By virtue of their PERT experience, they quickly agreed they would not impose any
specific "management control system" on private industry. Rather, they conceived the
notion of merely requiring that contractors satisfy broadly defined "criteria" with their
existing management control systems. A subtle departure from the PERT experience,
but it made all the difference between success and failure for the new approach.

The criteria concept simply required responses from industry to some rather
basic questions, but based on sound project management principles. One individual
who was a part of this early process described what answers he hoped to obtain from
industry:

Does the contractor break down the work into short span packages that can
be budgeted, scheduled and evaluated? Do they have a cost accumulation
system? Do they measure performance against those packages of work . . .
and do they then report status and variances to their own internal manage-
ment? We don't want to tell anyone how to manage.[16]

---

15 Office of the Secretary of Defense and National Aeronautics and Space Administration. (1962). *DoD and NASA*
    Guide PERT/Cost. Washington, D.C., p. 17.
16 Lt. Gen. Hans Driessnack. (1990, March) How it Started. *PMA Newsletter,*

By December 1967, the DoD was ready to formally issue what they then called their Cost/Schedule Control Systems Criteria, shortened to simply C/SCSC. The C/SCSC carefully incorporated the earned value concept in the form of 35 criteria that were imposed on any private contractor wishing to be chosen for a new major systems contract or subcontract which exceeded given funding thresholds. The DoD imposed these 35 criteria on a contractor's management control system any time a cost or incentive type contract was used.

Over the three plus decades since these criteria were put in place, the practitioners of the concept have developed a significant amount of scientific knowledge based on the employment of these standards. Much knowledge has been gathered about earned value, both scientific and simply empirical. These findings will be covered in our next chapters.

However, there is some bad news: The concept of earned value measurement as a part of the C/SCSC has been largely restricted to the acquisition of major systems by governments. Private industry, with but a few exceptions, did not embrace the full and formal criteria concept.

Earned Value Management as a part of the C/SCSC produced mixed results.

The utilization of the earned value concept within the C/SCSC produced some impressive results. A new body of scientific knowledge based on actual experiences with several hundred projects was developed. However, in other instances the experience was less than satisfactory, from the perspective of practitioners in private industry. We should candidly discuss these experiences so as not to repeat them in the future.

The C/SCSC went through some three decades of bureaucratic evolution, which took a departure from the original (unobtrusive) objectives set forth in 1966, when the criteria were first defined. Esoteric interpretations subsequently led to the development of formalized (rigid) implementation guidelines, surveillance manuals, and implementation checklists containing hundreds (at one point 174) of questions for the use of the practitioners.

The guidance checklists themselves became absolute requirements to impose on contractors' management control systems. In some cases there were reasonable applications of these checklists. But in other instances the implementation rules were arbitrary and perhaps dogmatic.

The criteria checklist questions were intended by the originators to be used as a guideline only, to be exercised with good professional judgment. However, some government practitioners elevated the checklists and associated questions to a position on a par with the original 35 criteria. Contractor personnel understood the importance of having to meet certain oversight standards. But they resented many of the minor peripheral interpretations which were raised to the level of absolute requirements.

By the 1980s, a sort of cultist society of C/SCSC professional practitioners emerged, which did not sit well with many of the project managers in the private sector. Project managers look for simple tools to assist them in meeting their primary mission of completing their projects on time, within the authorized budget, and while achieving all technical objectives.

C/SCSC was a success from a government perspective because they permitted the oversight of contractor performance whenever the risks of cost growth rested squarely with the government. Government applications of C/SCSC have been consistent and have met the test of time. The original 35 criteria have remained consistent and unchanged. However, earned value management as a part of the original C/SCSC was never completely accepted or adopted by private industry for use in the management of its internal projects.

Phase 3—Earned Value Management (ANSI/EIA 748): 1996 to the present

In spite of the overall impressive results from the use of earned value within the C/SCSC, there was concern from both private industry and the U.S. Government, particularly the DoD, that perhaps some changes needed to be made. Earned value had to be made more "user-friendly" if the concept was to be applied to projects beyond simply government-imposed mandate.

On April 18, 1995, in Phoenix, Arizona, at a meeting of the Management Systems Subcommittee of the National Defense Industrial Association (NDIA), the subcommittee accepted the task of re-examining and rewriting the DoD's formal earned value criteria. Their objective was to make the criteria more compatible with the needs of private industry.

Over the next few months, members of the NDIA subcommittee met, discussed, and established their own version of the 35 C/SCSC. They called the new industry version the "Earned Value Management System" (EVMS) criteria, and it contained just 32 criteria, each of them rewritten in a more palatable form. Gone were the ambiguous terms of BCWS and BCWP, and in their place were "planned value" and "earned value." The goal was to make earned value a more useful tool for project managers.

On December 14, 1996, the Under Secretary of Defense for Acquisition and Technology accepted the 32 EVMS criteria, verbatim, and they 32were later incorporated into the next revision of the DoD Instruction 5000.2R in early 1997.

The Management Systems Subcommittee of the NDIA was not content to simply allow EVM to be restricted to the DoD. The NDIA subcommittee then obtained approval for these 32 EVM criteria to be formally issued as an American National

Standard Institute/Electronic Industries Alliance (ANSI/EIA) document. In June 1998, the ANSI/EIA-748-1998 Guide was officially issued to the public.

The significance of these moves does not lie in the revised wording of the criteria, or in the minimal reduction in their number from 35 to 32. Rather, the important change was in the attitude of all parties to the process. During 1997, there was a sort of shifting of the earned value management system responsibility from that of a government mandate to the ownership of earned value by private industry. Private industry was adopting the earned value management technique not because it was a government requirement, but because it represented a viable best practice tool which project managers everywhere could use.

Author's Note: In an Appendix to this book, there is a description of the 32 EVM criteria and the author's unofficial description of the meaning of each.

In Summary

Although many positive steps have been recently taken to make the earned value concept more user-friendly, much work remains to be done. We now have the opportunity to transfer earned value into a widely accepted tool for broad-based project management applications. But we must go back to the simple basics.

Figure 4.1 is a chart that depicts the evolution of the earned value concept. It all started in the industrial factories over a hundred years ago. The industrial engineers who conceived of the concept used it as a simple management tool. We in private industry should now do likewise. What we suggest is a return to the original approach used by the industrial engineers, but while incorporating the critical success results from applications of the formal C/SCSC and EVMS. In our opinion, a simple form of earned value should be used to manage *all* projects within the private sector.

Figure 4.1 *Getting back to earned value basics*

5

THE EARNED VALUE
BODY OF KNOWLEDGE

THIS CHAPTER might well have been entitled: "Ten compelling reasons why earned value should be employed on all projects." The empirical data on the actual employment of earned value would suggest that it has truly become a "best practice" project management tool. Earned value provides a project manager with the status of their project . . . available with no other tool.

In a manner somewhat resembling the approach used by PMI as they have carefully documented the evolution of project management, resulting in the publication of their *PMBOK® Guide*, there has been a similar but less formal accumulation of data on the subject of earned value management. The authors have elected to call these empirical findings "the earned value body of knowledge."

First, we need to candidly acknowledge what many feel is a negative aspect of the earned value experience: Most of the gathering of empirical data on earned value management has been done by practitioners operating within the U.S. Department of Defense (DoD). That single fact disappoints many professionals, and they often flatly reject the findings by suggesting that: "My project is not a military weapon system."

That fact may be true. Most projects are not within the DoD or even U.S. Government sponsored. However, the authors are of the belief that a project is a project, and all projects have similar generic characteristics. Fundamental project management principles apply to any project. For example: Scoping the project before you begin work, scheduling, budgeting, obtaining formal authorization before starting work, performing risk analysis, base-lining, monitoring performance, taking corrective actions, etc., are all fundamental principles which should apply to any project. While the concept of earned value began with the industrial engineers in the factories at the turn of the last century, the actual collection of scientific knowledge has centered on its practical applications on projects over only the past four-plus decades.

Since the implementation of earned value as an integral part of the Cost/ Schedule Control Systems Criteria (C/SCSC) starting in 1967, the criteria concept has been consistently applied to virtually all new major government development projects. There have been no substantive changes to the earned value criteria for over forty years. Therefore, the findings and the conclusions reached can reasonably be considered to represent valid empirical project data. These findings have evolved into what is becoming a creditable earned value management science.

In particular, we would like to acknowledge the outstanding work of performance management personnel within the Office of the Under Secretary of Defense for Acquisition, Technology and Logistics. These individuals have been responsible for the scientific analyses of several hundred contracts (projects) where the earned value criteria have been employed.[17] They have formulated some rather sophisticated scientific conclusions based on the consistency, predictability, and reliability of the earned value data. Their findings should not be ignored by anyone managing projects in the private sector. Quite possibly, the project managers in industry may discover a valuable tool for their use in the management of commercial projects.

The DoD effort has been augmented by studies done at the Air Force Institute of Technology (AFIT) in Dayton, Ohio, which has expanded the empirical conclusions on this evolving management science.[18] It might be beneficial to also review some of these findings to see if they might apply to more universal applications to all projects— yes, even projects in the private sector, and perhaps even on software projects! What a radical notion.

Why do the authors feel the empirical data from DoD projects might be valid for any project? Answer: Because the DoD data contains the results from all types of projects—the GOOD projects, the BAD projects, and even the downright UGLY projects! In the commercial sector, when companies "benchmark" their results, somehow they include data from *only* their GOOD performing projects. The BAD performing projects are somehow missing from their databanks. And any information accumulated on their UGLY performing projects no longer exists, because such performance results have been carefully removed. An unfortunate fact is that management doesn't like to talk about cost overruns, schedule slippages, missing technical features, the numbers of design changes, the testing failures, the bugs, the undocumented features, and so on.

However, to their credit, the DoD has systematically tracked the performance results of hundreds of projects, good, bad, and otherwise. It also protects the names of the individual companies and simply uses the data to look for overall trends not associated with any one project or any one company. If you accept the premise that a project is a project, and that they all contain basic characteristics, then what actually happened in the performance of DoD projects may well be compared to other, non-government projects.

---

17 In particular, we would like to acknowledge the work of Robert R. Kemps, Gary E. Christle, and Wayne Abba.
18 In particular, the work of Dr. David S. Christensen, USAF retired, now with Southern Utah University.

THE LEGACY OF EARNED VALUE AS A PART OF THE C/SCSC

We would like now to focus on what we consider to be the emerging earned value body of knowledge that has been accumulated by individuals working within the DoD Pentagon and the individual branches of the military services. Truthfully, the authors have not attempted to reach any type of broad consensus on the following ten points. Rather, we have compiled our listing of the issues we feel to be the most important accomplishments resulting from the employment of earned value. To us, these ten findings constitute the beginnings of a valid management science.

1. The employment of a "single management control system" which provides accurate, consistent, reliable, and timely data to management at all levels, allowing them to oversee the performance of all projects and production work within their enterprise.

One of the primary benefits of employing earned value is that it allows for the use of a single management system which can be applied to both projects and production (batches or lots) work within any given organization. The relationship of what work was scheduled to what work was accomplished provides an accurate indicator of whether one is meeting the time expectations of management. Additionally, the most critical relationship of what work was accomplished to how much money was spent to accomplish the work provides an accurate reflection of the true cost performance.

Far too often, companies in private industry will employ multiple management control systems to monitor various activities. One approach may be used to monitor the work on their big projects, another for the smaller projects, and still another approach used to oversee the production work, and so forth. Earned value data is somewhat analogous to measuring the temperature of the human body. If the human body temperature is higher or lower than the standard of 98.6 degrees, the doctor will know to look further. Likewise, earned value performance data which exceeds or falls below pre-set thresholds should be explained to management. Earned value performance data is consistent and can be applied to all projects and production work within the enterprise.

By employing a single management system on all work within an organization, the temptation to try to put a positive spin on negative results can be minimized. Often companies will allow their various managers to make different interpretations of the same actual results. The project manager, executive management, functional management, the chief financial officer, and others would each interpret the same performance results to reinforce their own parochial, self-serving positions.

Therefore, one person's interpretation often would not match another's. Earned value provides for one set of books and one set of reliable metrics, thereby reflecting accurate performance data.

2. A management approach that requires the "integration of the triple constraint"—the scope of work, the schedule commitment, and the authorized budgets—allowing for the accurate measurement of integrated performance throughout the full life cycle of a project or production run.

While most management theorists may be quick to express support for any approach which integrates the work to de done with the necessary time and resources, in practice such integration actually happens rarely. Typically, the contract administrators will define a project one way, the technical staff implement it another way, and the resource controllers will view the same requirements in still a different way. The scheduling community, not to be outdone, has always had their own unique perspective of what is important, which likely will be at odds with what others have determined to be important. The result is that any given project or production effort will often be implemented by the sum of various individual and sometimes conflicting perspectives. Each function may well measure and report on their own performance in a manner which is in conflict with how other functions are tracking their performance. Whether we like it or not, will admit it or not, most projects and production work are defined and then performed in a non-integrated manner.

Sometime in the early 1960s, a new concept called the Work Breakdown Structure (WBS) was introduced. The WBS provided an opportunity for all key functions on a given project to view the same project in a like manner and to speak with a common project language for the first time. Collectively, all functions would have the opportunity to define a given project in a similar manner, which would then relate to other functional perspectives.

With use of a WBS, key functions would be expected to define and decompose a new project into progressively smaller units, down to the work task level, at which point they would relate the technical work to be done, add the estimated resources, and set the time frame for each task. With use of the WBS, all critical functions would be required to work to an integrated project plan. Performance could then be measured at the lowest task level, allowing the project manager to ascertain how much work had been planned, how much work was accomplished, and how much money was being spent to accomplish the authorized work. The use of a WBS allowed for performance measurement to take place within an integrated baseline.

Figure 5.1 is a comparison of the two management approaches just discussed. The left side shows the more traditional functional matrix approach which has been employed in most projects and production work. Here, each of the various functions is allowed to make their own peculiar interpretation of project requirements, according to their own unique perspective. This approach allowed, and actually encouraged, projects to be implemented in a non-integrated manner.

Figure 5.1 *Earned Value requires an Integrated Project Baseline*

By contrast, the right side displays an integrated management approach, which is required for the employment of earned value management. Each function must work in concert with all other functions on the same defined work, all within the project's WBS. Multi-functional work is defined, authorized, performed, and reported within management control points, typically referred to as Control Account Plans, or CAPs. Each CAP is placed at the appropriate position within the WBS. The WBS has thus provided the mechanism for the integration of all project and production work.

3. *"Scientifically documented empirical evidence" collected from over 700 DoD contracts (projects) which have employed earned value management, demonstrating a pattern of consistent and predictable performance history.*[19]

Since the mid-1970s, the performance management practitioners within the DoD Pentagon have been empirically tracking the actual results of all contracts (projects) that have employed earned value management as a central component of the C/SCSC Criteria. They have documented their findings, analyzed the results, and hypothesized final performance patterns for contracts (projects) which employ earned value.

Their findings have been spectacular in that they have demonstrated a pattern of predictable project performance which can be used to scientifically forecast future performance results. Figure 5.2 shows the summary displays of these findings. This same summary was initially prepared by the DoD practitioners in the early 1980s, with only the number of sample projects increasing from an original base of 100 projects. Now, well over 700 projects are represented, and this figure summarizes

19 Chester Paul Beach, Jr., *"A-12 Administrative Inquiry,"* citing studies by Gaylord E. Christle, et al., Office of the Under Secretary of Defense for Acquisitions, Washington, D.C., November 28, 1990. This study at the time cited 400 projects from 1977 on, but has since been increased to 700 projects without a change in their findings.

GIVEN:

Contract more than 15% complete
1. Overrun at completion will not be less than overrun to date.
2. Percent overrun at completion will be greater than percent overrun to date.

CONCLUSION:

You can't recover!

WHO SAYS:

More than 700 major DoD contracts since 1977.

WHY:

If you underestimated the near, there is no hope that you did better on the far term planning.

Figure 5.2 *The DoD Earned Value Body of Knowledge*

the most impressive empirical findings.

The hypothesis of this summary is that as early as the 15 percent completion point in a project, the actual performance results (the earned value results) will provide an "early warning" indicator to management. Such results can be used to predict the final costs and time requirements within a finite range of values. The results of work accomplished against a given plan can be used to forecast the final project or production results. The DoD practitioners' empirical conclusions are simple: If a project has overrun the work it has accomplished to date, that initial overrun will not likely be recovered on the remaining work. In fact, they conclude, that overrun will typically get progressively worse, not better, with the passage of time.

Without attempting to explain the reasons behind these conclusions, the suggestion is that there is a natural tendency for any project team to provide its best scope definition, planning, scheduling, estimating, etc., for the near-term work. And as the project plans extend into later periods, things like scope, schedule, and budget will become progressively more vague and imperfect. Thus later performance trends will likely deteriorate as the project continues through to completion.

4. The development of a key metric called the "Cost Performance Index" CPI, reflecting that critical relationship between the physical work actually accomplished and its corresponding budget, versus the actual costs expended to accomplish such work, thus allowing management to continuously monitor the true cost performance of any project or production run.

The DoD practitioners' empirical findings: As early as the 15 to 20 percent completion point of any project, the cumulative cost performance efficiency factors (earned values versus costs) have been demonstrated to stabilize, and the data provided can be used to accurately predict a final range of costs for any given project. This index is sometimes referred to as the CPI(e), with the "e" representing the cost efficiency.

A note of caution: These same forecasting results are not possible using periodic or incremental performance data. Periodic data has been found to fluctuate widely. Periodic performance data thus have limited utility as a long-term trending tool. However, periodic data are obviously needed to continuously monitor the most immediate results on a project. In short, periodic earned value data can be used to monitor current performance status, and the cumulative data can be used for predicting the final performance results.

Individuals working at the U.S. Air Force Institute of Technology (AFIT) have been instrumental in extending the scientific knowledge begun at the Pentagon. One significant study provides us with insight into these findings:

> *Using data from a sample of completed Air Force contracts, Christensen/ Payne established that the cumulative CPI did not change by more than 10 percent from the value at the 20 percent contract completion point.*

> *Based on data from the Defense Acquisition Executive Summary (DAES) database, results indicate that the cumulative CPI is stable from the 20 percent completion point regardless of contract type, program, or service.*

> *Knowing that the cumulative CPI is important . . . the government can now conclude that a contractor is in serious trouble when it overruns the budget beyond the 20 percent completion point.*[20]

Let us reflect on the significance of these empirical findings. No longer must management wait until all the funds have been spent to conclude that additional budget will be needed in order to complete the full scope of a given project. The CPI thus represents the project manager's "early warning signal" and is perhaps the most compelling reason why any project should employ some form of earned value. No other project management technique provides these metrics.

By monitoring the cost performance against a detailed project plan, and by relating the value of the work performed against the costs of doing that work, a predictable pattern becomes available to management early in the life cycle of the project. Such patterns can be used by management to both assess the performance to date and to predict the final performance results.

---

20 Major David S. Christensen, PhD, & Captain Scott R. Heise. (1993). Cost performance index stability. *National Contract Management Association Journal, 25,* 7 and 13.

Figure 5.3 *Project performance: Watch the cumulative CPI(e)*

The CPI (based on cost efficiency) is determined by simply dividing the value of the work actually performed (the earned value) by the actual costs needed to accomplish the earned value. The use of the cumulative CPI is displayed in Figure 5.3. Perfect cost performance would be 1.00. Results of less than 1.00 performance reflect the condition typically called an "overrun" of costs.

One more point needs to be made about the utility of the cumulative CPI for universal project management. The above findings reflect data produced by major DoD acquisition projects. Major projects will often take months to establish a baseline against which performance can be measured, and thus the CPI results known.

But what about the typically smaller projects of perhaps only one year or less in duration? Such projects can easily be defined and planned with a performance measurement baseline before go-ahead is given by management. Such projects can measure performance from the start of the project. Thus, accurate CPI readings could become available as early as perhaps 5 to 10 percent into the life cycle of any project, which is a way of employing a simple form of earned value measurement.

5. The development of a metric called the "Schedule Performance Index" SPI, reflecting that important relationship between the physical work actually accomplished and the authorized baseline schedule, thus allowing management to focus on and manage their schedule time obligations to completion.

One of the more important benefits of employing a performance measurement system is the ability to determine how much of the originally scheduled work has been physically accomplished at any point in time. The fundamental issue: Is the project performing on its authorized schedule, ahead of schedule, or behind the work the team planned to do? And if there are deficiencies in the schedule performance, what is the value of such work?

Such schedule performance knowledge is particularly powerful for any project when it is compared against the project's critical path position. Both the earned value SPI and Critical Path Method (CPM) indicators when used in concert will accurately assess the true schedule position of any project.

Even though the SPI may have little (or no) relationship to the project's critical path, falling behind in accomplishing the work scheduled is one of the first indicators of potential future problems. Project managers do not like to get behind in their scheduled work, even though a more important indicator will perhaps be performance against the project's critical path.

The natural tendency when one falls behind the planned work is to add unplanned resources in an attempt to catch up— effectively doing the same work as was planned, but by spending more money to accomplish the same effort. Arbitrary decisions to catch up on the planned work, to improve the SPI performance, can cause non-recoverable damage to the project's cost performance. The SPI is a useful schedule monitoring indicator that should be used in conjunction with other scheduling techniques, particularly critical path methodology.

The SPI is determined by dividing the value of the work performed (the earned value) by the value of the work planned to be accomplished (the planned value) as of any point in time. It is a valuable indicator of schedule performance and also can be used in conjunction with the CPI to predict the final required project costs.

6. The utility of the cumulative CPI to statistically forecast the "low-end" range of final required costs at completion.

The cumulative CPI has been scientifically demonstrated to be a stable early indicator of project cost performance. Perhaps its most significant utility is the ability to use it to statistically forecast the final cost requirements for any project.

A statistical forecast of the total final required funds may be determined by simply dividing the total project Budget at Completion (BAC) by the cumulative CPI. This approach assumes that the actual cost performance results to date will likely continue to the end of the project. Many consider this to be the "best case" or a "low-end" forecast for a project within a statistical range of final cost estimates.

7. The utility of the cumulative CPI when used in conjunction with the cumulative SPI to statistically forecast the "high-end" range of final required costs at completion.

The combination of the cumulative CPI when used in conjunction with the cumulative SPI provides the ability to also statistically forecast the final cost results of a project. Some individuals with the DoD consider this technique to represent the "most likely" final forecast, while others feel it represents the "high-end" in the range of statistical possibilities. Either way, it is an important final costs indicator.

The rationale for this combination is that if a project is both behind its planned schedule position and is overrunning its initial costs, these two conditions will combine to exacerbate the final results. The use of the CPI alone, and/or the CPI with the SPI as forecasting tools will be discussed in detail in a later chapter on forecasting the final cost results. Both are specifically called out in the Fourth Edition of the *PMBOK® Guide.*[21]

8. The development of a metric called the "To-Complete Performance Index" (TCPI) to monitor the remaining effort against specific management financial goals, with such goals representing either the original authorized Budget at Completion (BAC), or the project manager's latest Estimate at Completion (EAC).

The remaining (to-complete) project work constitutes the only area where a project manager can influence the final cost results. Costs already spent or committed are effectively "sunk costs," meaning they are non-recoverable. Therefore, it is useful to any project to determine what performance factors will be needed to accomplish the remaining effort in order to achieve a specific management objective. Such management goals can be variable and can reflect the original project budget, or if actual results so dictate, can also represent an increased financial goal reflecting a more realistic and attainable objective.

The TCPI focuses on the remaining project tasks. It is effectively the mirror opposite of the cumulative CPI in that it reflects what it will take in future performance to recover from a negative actual cost position. The TCPI takes the work remaining (the total budget less the earned value accomplished) and divides that amount by the funds remaining (the latest management financial goal less funds spent) to determine what performance results it will take to meet such goals. The TCPI can be an effective indicator for management at all levels to monitor the remaining project tasks. More will be covered on this subject in a later chapter.[22]

9. The utility of a "weekly" (or a periodic) industrial engineering Cost Performance Index, or CPI(p) to monitor performance results for production, or repetitive type work.

Although the use of cumulative data has been found to work well to determine the long-term trend or direction of a project, industrial engineers monitoring production work have often used periodic or weekly data to track the cost performance achieved against an established production standard. By breaking down a total production effort into detailed sub-parts (lots or batches) and then establishing a weekly production standard (a planned value) for each part, the tracking of production effort has been successfully employed with use of what is called a Cost Performance Index-CPI(p).

Figure 5.4 *Production performance: Watch the weekly CPI(p)*

The "p" in CPI(p) refers to "performance," and the formula is the exact reverse of the more widely used CPI(e). It is determined by dividing the actual costs incurred to accomplish the earned value by the value of the physical work performed (earned value) during the measured or incremental period. Displayed in Figure 5.4 is an example of the CPI(p) plotted weekly against the established "equivalent unit costs" (EUC) for a given manufactured part, component, or assembly.

Compare the two earned value indices displayed in Figure 5.3, a project cost efficiency CPI(e), with Figure 5.4, a weekly production CPI(p) against an industrial standard. Since the CPI(p) is limited to production work, not projects, we will not discuss it further here.

> **10. The employment of a "Management by Exception" (MBE) approach, allowing busy executives to focus exclusively on only the exceptions to key earned value metrics (CPI, SPI, TCPI, EAC), thus allowing senior management to effectively control a portfolio of projects or production work within their enterprise.**

The last, and perhaps the ultimate, utility in the use of earned value performance measurement is that it allows for the employment of the Management by Exception (MBE) principles with established and authorized project or production baseline plans. Executives employing earned value need not follow each and every detailed task in order to effectively oversee the performance of all authorized work. Rather, by focusing on only those exceptions to the authorized plans in accordance with specified variance thresholds, management can effectively monitor all critical aspects of performance against their project or production plans.

○ ○ ○

These ten items represent to us the more significant findings of the body of knowledge which has resulted from over four decades in the employment of earned value management. We will use these findings as a basis to suggest a simplified form of the earned value for use with the other more established project and production management tools. We hope to describe a simple form of earned value—earned value for the masses—for use on all projects and production work, of any size, in any industry.

6

SCOPE THE PROJECT

THERE IS LIKELY no single factor which would contribute more to the success of any new project than starting off with a solid and complete definition of the work to be done, typically called the project's scope of work. Conversely, there is probably no factor which would contribute more quickly to the demise of any new project than to initiate a new effort without having a full understanding of the work to be done.

To paraphrase a saying from *Alice in Wonderland*, "If you don't care where you get to, it doesn't matter which way you go."[23] Project managers need to know where their projects are going so they know when they have arrived. Project managers also need to define the scope of work to the best of their ability.

Interestingly, the earned value technique cannot be employed on any project unless the project manager has defined the job, the total job, to the greatest extent possible. Reason: The purpose of employing the earned value technique is to monitor the physical completion of work together with management's budget for the completed work, which we call the "earned value." Such monitoring takes place from as early as possible until all the physical work has been completed. Scope creep, if allowed to happen, would negate the ability to accurately measure project performance and predict the final cost and schedule results along the way.

UNDERSTANDING THE PROJECT (KNOWING WHAT'S IN . . . AND WHAT'S OUT)

Planning a new project that employs earned value performance measurement is no different from the planning necessary to implement any project. It always helps to know what makes up the project, the whole project, and particularly the outer boundaries of the project. We can think of at least three reasons why this might be important to any project manager.

---

23 Lewis Carroll. (1960). *Alice's Adventures in Wonderland* and *Through the Looking Glass*. London: Bramhall House, p. 88.

First, you will need to know at the outset when the project will be over. You need to know when all of the work that you originally agreed to do will be considered complete, and you need to have tangible metrics for any project called "done." You also need to know when you may start work on the next project.

Second, you will need to know the difference between the agreed-to work and any new work requested of you—that is, whenever someone brings in more work for you to do than you had originally agreed to do. For example, if you agree to peel ten bushel baskets of potatoes, and someone brings in an eleventh basket, you will want to ask for some additional compensation (adjustment in the project's budget) for doing that eleventh basket. You may also need some additional time. Unless you had sufficiently defined the scope of work in the first place, you may not be able to tell the difference between basket ten, or eleven, or twelve, etc.

Third, and this is most critical to the earned value performance management concept, you will need to know how much of the entire job has been accomplished at any given point in time. The issue is fundamental: If you do not know what constitutes 100 percent of a project, how will you ever know if you are 10, 20, or 35 percent done? You must know what constitutes 100 percent of the project scope in order to tell how much of it you have performed during the life of the project. PMI's cranky "Olde Curmudgeon" wrote about this very issue a few years back:

> *Failure to define what is a part of the project, as well as what is not, may result in work being performed that was unnecessary to create the product of the project and thus lead to both schedule and budget overruns.*[24]

This isn't a new concept. In 1996, in Chapter 5 of the original *PMBOK® Guide*, the subject of scope management was addressed nicely. The opening paragraph describes well the importance of knowing what was agreed to be done and, perhaps of equal importance, knowing what was not agreed to be done, together constituting the project boundaries:

> *Project Scope Management includes the processes required to ensure that the project includes all the work required, and only the work required, to complete the project successfully. It is primarily concerned with defining and controlling what is or is not included in the project.*[25]

One of the key pillars of the earned value concept is that the project manager must know at all times what percentage of the physical work has been accomplished,

---

24 The Olde Curmudgeon (Dr. Francis M. Webster). (1994, December). PM 101, in *PM Network®*. Upper Darby, PA: Project Management Institute.
25 *PMBOK Guide®* (1996), p. 47.

or the percent complete, as it relates to the total job. This information is needed in order to compare the physical work done against the actual costs spent to perform that work in the same period being measured. The relationship between the total physical work accomplished and the total dollars spent provides the answer to the question: *What did we get for the money we spent?* For example, if you spent 30 percent of the project's total budget but had accomplished only 25 percent of the total project's physical work, what do you call this condition? Answer: *a 20% overrun!*

Using a Work Breakdown Structure (WBS) to Scope the Project

Starting sometime in the early 1960s, a school of thought developed which centered on the belief that project managers needed a new device, a tool similar in utility to the company organizational chart. For years, corporate executives have been using their organizational charts to conceptually define in graphical form: (1) who does what in the company, (2) who is responsible for what, and (3) who reports to whom within their organization.

This notion that project managers needed a special tool led to the introduction of the Work Breakdown Structure (WBS) concept. The WBS is to the project manager what the organizational chart is to the company executive. It is a tool used by the project manager to define a project and give it cohesiveness so that it can be managed as a unique one-time effort, a transient unit of work passing through the firm's permanent organization. At any point in time a given company will have many projects in progress, each competing for limited company resources. The WBS is the device that integrates the project effort and sets one project apart from all other projects within the same organization.

An important point often missed by some is that, although the WBS looks like an organizational chart, it definitely is _not_ an organizational chart. Unfortunately, some people get confused about this issue and draw a project organizational chart which they then incorrectly label as their WBS. The project WBS represents the project work to be done, the deliverable products, both tangible and intellectual, rather than the project's organization chart. However, it can be used to first define the work and then to assign responsibility for conducting the work.

An important point to remember is that a company's internal reorganization should never change a project's WBS. A reorganization may well change who actually performs the specified project work, but it should not change the project's unique WBS.

An example of a typical project WBS is shown in Figure 6.1, which is a diagram of a U.S. Department of Energy (DOE) project. Note that this is a "product" oriented

Figure 6.1 *WBS for an energy project*

hierarchy that progressively breaks out the work elements downward from the top WBS box, called WBS Level 1.0.

The owner of a project will sometimes specify the top three levels of the "Project WBS" to define the desired reporting requirements. Then the performing project manager will extend the "Contract WBS" down to lower levels to assist in the management of the project by integrating the technical work, costs, and schedule. A key point is that the WBS must reflect how the project manager plans to manage the project. Much initial thought must be given to the WBS by both the owner/management and the performing project manager. The WBS should be owned by the sponsor and the project manager, although all functions will have a vested interest in it.

The emphasis for the WBS must be on the project, the project tasks, and the unique work to be done to accomplish the project objectives, including the specification of the project deliverables. Some of the key words that should be a part of any viable WBS definition are: *project end-items, project deliverables, project tasks* and *project sub-tasks.*

One of the best definitions of the WBS was published in 1976, when its author described what he then called a Project Breakdown Structure (PBS). In retrospect, PBS is perhaps a more descriptive name than WBS. However, WBS stuck, and the earlier name of PBS did not:

> *The PBS is a graphic portrayal of the project, exploding it in a level-by-level fashion, down to the degree of detail needed for effective planning and control. It must include all deliverable end items ... and include the major functional tasks that must be performed.*[26]

The PBS would appear to have its primary focus on the product, whereas the WBS often has its focus on the project's work tasks. Since the *PMBOK Guide®* and most of the project managers of the world use the term WBS, we will do likewise.

From its first edition in 1996, the *PMBOK® Guide* has always provided us with a solid definition of a WBS. However, in the third edition, issued in 2004, it gives us a

---

26 Russell D. Archibald. (1976). *Managing High-Technology Programs and Projects.* New York: John Wiley & Sons, p. 141.

modified definition of the WBS which (to the authors) is the most complete one we have seen thus far. The WBS is now defined as:

> ***A deliverable-oriented hierarchical decomposition of the work to be executed by the project team to accomplish the project objectives and create the required deliverables. It organizes and defines the total scope of the project.*** [27]

The project team is essentially forced to define its necessary work tasks into progressively greater detail with use of a WBS, including making the important make or buy choices.

The WBS in total will define what is to be performed inside and what is outside of any given project. Returning once again to the wisdom of PMI's cranky Olde Curmudgeon:

> ***A project consists of the sum total of all the elements of the WBS. Conversely, an element that is not contained in the WBS is not a part of the project. Any work that cannot be identified in the WBS requires authorization to proceed, either as a recognized omission or as an approved change order.*** [28]

At the lowest WBS element, a project manager will want to expand the brief task titles into a descriptive narrative that can then evolve into what is referred to as the "WBS dictionary." The WBS dictionary in total will typically comprise the project's technical statement of work. It may also be used to relate the defined work tasks directly to a specific organization responsible for performing the actual work. This summary is often referred to as a project's Responsibility Assignment Matrix (RAM). The project's contractual specialists will also have use for the WBS dictionary to serve as the basis for creating the contractual Statement of Work (SOW) between the owner/customer and the project manager.

A WBS CAN HELP MANAGE PROJECT SCOPE CREEP.

One of the most challenging projects ever was the World War 2 "Manhattan Project" to develop the first atomic bomb. The Allies had to develop this weapon first, ahead of the enemy Axis, or face the distinct possibility of losing the war. The hero for this

---

[27] *PMBOK® Guide — Fourth Edition*, 2008, Glossary.
[28] The Olde Curmudgeon (Dr. Francis M. Webster). (1994, December). PM 101, in *PM Network®*. Upper Darby, PA: Project Management Institute.

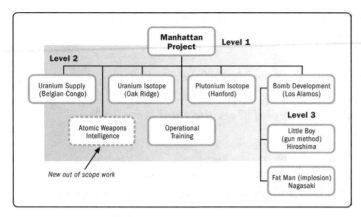

Figure 6.2 *The WBS Dictionary becomes a project Statement of Work*

effort was a project manager by the name of General Leslie R. Groves. His overall mission was to define and then organize this massive, never-been-done-before project undertaking.

Realistically, the Manhattan Project took place some two decades before the project management community was first introduced to the WBS concept. Thus, that concept, in place today to help define new projects, has given contemporary project managers an advantage over General Groves. However, it is likely that the general followed the same processes, though they were not called a WBS then.

Figure 6.2 illustrates an imaginary WBS for the Manhattan Project. Level 1 of the WBS always represents the total project. Next, Level 2 must reflect the principle subdivision of the total effort: obtaining uranium ore from Africa, developing two types of isotopes, developing the actual bombs, and, finally, training the flight crews to use this new weapon. The WBS provides an excellent vehicle for achieving a complete definition of project scope. And when a narrative description is added to each WBS element, the WBS dictionary in essence becomes the project's official Statement of Work (SOW).

But WBS also provides an excellent vehicle for defining the outer limits of one's commitment to a project. This can also be called managing project scope creep. Note in Figure 6.2 the WBS element to the left with the arrow and the notation "New out of scope work." About one year after General Groves was first designated project manager for the Manhattan Project, he was given additional work responsibilities: that of managing Atomic Weapons Intelligence. This new effort made him responsible for not only developing the new weapon system, but also determining how far along the enemy Axis was in developing its own atomic bomb. The intelligence-gathering function was clearly new work for the Manhattan Project.

Realistically, in the case of the Manhattan Project the effort was so critical to the war effort that the addition of new work likely did not matter. General Groves essentially had a carte blanche, an unlimited budget. But most projects today operate under a finite amount of funds, and the use of a WBS can help any project manager maintain the delicate relationship between authorized work and appropriate funding.

By starting out with a complete project definition in the form of a WBS, and with a buy-in to the WBS by all key functional organizations, any project manager will have better assurances that the work being done will represent what his or her customer and or management desires to be done. And if the customer or senior management should ask for more work or changes the work, as they often must do, the use of the WBS to define project scope will help the project manager make the case for more budget, more time, etc.

SOME SPECIFIC EXAMPLES OF WBS FORMATS

Perhaps the best way to illustrate the utility of the WBS is to review some specific examples. Shown earlier in Figure 6.1 was a WBS for an energy project. This illustrated a product type breakout exploding the project from the top down into progressively smaller units.

By way of contrast, Figure 6.3 illustrates another energy project, but this time for a construction job. In this case the WBS reflects the critical phases of the construction effort and the manner in which the project manager plans to implement that effort.

The design work will sometimes be sent to an outside company, as indicated in the box at the top left, designated *Design 1.1*. The project team will procure the high value and or common materials to achieve a cost savings, as indicated in the box designated *Procurement 1.2*. The actual construction effort will be contracted with still another firm, as reflected in box *Construction 1.3*. In this case the WBS reflects how the major project segments will be managed at Level 2: *design, procurement, and construction.* This is a fairly typical WBS for a construction job.

Figure 6.3 is a chart from the DOE *Project Control System (PCS)*, and a key point is contained in the quote from their PCS Manual which is shown at the bottom left of Figure 6.3: *The WBS always reflects the way a project has been planned, cost estimated and will be managed.* The message here is that the WBS must be owned by the

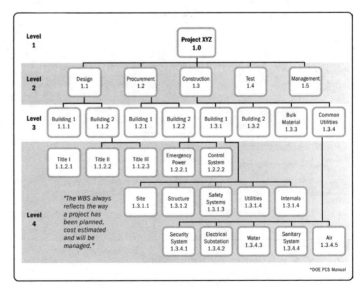

Figure 6.3 *WBS for an energy construction project*

project manager and the project management team and reflect the way they plan to perform the effort. The WBS should not be the property of any single function, although all functions working on the project should have a say in its formation and buy into the final WBS.

Sometimes we see the finance and contracts organizations trying to take control of the project WBS, particularly when there are different sources of funding for the project (federal, state, local, private, etc.). However, funding sources should never influence the composition of the WBS, and it must ultimately be the exclusive property of the project manager, used to define the project scope of work.

Continuing with specific examples of WBS, the DoD took the lead in the mid-1960s in defining a WBS standard for their industry. This was both good and, frankly, bad for project management. The DoD's WBS document was then called Military Standard 881 (MIL-STD-881), and it described in very specific detail the format in which the WBS was to be used. MIL-STD-881 defined seven specific systems to be managed: aircraft, electronics, missiles, ordnances, ships, spacecraft, and surface vehicles. Interestingly, at least three of our more prominent project challenges (or opportunities) today are missing from this listing of seven systems: construction projects, environmental cleanup projects, and computer software projects.[29]

Figure 6.4 shows an example of just one of the seven specific DoD WBS formats, this one covering an aircraft system. Level 2 of any WBS is most critical, because at this level the project manager will usually indicate the approach planned to manage the project. With MIL-STD-881, the particular system would be displayed to the extreme left of Level 2, and then a series of common elements would be listed going from left to right. MIL-STD-881 was very specific in defining the remainder of the authorized elements allowed at WBS Level 2: systems engineering and program management, systems test and evaluation, training, data, peculiar support equipment, common support equipment, operational site activation, industrial facilities, and spares/repair parts.

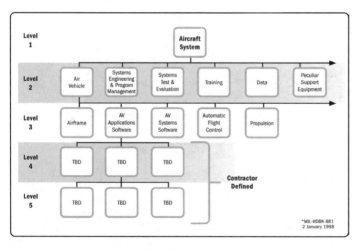

Figure 6.4 *WBS for an aircraft system*

---

29 As we are updating this book the DoD is revising its MIL-STD 881 again for release later this year or next. This will be a major event for the project management community in the military to follow.

There was nothing unreasonable or anti-project management contained in these nine common elements as precisely specified in the DoD's MIL-STD-881. However, project managers are unique individuals who do not take kindly to being told by anyone how they must define or manage their projects. Considerable friction surfaced over the years between the project managers and the U.S. Government buyers when the project managers were told that they must structure their project WBS to conform to the specific breakouts contained in this military standard. The DoD's rigid standard WBS encroached on the creative territory of project managers, and they often resented this intrusion.

We are fortunate now to have the use of relational databases and project management software coding sufficient to make these earlier WBS problems somewhat a non-issue today. The principles that should guide us are that: (1) the WBS always belongs to the project manager, and (2) the WBS should represent the way the project manager plans to manage the project, period.

Illustrated in Figure 6.5 is a simple WBS to build a house. Shown at the left on Level 2 are three critical elements of work which will precede the actual physical construction of the house: *design plans*, a *building permit*, and a *loan*. After these critical items are secured, the project manager will divide the project into three distinct categories to manage as shown next at Level 2 of the WBS: *grounds*, *structure*, and *subsystems*. All other categories of the project will be lumped into the general category to the extreme right, called *project management*.

Another WBS example is shown in Figure 6.6, this one for a transportation vehicle. Although this might be a commercial venture, the WBS as displayed is consistent with

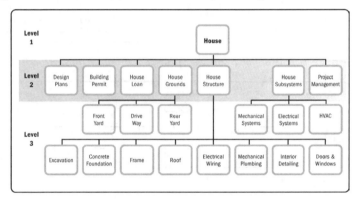

Figure 6.5 *WBS to build a house*

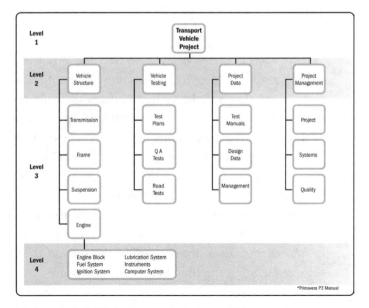

Figure 6.6 *WBS for a transportation vehicle*

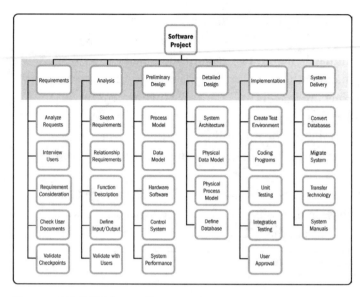

Figure 6.7 *WBS for a software project*

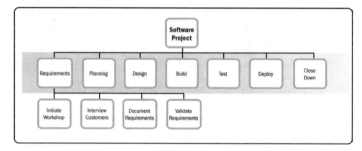

Figure 6.8 *WBS for a software project*

the DoD WBS standard, in that Level 2 breaks out: *vehicle structure, vehicle testing, project data,* and an all-other category called *project management.*

The last three illustrations of WBSs are shown in Figures 6.7, 6.8, and 6.9 and represent examples of software projects. Software projects are gaining in importance and would appear to represent a new challenge for project management. As of this writing, there appears to be no universal agreement as to what might constitute an acceptable WBS format for software projects.

ISSUE: MAKE OR BUY CHOICES: A CRITICAL PART OF SCOPE DEFINITION

One last point must be made about using a WBS to define a new project. The WBS must reflect the way the project management team intends to manage the project, which should include the project manager's make or buy decisions. Final make or buy choices typically come after the project has been initially defined, and they are an integral part of the project definition process. Stated another way, project scope definition is incomplete until the determination has been made as to who will be performing the effort: one's own organization (company make), or procured (bought) from another company.

It does make a difference. Procured project scope creates a legal relationship which if not managed correctly can lead to energy-absorbing claim demands, negotiations, and the claims settlement process. The procurement of project scope is a subject of critical importance to the project manager. Make or buy choices should be reflected in the final WBS for a given project.

The WBS at Level 2 often reflects the most critical part of the scope definition process. Shown in Figure 6.10 is an illustration of a WBS for a single construction project, but with three distinct management approaches. Each approach needs to be understood because it illustrates the project manager's make or buy choices and hence the way the project will be managed.

To the left side of Figure 6.10 in section [-A-] is displayed one approach reflecting the project manager's make or buy choices. Under approach [-A-] the design effort will be procured from an external company. The common and or high-value materials will be purchased by the internal project team, perhaps to achieve a price advantage by the pooling of requirements from multiple projects. Finally, the construction effort will be separately contracted to another firm. This display is similar in approach to the WBS for the energy construction project shown earlier in Figure 6.3. For purposes of simplicity, other important project work (final site check-out and project management, for example) is not displayed in the Figure 6.10 WBS.,

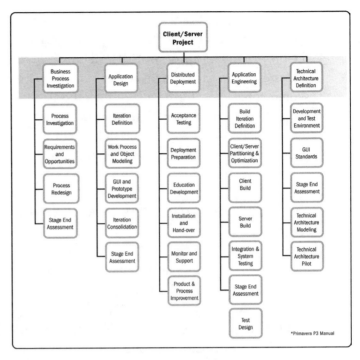

Figure 6.9 *WBS for a client/server software project*

Figure 6.10 *WBS Level 2 reflects how the project will be managed*

Shown in the center section, [-B-], of Figure 6.10 is a second approach in which the major project effort is divided into only two major parts: the design effort and a construction effort, both of which will be procured. In this case, the construction contract will include the purchase of all materials.

The third approach is shown to the right, in section [-C-], in which case a single design-build contractor will be selected to perform the total design, procurement and construction job on behalf of the owner.

The point of this discussion is that the WBS is a critical tool for the project manager's use in the initial definition of the project, and then in describing to everyone how the project will be implemented, including reflecting the make or buy determinations. All functions must have a say in the formation of the project WBS and, once approved, should conform to the format of the official WBS. This is vital in order to achieve an integrated project management approach and to measure project performance during the full life of the project. While all levels of the project WBS are important, Level 2 in particular will typically describe the project management approach being implemented.

THE WBS PROVIDES THE FRAMEWORK FOR EARNED VALUE MANAGEMENT.

From the beginning, the WBS has always been an integral part of the earned value concept. A hierarchical structure defining the project is required in order to integrate the various functions into a common project mission and then to relate the requirements of the project to the company's permanent organizational units.

When the earned value concept was first introduced to industry as a part of the Cost/Schedule Control Systems Criteria in 1967, the DoD mandated 35 management control system standards, or criteria, which had to be met by any firm wanting to contract for a new major government acquisition. Interestingly, the very first of these 35 criteria addressed the issue of defining the project with use of a WBS. This 1967 criterion read:

> **Define all authorized work and related resources to meet the requirements of the contract, using the framework of the contract work breakdown structure (WBS).**[30]

In practice, under cost reimbursable type contracting, the owner of the project would typically define the first two or three levels of the WBS, representing the way performance was to be monitored and reported during the life of the project. Typically the project manager and the team would then define the lower levels of the project, extending the WBS to represent the way the work was to be performed. Under fixed price or lump sum contracting, where the cost growth risks rest totally on the project manager, the project management team will define all levels of the WBS, representing how they intend to implement and manage their project.

Management control points are defined at the appropriate level of each WBS element. These control points initially went by the term "cost account" but are now called a "control account." Different name, same concept. The "control

---

30 U.S. Department of Defense. (1967, December 22). *Performance Measurement for Selected Acquisitions* (Instruction DoD 7000.2). Washington, D.C.

account" is a critical point in the WBS where performance measurement must take place. The control account is also where the integration of scope, schedule, and resources (budget) happens, and where the project will measure its performance throughout the duration of the project. The control account is thus the fundamental building block for earned value performance measurement. It was defined some three decades ago as:

> ***A management control point at which actual costs may be accumulated and compared to the budgeted cost of work performed . . . a natural control point for cost/schedule planning and control, since it represents the work assigned to one responsible organizational element on one contract work breakdown structure (CWBS) element.***[31]

Initially, the control account was defined as the intersection point of a *single* WBS element with a *single* organizational unit. More recently, with the increasing popularity of integrated multi-functional project teams, the requirement for a single organizational unit has been expanded to represent multi-functional teams. Additionally, while the scheduling of activities may continue to take place deep within detailed WBS elements, the use of multi-functional project teams has resulted in larger segments of defined work being done within control accounts, at higher levels of the project WBS.

Thus, under the multi-functional project team approach, project management will monitor the performance of less management control points—a more logical approach, and one which has led to a reduction of some 90 percent in the total number of management points. This is a most positive move.

PROJECTS SHOULD USE A WORK BREAKDOWN STRUCTURE (WBS).

One last issue needs to be carefully emphasized. There is sometimes an organizational conflict between the best interests of the projects and the best interests (or parochial objectives) of the functions who supply the resources to the projects. Because the functions will frequently support multiple projects at the same time, they may well have other priorities that compete or conflict with the requirements of any given project. Functions typically support multiple projects and employ a matrix form of organization. Individual functions often do not appreciate the importance (to them) of operating within the confines of the project WBS, perhaps even requiring that they relax their functional perspective.

---

31 Ibid.

For example, the cost estimating function will typically have its historical cost data available in great detail, but will likely be collected and formatted along company functional organizational lines. Unless specifically directed by senior management, these functions may not see the utility (to them) of structuring such data simply to match a given WBS for a single project.

Often the scheduling function will find a project WBS environment too confining. Scheduling is a critical project function, and the people who perform this important role are unique individuals who will often perform their creative work best without restrictions of any sort. However, unless this critical function operates within the overall envelope of the project WBS, the opportunity for the project to integrate its work scope with the costs and schedules will be lost.

From an enterprise standpoint, only if all key project functions perform their work within the framework of the agreed-to project WBS, and most particularly the contracting, scheduling, estimating, and budgeting functions, will the project be in a position to adequately integrate its functional work and maximize project performance. Since many (perhaps most) organizations often consist of the sum of their individual projects, the successful performance of each project should be of major consequence to the firm, overshadowing the parochial interests of individual functions. The WBS, if properly defined at the outset, can constitute the mechanism to negotiate functional resources, to set project priorities, and then to measure performance in an integrated fashion throughout the full life cycle of a project.

One final point. We have been attempting to make the case for the use of a WBS for two important purposes: (1) to define all project work down to detailed discrete tasks that can be individually managed, and (2) to integrate the various functional efforts into a common project framework. We can think of no better vehicle to accomplish this objective than the use of a WBS. However, it would be misleading to suggest that the WBS must be used, or that it is the only vehicle to accomplish these goals. We know of projects that have been successfully performed through the employment of the earned value concept and have not used a WBS. But they have substituted another vehicle for the WBS.

A company's organizational structure, if it is stable for the full project duration, may sometimes be used as a WBS substitute to integrate scope, schedule, and costs. The construction industry, which typically employs a simple form of earned value but does not call it as such, often uses construction historical standards, the Construction Specifications Institute (CSI) Codes, or other hierarchical standards as a method to integrate project tasks. Bottom line: The WBS seems to work best, but other hierarchical structures may on occasion be used as a substitute for the WBS. However, our recommendation is that all projects use the WBS to define, and then implement and control their work.

In Summary

We have been making the case for defining the total project effort before starting to perform the work. Reaching an agreement between the owner and contractor, between the buyer and seller, between the project and the functions, on what constitutes the project scope is important to the success of any project. It is also critical to the employment of the earned value concept.

All this discussion reminds us of a remark made by a person who worked in project management. When asked if the projects at his site ever overrun their costs, he immediately replied:

> **We never overrun our project costs . . . all unfinished work gets moved into next year's projects.**[32]

Think about this remark for a minute. If one is given a budget to do a certain amount of work, then spends all of the money but only completes part of the work, and then moves the unfinished work into next year's projects, what do you call this condition? Answer: *an overrun!*

Scope management is vital to the effective management of any project. Understanding the scope of a project is perhaps of even greater importance when earned value is employed, because project performance must be measured throughout the life of the project, from implementation until project closeout.

Scope management is likely a project manager's greatest challenge, and it is also fundamental to the employment of the earned value management concept. Unless the full scope is properly defined and then managed throughout the life of a project, the ability to meet the objectives of projects will be severely compromised.[33]

---

32 Anonymous quote.
33 An important reference when developing a project WBS is the Project Management Institute's Global Standard, *Practice Standard for Work Breakdown Structures*, Second Edition, published by PMI in 2006.

7

PLAN AND SCHEDULE THE PROJECT

IN ITS MOST FUNDAMENTAL FORM, employing the earned value concept requires nothing more than managing a project with a good schedule—a schedule which represents the defined scope and has the authorized budget embedded task by task into it. Earned value is thus managing projects with a resource-loaded schedule. Not a difficult concept.

Management will then focus on the authorized work which has been completed, and measure performance by crediting management's official budget for the completed work. But earned value does require a defined and measurable baseline made up of all the authorized work, tightly controlled for the duration of the project. After adequately defining the scope of the project, the next critical steps are to plan and then to schedule the work. Fundamental stuff.

UNDERSTANDING THE PROJECT

Previously, we emphasized the importance of completely defining the full scope of any new project and suggested that this effort is best accomplished using a generally accepted technique called the Work Breakdown Structure (WBS). We recommended that the full project management team collectively define what work it needs to perform, including specifying the outer limits of the project's commitment. The WBS is a vehicle that allows for the progressive detailing of project tasks and for the integration of such tasks with various organizational functions, in particular the technical, contracts, estimating, budgeting, and scheduling functions, as well as those line functions which will be performing the defined work.

We refer to the WBS as a generally accepted technique because, while some industries have enthusiastically embraced the WBS as a project management tool, other industries have not. The construction industry, as an example, frequently relies on other methods to define its projects. Perhaps most notable is the use of the Construction Specifications Institute (CSI) standard codes in lieu of using a WBS. Some construction projects use both.

Of equal importance is the fact that, by having a clear understanding of what scope of work the project manager has committed to do, he or she has also effectively defined what work has not been agreed to. Project managers must be cognizant of the full scope (and the outer boundaries) of the projects they set out to accomplish. They must be able to discern when the project effort has been completed, and know precisely when out-of-scope tasks are being requested. There is nothing wrong with doing out-of-scope work, as long as one gets paid extra for doing the added tasks. This is called managing "scope creep," and such creep must be quickly identified in order to avoid cost and schedule problems.

Once we have an understanding of what we are going to do and the project has been defined, it is time to take the next logical step in the process of implementing a new project that employs the earned value concept: we must formulate a detailed plan, and then schedule all the specified project tasks. The process of planning for any new project is no different with earned value. A detailed, bottom-up plan is always required.

PLANNING THE PROJECT

Perhaps a good way to start a discussion on project planning is to borrow a quote from Rudyard Kipling, a man who knew nothing about project management . . . or did he? A century ago, this Englishman who was born in India gave us these profound words, which define nicely the key processes of project planning:

> *I keep six honest serving men (they taught me all I knew); their names are WHAT and WHY and WHEN and HOW and WHERE and WHO.*

Any project manager who could enlist the services of these six honest serving men would be well on the way to defining a viable project plan.

Just what is the project planning process? Well, it all depends on whom you ask. One of the best descriptions of this process was given to us three decades ago by a founding PMI member assigned the membership number of 007, a PMI Fellow, and a certified PMI Project Management Professional (PMP)®. We can think of no better description of project planning than that provided by this expert in his book. He defined the project planning as requiring ten iterative steps:

1. Define the project scope and identify specific tasks with use of a WBS.
2. Assign responsibility for performance of each of the specific tasks.
3. Identify the interfaces between tasks.
4. Identify the key project milestones.

5. Prepare the master schedule.
6. Prepare the top budget.
7. Prepare detail task schedules.
8. Prepare detail task budgets.
9. Integrate task schedules and budgets with the project master schedule and top budget.
10. Set up the project files.[34]

Now what does all this mean? Well, to us it suggests, first, that project planning is an iterative process. It will continuously evolve. Planning becomes progressively more definitive with each completed cycle. Each iteration serves to reinforce the viability of the overall plan. The process works best when the full project team gets involved, including, if possible, the project's owner or buying customer, or perhaps senior management. Customer involvement not only brings out good ideas, but also leads to a customer buy-in or approval of the resulting plan. The final project plan should identify by name specific individuals who will be held accountable for the performance of each of the specified project tasks.

We particularly like the inclusion of the last item, the setting up of project files. All too often this work is considered to be mundane, and it is often overlooked . . . until the supplier claims show up and a team of people must then set out to sift through a multitude of old project documents in an attempt to make some order out of the chaos. Better to start accumulating these critical files early and maintaining them throughout the full life cycle of the project.

The one additional step we would like to add to the above listing of project planning tasks is that of project "risk management." Risk identification, risk assessment, and risk mitigation planning are of vital importance to completing the project planning process, and to the ultimate success of any project.

The risk management process will typically begin with an identification and assessment of the potential risks as envisioned by the project team. They will focus on the known and anticipated risks for the project. Teams will often use the framework of the WBS to display and conduct their initial risk assessment. After the project risks have been identified, they are then normally subjectively quantified as to the likelihood (and the probability) of the risk actually happening, and to the impact (the consequences) to the project should such risks materialize.

A risk mitigation plan will begin to take form, often not necessarily eliminating such risks altogether, but hopefully reducing them to acceptable levels. Risk mitigation planning will often impact the planned allocation of project resources and sometimes requires adding (redundant) tasks to the project. Added resources, task

34 Russell D. Archibald. (1976). *Managing High-Technology Programs and Projects.* New York: John Wiley & Sons, p. 141.

redundancy, and what-if analysis will typically help to bring the project risks down to acceptable levels. Admittedly, we have tried to describe a rather simple form of risk management. Some more complicated projects will want to employ more sophisticated approaches to the management of their risks, perhaps using the various software tools available to them.

Additionally, it should be mentioned that the project managers of today have available to them the finest array of software tools to help perform these critical tasks. These state-of-the-art tools allow them to quickly plan their new projects, lay out the expected tasks, show the task interrelationships and constraints, expose potential risks, and model various "what-if" scenarios. There are numerous planning, scheduling, and critical path method (CPM) software packages available to the general public. The project CPM network serves to reinforce the viability of any new project plan, and if reflected in a formal project master schedule (PMS), it will provide assurances that the project will accomplish the project plan to the satisfaction of all vested parties.

Scheduling an Earned Value Project

There is probably no single issue which has greater universal acceptance with project managers than the need for and the benefits to be gained from formally scheduling every project. All projects need a schedule for the reflection and implementation of project plans. Larger projects may have multiple schedules requiring a formal scheduling system. But even the smallest of projects need at least a one-page project master schedule (PMS) to guide them.

The project schedule is likely the best tool available for managing the day to day communications on any project. And further, one of the best ways to control a project plan is to monitor performance regularly with the use of a formal scheduling routine.

In 1967, when the U.S. Department of Defense (DoD) initially released their 35 C/SCSC criteria, thus formally implementing earned value, three of these criteria specifically dealt with the requirement to employ a formal scheduling system. Earned value thus relies on the project schedule to provide a framework for allocating the authorized resources—that is, the authorized budgets.

The original 1967 DoD earned value criteria were rewritten by private industry in 1996, but identical requirements for a formal scheduling system were maintained in three of the criteria, as the following quotes:

6. Schedule the authorized work in a manner which describes the sequence of work and identifies the significant task interdependencies required to meet the requirements of the program.

7. Identify physical products, milestones, technical performance goals, or other indicators that will be used to measure progress.

23. Identify, at least monthly, the significant differences between both planned and actual schedule performance and planned and actual cost performance, and provide the reasons for the variances in the detail needed by program management.[35]

Question: Are these three criteria unique to the management of earned value projects only? Answer: absolutely not. These three criteria lay down fundamental scheduling principles which would apply to any project, in any industry, anywhere in the world. It is also interesting to note that these same three criteria were incorporated verbatim into the ANSI/EIA-748 industry standard which applies to the private sector in general.[36]

Since the earned value criteria were initially released, there have been several interpretations of what may be required from projects in order for them to comply with these three scheduling criteria. The requirements for a formal scheduling process specified in these criteria can generally be reduced to meeting the three obligations conceptually displayed in Figure 7.1.

First, all earned value projects must have at a minimum a single top-level summary schedule which completely defines the broad parameters of the project. These schedules typically go by the title of "master schedule" or "project master schedule." They will be the exclusive property of the project manager and issued under the direction of that individual.

All master schedules must be controlled documents which are formally issued to all key functions, individuals and suppliers supporting the project. Important note: All the task completion dates as specified on a project master

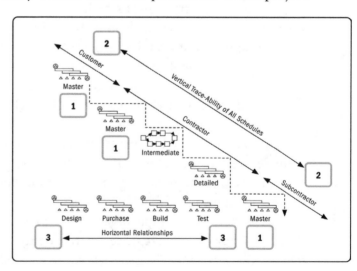

Figure 7.1 *Earned Value requires a "scheduling system"*

35 U.S. Department of Defense. (1996, December 14). *Earned Value Management Implementation Guide.* Washington, D.C.

36 American National Standards Institute/Electronic Industries Alliance. (1998, May 19). ANSI/EIA-748-1998, *Earned Value Management Systems.* Arlington, VA.

schedule must be respected, and such end dates cannot be altered by anyone other than the project manager. If individual functions or suppliers run late with respect to the specified master schedule dates, such late conditions will not change the required dates contained in the master schedule. While it may be necessary to be late in meeting master schedule dates, it is unacceptable to ignore (or reposition) the specified dates in a master schedule.

On a smaller project there may only be a single one-page master schedule needed. But as projects increase in size and complexity, with the possible involvement of the customer, contractor, and multiple subcontractors, the necessity of having a top controlled schedule to specify the outer time parameters is of critical importance. The requirement for having a master schedule is displayed as items [1] in Figure 7.1, reflecting a master schedule from the buying customer, the performing contractor, and the subordinate subcontractors. All master schedule dates for a given project must be in concert with each other. Any lower-tier intermediate and or detailed functional schedules would by definition be subordinate to the project manager's master schedule.

The second requirement for scheduling earned value projects is that the tasks or milestones described in all subordinate schedules must be in concert with the specific requirements contained in the project master schedule. All of the tasks and events depicted on lower-level project schedules must be relatable to the project master schedule, that is, there must be what is called "vertical" trace-ability [2], going from the lower detailed schedules up to the requirements defined in the top schedule. It may be acceptable to be behind relative to the requirements of the top schedule. However, it would be unacceptable to not know one's position as it relates to the requirements of the project master schedule. The project manager's master schedule must be supreme, and it must be followed on any project.

Vertical trace-ability simply means that all individuals working on a given project must know when the project manager requires their particular task(s) to be completed and deliverables made, consistent with the project master schedule. For example, on a construction type job all project schedules must support the same substantial completion date. On an aircraft development project all schedules must support the same first flight date, and so forth.

When there are multiple organizational levels involved on any given project, as shown in Figure 7.1, where three separate entities are displayed (the customer, contractor, subcontractor), the issue of vertical traceability becomes critical. For example, the buying customer will specify their requirements in the form of a master schedule, which is typically incorporated as an exhibit into the prime contractual document. Then the performing contractor's master schedule must be issued consistent with the requirements of the customer's master schedule. Further, all subordinate subcontractor schedules must likewise be in concert with the requirements contained in the highest level master schedules. This concept is displayed as item [2] in Figure 7.1.

On projects of major size or complexity, where multiple sites and companies are frequently involved, project managers have gravitated to a more formally controlled scheduling process out of necessity. On such major projects, they will frequently employ some type of a scheduling hierarchy document to pull together the various schedules.

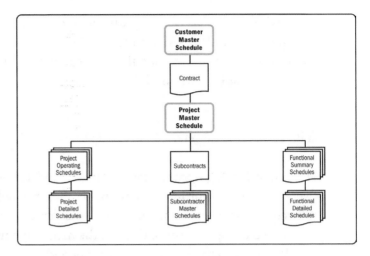

Figure 7.2 *A "Schedule Tree" vertically integrates schedules*

Shown in Figure 7.2 is what is called a project "scheduling tree," which is used to vertically link and integrate all project schedules. Each subordinate schedule represents a subproject to the master schedule and, ideally, major project milestones can be linked within each of the respective subordinate schedules.

Figure 7.2 reflects the hierarchy of the buying customer, the prime contractor, and the various subcontractors. It also displays the project's peculiar schedules (e.g., test articles) on the left side and the functional organizational (e.g., engineering, procurement) schedules on the right side. The functional schedules for the various departments (engineering, for example) will also contain the tasks necessary to support each project. The various subcontractor schedules are listed in the center. These schedules will also help to prevent an over-commitment of scarce resources.

The third [3] and final requirement of scheduling in an earned value project environment is that there be "horizontal" relationships identified between all dependent project tasks. Simply put, as shown in the lower left-hand corner of Figure 7.1, the design must be available before materials can be purchased, and the materials must be available before the project deliverables can be built, tested, etc. Relationships and constraints between project tasks must be identified. Most call this requirement critical path methodology (CPM).

Interestingly, the creators of the original C/SCSC requirements and the more recent industry Earned Value Management (EVM) System rewrite have carefully avoided imposing any requirements for employing a specific scheduling methodology. Rather, they have taken the approach of merely specifying broad general requirements. Most particularly, they avoided requiring the use of the Critical Path Method (CPM). And yet, we know of no other way to adequately isolate the "horizontal" task relationships and constraints, particularly on a complex project, other than with the use of critical path method scheduling. It is interesting to note that two more recent U.S. Government initiatives of the early 1990s (to be covered next) were very specific in defining their scheduling requirements. They both required the use of Critical Path Methodology (CPM).

GOVERNMENT MANDATES REQUIRING CPM

Two (non-DoD) governmental initiatives mandated several years after the initial criteria were released are worthy of mention, because they both imposed rather specific schedule requirements on the private sector when employing the earned value concept. Both required the employment of CPM in the management of earned value projects.

When the U.S. Department of Energy (DOE) first issued its Project Control System (PCS) guidelines document in 1992, they specifically required CPM scheduling as a required technique to be employed on all DOE funded projects. Also, CPM networks were required to be an integral tool in the management of all DOE projects. This same policy was restated in the year 2000, with the acquisition of DOE capital assets:

> The Department of Energy (DOE) prime contractor's project management system must satisfy the following requirements:

> 1. The industry standard for project control systems described in American National Standards Institute (ANSI) EIA-748, Earned Value Management Systems, must be implemented on all projects with a total project cost (TPC) greater than $20M for control of project performance during the project execution phase.
> 5. A critical path schedule and a project master schedule must be developed and maintained.[37]

Thus on projects in excess of $20 million (Total Project Cost), the DOE required both EVM and CPM.

Also of note, when the Government of Canada first released its new earned value management control system guidelines in 1993 for private industry to follow, they required the use of CPM scheduling. The Canadian EVM project guidelines were patterned after the U.S. DoD C/SCSC, but specifically required that EVM be used in conjunction with CPM network scheduling.[38]

---

37 U.S. Department of Energy. (2000, October 13). Order, DOE O 413.3, *Project Management for the Acquisition of Capital Assets.*

38 Canadian General Standards Board: 1993 "Policy 187-GP-1" (August) *Cost/Schedule Performance Management Standard.*

While the initial DoD 1967 earned value criteria remained silent about which scheduling methodologies had to be employed, these two more recent mandates for governmental project management specifically called out the use of CPM as a required scheduling technique.

EARNED VALUE PROJECT MANAGEMENT REQUIRES A SCHEDULING SYSTEM.

Two absolute rules for the implementation of any form of earned value project management have been discussed so far. First, you must define what it is you are about to do; that is, you must scope the entire project to the best of your ability. The second requirement deals with the placement of the defined scope into a fixed time-frame so that time performance can be measured throughout the life of the project. Some might suggest that these two rules are not unique to earned value project management, and that they are fundamental to all good project management, period. We would agree completely with this assertion. Earned value simply requires that fundamental project management principles be employed. Just how important, though, is scheduling to the management of earned value applications? We need to understand this issue in order to put earned value implementation on a proper footing.

In 1967, some four months prior to the formal release of the DoD's earned value C/SCSC, an industrial engineer with the U.S. Air Force, and one of the early architects of the modern day earned value applications, wrote a paper in which he described the importance of scheduling. He was specifying the requirements for the employment of earned value, emphasizing the need for a controlled scheduling process. His message to us read:

> *As of a given point in time, we need answers to these questions:*
>
> *What work is scheduled to have been completed?*
>
> *What was the cost estimate for the work scheduled?*
>
> *What work has been accomplished?*
>
> *What was the cost estimate of the completed work?*
>
> *What have our costs been?*
>
> *What are the variances?*[39]

---

39 A. E. Fitzgerald. (1967, August 29). *The Air Force Cost/Schedule Planning and Control System Specification: Experience and Outlook.* From a speech given to the Armed Forces Management Association.

Items 1 and 2 in the list above cover the baseline work scheduled plus the budgeted costs for doing this work. We now call this the "Planned Value." Items 3 and 4 cover the work actually performed plus the original budgeted costs for doing this work. We now call this the "Earned Value." Item 5 represents the actual costs incurred in converting the Planned Value baseline into Earned Value. Note that Item 5 has nothing to do with either establishing the Planned Value baseline or in determining the Earned Value accomplished, but it must be related to the Earned Value thus performed.

It should be clear by now that in order to employ some form of earned value measurement one must understand the authorized work to be done, and then manage that effort within a tightly controlled timeframe, that is, a scheduling environment.

There is one additional earned value criterion that should be mentioned, because it requires that a formal scheduling process be in place in order to, first, synchronize, the Planned Value of the work scheduled with the Earned Value of the work actually performed, and second, relate the Earned Value against the Actual Costs for performing the work. This important criterion reads as follows:

22. At least on a monthly basis, generate the following information at the control account and other levels as necessary for management control using actual cost data from, or reconcilable with, the accounting system:
    (1) Comparison of the amount of planned budget and the amount of budget earned for work accomplished. This comparison provides the schedule variance.
    (2) Comparison of the amount of the budget earned and the actual (applied where appropriate) direct costs for the same work. This comparison provides the cost variance.[40]

Item 1 in this criterion requires the synchronization of the Planned Value with the Earned Value in order to isolate any schedule variance from the baseline. The Schedule Variance (SV) formula is thus: "Earned Value less Planned Value."[41] A negative earned value schedule variance simply indicates to the project manager that they are falling behind their scheduled baseline work.

Please note that the earned value schedule variance may sometimes have no relationship to the project's critical path position. The critical path position is likely a more important indicator for monitoring any project's time position. Being behind

---

40 U.S. Department of Defense. (1996, December 14). *Earned Value Management Implementation Guide.* Washington, D.C.
41 *PMBOK® Guide* — Third Edition (2004), section 7.3.2.2.

in the work the project team set out to do will probably cost more later on in the timeframe, but it may not extend the duration or completion date for the project. However, the critical path, if not managed aggressively, could extend the duration of the project and cost dearly in added resources to complete the required work. Both the earned value schedule variances and the project's critical path must be monitored closely by the project team.

Item 2 of this criterion is the more serious of the two earned value variances. It is called the "cost variance"(CV), and it represents the relationship between the earned value accomplished and the actual costs it took to generate the earned value. The CV formula is thus "Earned Value less Actual Costs."[42] A negative cost variance can result in a permanent, non-recoverable damage to the project's final cost position.

If more funds are spent to perform the planned work of a project than was budgeted, the resulting condition is plainly an overrun. Overruns, even early ones, have been proven to be non-recoverable. Overruns are rarely, if ever, completely offset by subsequent performance, although many project managers and technical people have trouble with this fact. They have a tendency to be optimistic about their ability to recover such losses. However, experience suggests that performance in later periods tends to get worse, rather than better, with the passage of time. The reason: The planning for later project periods tends to be progressively vague, less well-defined, and thus more subject to negative cost performance. The earned value cost variance is a critical indicator for any project team to watch.

The Earned Value Baseline Versus the Project's Critical Path

In any project that employs earned value management (EVM), the project's time-phased performance plan may go by several titles: the Performance Measurement Baseline (PMB), the sum of the Planned Values, the Budget at Completion (BAC), or simply the project baseline. Such baselines will be a reflection of all of the work authorized, as delineated in the project master schedule, plus management's budget for the authorized work. Note: Management or contingency reserves, if any, will reside outside of the PMB—not planned or scheduled, but simply a set-aside until needed. A scheduling system is vital to employing EVM.

But there is an important point to make with respect to performance measurement with EVM. While a negative "cost" variance, reflecting perhaps a non-recoverable cost overrun, is always a serious matter, a negative "schedule" variance may or may not be a serious issue. Reason: A negative earned value schedule variance is a temporary reflection of falling behind in the project's baseline PMB. The issue we must address is: What does the PMB represent? Does it represent early starts, late starts, or something else?

42 Ibid.

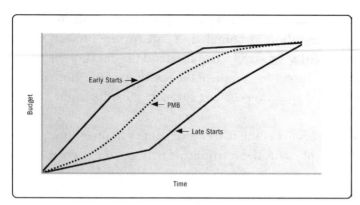

Figure 7.3 *The Performance Measurement Baseline (PMB)*

To help us discuss this issue, we need to review to Figure 7.3. When creating the initial project baseline, each and every task manager will decide precisely where to place their tasks in a timeframe consistent with the project master schedule. But there is often wide latitude allowed in the placement of each scheduled task. Some individuals are optimists, others are pessimists, and others, well, who knows?

The issue is that some of the tasks will be placed in an "early start" position, with respect to the critical path. Or some of the tasks may be placed in a "late start" position, putting each task on or near the critical path. Unfortunately, today the critical path positions of many projects are likely not known, and the calculations have never been done, so the placement of each task represents a best guess. These best guesses will constitute a "most likely" guess position with respect to the project's critical path(s). Thus, the earned value PMB will probably constitute some timeframe set in between the project's earliest starts and latest starts for each and every task.

Subsequently, any negative earned value schedule variance (SV = EV − PV) that may result from actual performance must be carefully assessed, task by task, to determine its true impact on the project's final completion date. A late performing task with considerable positive float may not be serious. But a late task with zero float, or one carrying high risks to the project, can be a very serious matter. It all depends on the placement of each and every task in the PMB.

8

ESTIMATE THE RESOURCES AND AUTHORIZE BUDGETS TO FORM CONTROL ACCOUNT PLANS (CAPS)

ONCE THE TECHNICAL REQUIREMENTS of the project have been properly defined, and all of the identified work planned and scheduled, the next logical step in establishing the project's baseline is to estimate how much each task or work package will likely cost. The required resources must be estimated, justified, and then specifically authorized by the project manager in the form of an official project budget. A cost estimate is only an estimate until it has been specifically authorized by the project manager. Every project needs the specific authorization of scope, schedule and budget by the project manager.

These initial steps are required in order to employ the earned value concept on a new project, but it is important to note that they are no different than the initial effort required to implement any new project. This is simply following fundamental project management. But these steps are particularly critical to an earned value project, because once the baseline has been put into place, the actual performance against the baseline will need to be measured continuously for the duration of the project.

However, there is one requirement that perhaps distinguishes earned value projects from most other projects. In order for performance measurement to take place during the term of the project, a project baseline needs to be created by detailed bottom-up planning. Performance measurement with earned value takes place within management control points which are sometimes called "Control Accounts" (CAs) or sometimes "Control Account Plans" (CAPs). The CA and CAP are synonymous terms. Within each CAP, the work to be done must be aligned with the authorized budget, within a precise timeframe specified in the project master schedule.

So that we are all clear on this important matter, let us bring in precise definitions of what we will be discussing:

Work Package. A deliverable or project work component at the lowest level of each branch of the work breakdown structure. See also control account.

Control Account (CA). A management control point where scope, budget (resource plans) actual cost, and schedule are integrated and compared to earned value for performance measurement. See also work package.[43]

Continuously, on a periodic basis (typically monthly, but sometimes weekly), the project manager will want to make an assessment of how well the project is performing against the authorized baseline. Project performance will be precisely measured employing earned value metrics, normally expressed as a cost or schedule performance variance from the baseline. Such variances will give an "early warning" signal of impending problems and are used to determine whether or not corrective action needs be taken in order for the project to stay within the commitment to management.

The process of taking these three initial steps to form an earned value project baseline is conceptually displayed in Figure 8.1. The project baseline must be established, typically done in the sequence as shown in the illustration. In Step 1, the project's scope of work must first be defined, often with use of a WBS, leading to a statement of work, which is then assigned to a functional organization or organizations for performance. In Step 2, the defined scope must be planned and scheduled down to the detailed work package or task level. Finally, in Step 3, the required resources must be estimated and subsequently authorized in the form of official project budgets.

Figure 8.1 *Steps to forming the project baseline*

It should be mentioned that in some organizations, particularly those managing software projects, this conventional sequence is often altered. These organizations will sometimes take Step 1 to define their work, then perform Step 3 to estimate the required resources, and finally take Step 2 to schedule their work. They will change the typical project implementation sequence because they may be constrained by the availability

---

43 *PMBOK® Guide* — Fourth Edition, 2008, Glossary.

of qualified resources to work on their projects. There is nothing inherently wrong with this approach ,as long as the organizations start with the project definition process in Step 1, and end up with the approved project baseline in Step 4, as displayed in Figure 8.1.

The end objective of taking the first three sequential steps, in whatever order, will be the formation of Step 4, the detailed project baseline. The earned value project baseline is made up of the sum of the CAPs. The CAPs provide the measurable performance control points for the earned value projects. The significance of the control account needs to be clearly understood in order to properly utilize the earned value concept. But next we need to emphasize the importance of working with an "integrated" project baseline.

INTEGRATING THE PROJECT SCOPE OF WORK WITH COSTS AND SCHEDULE

One somewhat unique aspect of employing the earned value concept is the fact that the technique requires there be an integration of all vital components of the project. What does the term "integration" actually mean? Simply put, integration in earned value means that the technical scope, authorization, planning, scheduling, estimating, budgeting, and cost accumulation of the work all must be aligned with the functions performing the actual work, and all integrated with use of the WBS. This concept was described earlier in Chapter 5, when we discussed the earned value body of knowledge illustrated in Figure 5.1. In that figure, the traditional non-integrated approach was shown on the left side, while an integrated earned value project approach was illustrated on the right side.

Rarely is the full integration of these diverse activities ever achieved on a typical project. However, an integrated baseline is an absolute requirement with earned value project management.

When the C/SCSC were first issued in 1967, and later updated by industry in 1996, the requirement for the integration of these processes was clearly mandated in the third criterion, which reads:

3. Provide for the integration of the company's planning, scheduling, budgeting, work authorization and cost accumulation processes with each other, and as appropriate, the program work breakdown structure and the program organizational structure.[44]

---

44 U.S. Department of Defense. (1996, December 14). *Earned Value Management Implementation Guide.* Washington, D.C.

The integration of an earned value project is achieved with the creation of detailed CAPs, which are the management control points placed at the desired levels of the project's WBS. The CAP is where the management and performance measurement will take place. Within each CAP, the planned tasks will be defined and then assigned to a specific functional organization or organizations for performance.

The cost, schedule, and technical performance within each CAP can be summarized and then reported either to the top levels of the project WBS, for the benefit of the project manager, or related to various functional units for the enlightenment of these managers.

CONTROL ACCOUNT PLANS (CAPs): THE POINTS OF MANAGEMENT CONTROL

At this time we need to cover what is perhaps the single most important feature that distinguishes projects which employ earned value from projects which do not. This unique feature is the requirement to develop a detailed, bottom-up performance measurement baseline. The earned value performance baseline is made up of the individual Control Account Plans (CAPs). Originally dubbed Cost Account Plans, also CAPs, by private industry, the DoD later substituted the term Control Account Plans. This was a good move, because the CAP is a management *control* point, a subproject, where the performance measurement must take place.

Additionally, and perhaps of greater importance, earned value is a technique for accurately measuring the costs against the physical work accomplished. This delicate relationship determines the cost performance efficiency factor being achieved on the project: what work was actually performed on the project relative to the costs that were actually spent. The cost efficiency factor is particularly critical, because poor cost performance is generally non-recoverable. It has been empirically demonstrated for over four decades that whenever more money is spent in a project than the value of the physical work accomplished, the overrun condition is not subsequently corrected. Historically, overruns only get worse, not better, with the passage of time.

Earned value requires that a detailed bottom-up baseline plan be put in place. The baseline in earned value is formed with the creation of self-contained, measurable CAPs. The earned value technique can be employed on projects of any size from as small as a few thousand dollars, to mega-projects valued in the billions of dollars. The earned value concept is scalable, as long as certain fundamental principles are followed and the performance baseline is formed with use of measurable CAPs.

A little background on the term Control Account Plan may be in order. In 1967, when DOD first issued its C/SCSC, they chose to call these measurement units by the name "cost accounts." A cost account was initially defined as the point of intersection of the *lowest* WBS element within a *single* functional unit. More recently, with the general acceptance of the concurrent engineering (often called integrated project teams) concept, the use of a single functional element has been broadened to include all functions working on a single WBS element. The subject of multi-functional teams will be addressed in the next section. Multi-functional project teams represent an important evolutionary development within the concept of earned value.

One important point on the use of CAPs: Four elements are necessary for earned value performance measurement. Each CAP must include, at a minimum: (1) a discrete scope of work, typically expressed with work package tasks; (2) a timeframe to complete each work package task, or the project schedule; (3) the authorized project resources, or the approved budget (which may be expressed in any measurable form, as in dollars, hours, units, etc.); and (4) a designated individual to manage the effort, typically called the Control Account Manager, or CAM. Most CAMs will have a dual reporting relationship: to the project manager for the project work, and to the functional manager in their permanent organization.

The CAP is the fundamental building block for performance measurement, and the summation of the CAPs will add up to the total value of the project. The project's master schedule determines the planned timeframe for each CAP, and then the earned value performance can be measured using the same metrics that established the plan.

On smaller projects of only a few thousand dollars in value, there may only be a few CAPs required for the project. However, on larger projects representing millions or even billions of dollars there will obviously be more CAPs required out of necessity. In every case, the project manager will determine the appropriate number of CAPs to be employed, their duration, and size.

There are no absolute standards to be recommended as to the appropriate size for CAPs. The determining rule of thumb should be whatever a manageable number for a given scope of work is. What is manageable will likely vary by the type of project being implemented. If the effort covers state-of-the-art research and development, or routine product testing, or continuous production, or a construction job, what will be considered manageable will likely vary in each case. Also, the amount of procured materials, the subcontracted work, the degree of personal supervision required, and the complexity of the effort, will all play into the determination of what constitutes a manageable CAP.

The current trend in most earned value projects would appear to support the employment of lesser numbers with larger size CAPs. It would also appear to support the use of multi-functional team CAPs, an important subject which will be covered next.

Multi-Functional Team Control Account Plans (CAPs)

The wisdom of earned value projects employing very small and detailed CAPs, representing the intersection of a *single* WBS element with a *single* functional organization, began to be questioned sometime in the mid-1980s. On larger multi-billion-dollar mega-projects, the numbers of individual CAPs often ran into the thousands. This approach was, frankly, both cumbersome and impossible to manage. The amount of energy it took to establish the initial detailed planning, and then to measure performance against hundreds or thousands of detailed CAPs, required more effort than any perceived benefit to management.

Certain individuals working with earned value questioned the need for the use of excessive, small, short-span CAPs. Why not combine larger segments of homogeneous work, perhaps representing higher levels of the WBS, and define it as a measurable CAP? As long as one maintained the critical relationship of authorized work to authorized budget, why not measure performance with larger groupings of work, and a lesser number of CAPs?

The integrity of the CAPs had to be maintained. This meant that once a given scope of work was defined for a CAP, and the budgets authorized for the work, the delicate relationship of "defined work to authorized budget" had to be maintained until performance was completed. Indiscriminate transfers of either budget or work, independent of the other between CAPs, would only serve to invalidate performance measurement. All work defined and authorized with a precise budget must remain in concert. Preventing the shifting of work without corresponding funds, or vice versa, is an absolute rule in order to maintain the integrity of performance measurement within CAPs.

In addition to questioning the use of small CAPs, these same practitioners also questioned the necessity of measuring a single function within each CAP. Why not take a given larger segment of homogeneous work, and measure the collective results of all functions performing such work? Would the performance of the full multi-functional team not be a more meaningful measurement than simply the performance of a single function?

Some initial resistance to the use of large multi-functional CAPs came from government C/SCSC review team directors. Perhaps they were concerned that the necessary discipline would not be present to prevent abuses. However, the DoD did subsequently endorse the use of integrated work-team CAPs in their 1989 supplemental guidance statement document:

A natural fallout of the work team concept may be the overall reduction in the number of cost accounts with a resultant increase in their size, duration, and resource composition. This will result from grouping organizational elements, WBS elements, or a combination of both into larger, higher-level cost accounts.[45]

This change of policy represented a significant advancement in the use of the earned value within the DoD. If properly implemented at the beginning of a new project, the use of larger multi-functional work-team CAPs resulted in the elimination of 90 percent of the total number of CAPs required for any project. Thus, with only 10 percent of the previous number of CAPs to monitor, management could then focus their attention on the CAPs as a viable management control point, a meaningful sub-project.

An interesting observation: Although the notion of employing larger, multi-functional, integrated cost accounts came from private industry, and was later approved for use by the DoD policy board, it was not implemented on new contracts to any significant degree. Rather, the entire approach was overtaken by other events during the same period. A new idea came along for the DoD project managers which seemed to incorporate the notion of larger multi-functional CAPs. The new direction was to be called Integrated Project Teams (IPTs), or Integrated Product Development Teams (IPDTs).

A product development management concept called "concurrent engineering" had been in existence for years and was starting to be noticed in both private industry and in certain quarters within the DoD acquisition community. In fact, the concurrent engineering initiative overtook the initiative for earned value multi-functional team CAPs. Management gurus were also beginning to coin exciting new terms to describe these phenomena, like "multi-functional projectization," [46] whatever that might mean. It sounds a little like the concurrent engineering concept, which was defined as:

"Concurrent" or "simultaneous" engineering . . . the means of carrying out the engineering process by forming a team whose members come from many disciplines . . . The normal activities of product design and development of manufacturing process are carried out in parallel rather than in a series, reducing the time it takes to perform both tasks.[47]

45 U.S. Department of Defense. (1989, July). *C/SCSC Supplemental Guidance*, Item #4. Washington, D.C.

46 Tom Peters. (1992). *Liberation Management*. New York: Alfred A. Knopf, p. 13.

47 Bernard N. Slade. (1993). *Compressing the Product Development Cycle*. New York: AMACOM Division of the American Management Associations.

Some of the military program managers enthusiastically adopted the idea of the use of concurrent engineering, which they were to later call IPDTs. As it was earlier with the initial earned value concept, the U.S. Air Force took the lead again in 1990 and issued the following policy statement urging, or perhaps demanding, the use of multi-functional integrated product development teams:

> *Integrated Product Development (IPD) Teams: the integration of all functional disciplines required to manage the definition, development, acquisition, training and support of systems for which we are responsible. The concept has been called "concurrent engineering," "integrated engineering," or "simultaneous engineering" in other organizations. Its principal feature is the merger of several functions in a single organization to ensure that all aspects of design, manufacturing, test, training and support are addressed at all stages of the acquisition cycle, but particularly at the front end.* [48]

Thus the private industry initiative which urged the use of multi-functional work-team CAPs for earned value applications was quietly made a part of the larger DoD procurement initiative promoting the use of IPDTs. Earned value benefited from the use of multi-functional CAPs, allowing management to focus on a more meaningful but lesser number of control points. Conversely, the DoD project directors have adopted and better accepted the earned value concept as their own valuable management tool and as a part of their initiative on using IPDTs. This has resulted in a win-win situation for all parties in the management process.

We also recommend the employment of earned value project management with multi-functional team CAPs on all projects within the private sector. To us, the integrated project team represents a natural sub-division of projects into meaningful sub-projects which align nicely with the project WBS.

The use of earned value multi-functional team CAPs is shown in Figure 8.2. Each CAP

Figure 8.2 *Form points of management control (CAPs)*

48   Lt. General John M. Loh, USAF Aeronautical Systems Division, Dayton, Ohio (a policy memorandum, *Organizational Alignment to Implement Integrated Product Development*, March 26, 1990).

must incorporate four elements to be viable: a precise scope of work, a schedule, a budget, and a team leader (the CAP manager) to manage the effort.

ESTIMATES VERSUS BUDGETS . . . AND MANAGEMENT RESERVES

Our opinion is that all project managers need some type of "just-in-case" reserves to carry out their challenging work. Such funds are sometimes called contingency budgets, other times called management reserves. These values are set-aside amounts over and above the allocated budget values that anticipate the misfortunes which too often befall projects; these misfortunes always have and they likely always will come. In scheduling, such management reserves will take the form of slack or float, which are time reserves, in addition to the cost reserves.

One important issue facing any project manager is, who should control (or own) these budgetary or time reserves? Our position is that, assuming such values can be uncovered—and this is not always an easy task—the project manager should always own and control the management/contingency funds and schedule float. Why? For this answer, we go to an established authority on the subject of project management, who commented on the issue several years back.

> *It is a natural tendency on the part of every person to provide a certain amount of cushion or reserve in his or her time and cost estimates . . . . If approved, then each person will tend to expend all the time and cost available . . . as Parkinson has said:*
>
> *• The work at hand expands to fill the time available.*
>
> *• Expenditures will rise to meet the budget.*[49]

If a project manager allows more time in the schedule than is needed to perform the tasks, somehow people have a tendency to take all the time which has been authorized, and the excess time will likely cost more money. Also, if more funds are approved than are needed to accomplish the defined work, somehow these funds will typically get spent.

We would now like to make a distinction between an estimate and an authorized budget. Authorizations will typically take the form of an approved budget or an approved schedule. An estimate may well represent the amounts the person feels will be necessary to accomplish a particular task. However, estimates sometimes, if not

---

49 Russell D. Archibald. *Managing High-Technology Programs and Projects.* New York: John Wiley and Sons. Quoted from C. N. Parkinson. *Parkinson's Law.* (1957). Boston: Houghton Mifflin.

always, contain the estimated value needed to perform a task, plus a just-in-case amount to cover contingencies, expected losses in negotiations, or possibly both.

Only the very young and inexperienced would seem to provide true, honest estimates of requirements. Stated another way, there would seem to be a high correlation between gray hairs and estimates which include contingency pads! Project contingencies may be needed, but the values must be owned and controlled by the project manager, or else they may be needlessly consumed. Most of the more astute project managers have learned to authorize only that which is needed to actually accomplish the work. Any differences are kept locked away by the project manager for potential problems which cannot be predicted in advance.

IN CONCLUSION

In a project that employs the EVM concept, the measurable performance plans will be formed with the creation of CAPs, placed at appropriate levels within the project's WBS. The WBS serves as an integrator of all activities for the project and allows the defined work in the CAPs to be assigned directly to the functional organizations performing the work.

As was stated earlier here, the formation of CAPs is the last of the four implementation planning steps necessary to form an earned value baseline: (1) define the scope, (2) plan and schedule the scope, (3) authorize the necessary resources to form CAPs, and (4) form the project baseline against which performance will be measured through to the completion of the project.

We have been describing the fundamental project management which should be applied to all projects, of any size or complexity, in any industry.

9

ESTABLISH THE EARNED VALUE
PROJECT BASELINE

INTRODUCTION

ALL PROJECTS NEED to establish some type of baseline against which their performance may be measured during the full life cycle of a project. This requirement is true for any project. But it is particularly critical for any project which employs the earned value technique. Once a project utilizing earned value is underway, a determination will need to be made of precisely how much of the authorized work has been physically accomplished, and management's authorized budget for the completed work will also need to be known, both in order to predict how long it will take to finish the project and how much the total bill will likely be.

A project baseline is needed to determine how much of the planned work has been accomplished as of any point in time. The completed (earned value) work is compared against the work the team originally set out to do in order to assess the planned schedule position. The completed (earned value) work is also compared against the actual consumed resources to reflect the true cost position.

Returning again to the experience gained from the DoD when they first issued the earned value criteria in 1967, and later when these same criteria were rewritten by industry in 1996, the requirement to establish a project measurement baseline has been consistent:

> 8. *Establish and maintain a time-phased budget baseline, at the control account level, against which program performance can be measured. Budget for far-term efforts may be held in higher level accounts until an appropriate time for allocation at the control account level. Initial budgets established for performance measurement will be based on either internal management goals or the*

external customer negotiated target cost including estimates for authorized but undefinitized work.[50]

The project manager must maintain the authorized baseline, and approve or reject all changes to that baseline. Each change once approved must be incorporated into the revised performance measurement baseline in a timely manner.

The term Control Account Plan (CAP), a management control point, represents the core measurement point for earned value measurement. CAPs are placed at selected elements of the WBS as determined by the project manager. As we discussed in the previous chapter, each CAP must contain three discrete elements in order to be viable: (1) a specific scope of work, (2) a timeframe for performance of the work, and (3) an approved budget to accomplish the work. The planned value of each CAP must be measurable against the earned value, and its earned value must be measurable against the actual costs. A project's total performance measurement baseline is therefore the summation of its individual control account plans.

We need to understand the makeup of the project baseline. Particularly, we should understand how earned value is initially planned and then measured within each of the CAPs and the various methods used to accomplish this.

INTEGRATED PRODUCT DEVELOPMENT TEAMS (IPDTs) VERSUS CAPs

In the previous chapter we described the concurrent engineering concept, or, as it is often now called, the Integrated Product Development Team (IPDT) approach. IPDTs have become a very successful project management approach, particularly when new product development is the primary deliverable. A question affecting the earned value baseline is: When an organization employs the IPDTs concept, what is the relationship between IPDTs and earned value CAPs? The answer: It all depends. The magnitude and complexity of the project will typically determine the project's hierarchy.

When an organization uses IPDTs on smaller projects, the IPDTs and CAPs may well be the same. The project forms IPDTs, which are in effect CAPs. They are points of management focus where performance measurement takes place. In Figure 9.1, the top section depicts a baseline for a smaller project of perhaps $100,000 in size. In this arrangement the designated IPDTs function as earned value CAPs.

---

50 U.S. Department of Defense. (1996, December 14). *Earned Value Management Implementation Guide.* Washington, D.C.

On larger projects, of perhaps $100 million or more, the IPDTs effectively become "super CAPs" which are the primary point of project manager focus. These IPDTs will typically have multiple CAPs performing work, subordinate to the IPDT team leader. In this case the CAPs are effectively sub-projects to the IPDTs. Individual performance will take place within the CAPs, which will roll-up to the IPDTs. The hierarchy of a major project is conceptually portrayed in the bottom half of Figure 9.1.

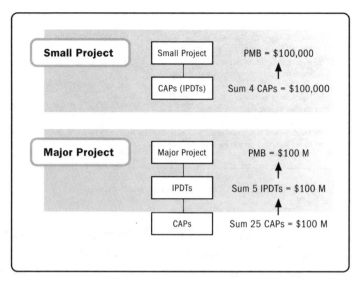

Figure 9.1 *The EVPM hierarchy . . . it all depends*

METHODS USED TO PLAN AND THEN MEASURE EARNED VALUE

Earned value is dependent upon the project's scheduling system to provide the mechanism for measurement of performance. Stated another way, without a scheduling system in place earned value performance measurement could not take place. A project scheduling system will by definition reflect the project's scope of work, and then place all the defined work tasks into a specific timeframe for execution. When one adds resources (management's authorized budget) to the scheduling system, and then the metrics to plan and consume such resources, the earned value performance plan is in place.

The determination of which metrics should be used to measure a particular application is an issue of personal judgment that will vary by project. But it is the job of the project team and the various work package and control account managers to ultimately select the appropriate measurement metrics which best support their particular needs. Planning, measurement, and consistent application are the keys to having a successful implementation.

Over the years since earned value was introduced to industry, a number of innovative methods have been employed for the measurement of performance. For purposes of summarization, we have grouped these various methods into eight

Figure 9.2 *Earned value measurement methods*

broad generic categories, which are displayed in Figure 9.2. We will review the various measurement method options and discuss their individual pros and cons, in order to provide an understanding of each.

Methods 1 through 6 as listed deal with what is called "discrete" types of performance measurement. Discrete measurement is always the preferred type to use. Method 7 is called an "apportioned" measurement, meaning it has some direct consistent relationship to another discrete base task as shown in methods 1 through 6. Method 8 is called "level of effort" work (LOE), which is *not* recommended for use by these authors, because LOE tasks will often give false readings.

1) Milestones with weighted values

This method of performance measurement works well and is typically used whenever individual work packages exceed a short span in duration, perhaps running two, three, or more performance periods (expressed in weeks or months). The longer work packages are converted into multiple measurable milestones to reflect finite

Figure 9.3 *Measure Earned Value with the project schedule*

divisions of work, preferably one or more milestones in each period being measured. Each designated milestone is assigned a specific budgeted value, which will be 100 percent earned upon the physical completion of the event. The total work package budget is divided up based on a weighted value assigned to each milestone. Once underway, values should not be changed.

The weighted milestone method is a preferred method used in performance measurement, but it is also a difficult method to initially plan and then to administer. This approach requires a close working relationship between the work package managers, the scheduling people, and the resource estimating function in order to set meaningful milestone values for all planned work. See Figure 9.3, Item 1, which displays Milestones with Weighted Values.

This approach is sometimes used to authorize interim progress payments to fixed-price sellers under a concept called "Performance Based Payments."[51] Performance Based Payments is in fact a simple form of earned value management. But interestingly, the term "earned value" is never mentioned in any government literature.

2) Fixed (start/finish) formula by task: 25/75, 50/50, 75/25, etc.

Item 2 in Figure 9.3 illustrates the approach which was most popular in the early years of earned value, but its use has somewhat diminished in more recent years. Conceptually, it is perhaps the easiest to understand, but it also requires very detailed and short-span work packages to successfully make it work. We have illustrated only three values for this type of measurement, but in fact any distribution which adds up to 100 percent may be used (10/90, 25/75, 50/50, 40/60, 90/10, etc.).

For example, the 25/75 method works well when applied to those work packages scheduled to start and be completed within the same one or two measurement periods. For example, 25 percent of the budget value is earned when the activity starts, and the other 75 percent of the budget is earned when the task is completed. Purchased materials often work well with this method: 25 percent is earned when the materials are defined and ordered, and the final 75 percent is earned when the materials arrive and are consumed.

One important rule to follow when using this method is that the defined tasks not exceed one or two maximum reporting periods, measured either weekly or monthly. You would not want to start a task in January, take credit for 25 percent of the work, then plan to complete the work in June, some five months later. No measurement would have taken place for five months. One or two reporting periods should be the maximum for this method.

3) Percent complete estimates

To follow this discussion best, see Figure 9.3, Item 3, which portrays both a long single task on the top, and a single task subdivided into three discrete tasks on the bottom. This discrete measurement method allows for a periodic (weekly or monthly) estimate of the percentage of work completed during the reporting period. Such (subjective) estimates are made by the individual in charge of a given work package. Generally, for ease of administration, such estimates are typically expressed as a cumulative value against the full (100 percent) value of the specified work package.

Typically, such estimates are made purely on a "subjective" basis, that is, on one's personal and professional but yet unsubstantiated estimate. Thus, when this method is used, if an individual wants to claim more initial earned value than he or she actually

---

51 Federal Acquisition Regulation (FAR) Subpart 32.10, Performance Based Payments.

has, the subjective percent complete estimate is where it will be revealed.

Over the years, the percent complete method of estimating performance has received increasingly wide acceptance within private industry. The reason is that it is the easiest to administer of all earned value methods. But it is also the method most subject to performance pressures from senior management and others with an individual bias.

There is nothing inherently wrong with the use of subjective estimates of results, as long as the work packages are well defined and senior internal management goes through periodic reviews of status to test the reasonableness of subjective estimates. Many a heated debate has taken place between work package managers and supervision (sometimes also involving colleagues) when it is felt that individuals were claiming too much value for their respective work packages. Rarely are such disagreements centered on too little value claimed, except perhaps at year-end bonus time!

If a company is genuinely utilizing the earned value method in the performance of a project, the individual professional integrity of both employees and supervision will often provide a sort of informal "check and balance" on the accuracy of the periodic estimates. Conversely, if a firm is intent on giving only lip service to earned value, periodic subjective estimates can have wide distortions in measuring earned value.

To minimize inflated subjective estimates, some firms have developed internal written procedures (operating guidelines) on specific segments of work to more accurately assign percent complete values based on actual work accomplishment. Providing such guidelines to work package managers thus incorporates some degree of objectivity into the subjective estimates. Examples of these guidelines may be: planning completed, lines of code released, drawings issued, materials ordered, parts received, tool orders released, and so forth.

Another good practice sometimes used to buffer excessive optimism when using the percent completion method is to set a "maximum ceiling" allowed for any work package until it is 100 percent complete. While such percentages will vary from company to company, an 80 to 90 percent ceiling is typically used by many firms. Thus, with an 80 percent ceiling in place, a given work package may earn only up to 80 percent of the manager's subjective estimate until the task is 100 percent complete, at which time the balance of 20 percent may be earned.

4) A combination of percent complete estimates, with milestones used as "gates"

See Figure 9.3, Item 4. Private industry has typically embraced the use of percent complete estimates to set earned value measurements, probably because it is easiest to use. The manager of a work package merely assesses the status of the work package, perhaps compares its progress with some personal metric, written or not, and estimates the cumulative value accomplished.

Whatever progress value is selected, the work package manager knows that he or she must defend the estimated value before fellow associates, and sometimes before senior management. Unduly optimistic assessments will ultimately come back to haunt the individual work package manager. If the project manager and company management have genuinely endorsed the earned value concept, the subjective progress estimates by individual work package managers have proven to be quite accurate. In fact, when a work package manager's personal reputation is at stake, and they know that management will hold them accountable for accurate earned value assessments, these managers tend to be on the conservative side and will often slightly understate performance values to give themselves a cushion for next month's status report.

However, over the years, many of the U.S. Government's earned value oversight teams have expressed great suspicion of the accuracy of purely subjective work package estimates. Perhaps they have valid reasons. Subjective estimates of earned value performance do work well, but only if there is a check and balance in place to challenge the artificial or overly optimistic estimates. It often depends on the degree to which the project managers and more senior management have accepted earned value as a management tool. If company management employs earned value simply because it is a government mandate, the validity of subjective estimates may well be questionable.

As a general rule, government oversight teams encourage the use of objective or tangible milestones for performance measurement. However, the difficulty with weighted milestones is that they require considerable time and energy to put a plan in place. Some feel that an inordinate amount of energy is required to plan a full baseline made up of weighted milestones.

Recently there has been an evolution in earned value applications that seems to have captured the best of both measurement techniques: the ease of subjective percent complete estimates, used in conjunction with difficult tangible milestones. Such milestones are placed intermittently as performance "gates" within long subjectively measured tasks. Subjective estimates of performance are allowed up to a certain preset value for each milestone. However, subjective percentage complete estimates cannot go beyond a given milestone until certain predefined and tangible criteria have been met.

This method seems to work well in any industry and with any type of project. Thus, the broad universal acceptance of earned value may well be the result of finding the right balance between ease of implementation and accurate performance measurement. Subjective estimates with milestones as "gates" may provide that balance.

Three specific examples will be discussed below as we cover the use of Control Account Plans (CAPs) in the private sector.

5) Equivalent completed units

This measurement method allows for a given planned value to be earned for each full unit of work completed, and also for a fractional equivalent of a full unit. The equivalent completed unit approach works well when the project periods are of an extended duration, and it is also used for the management of repetitive work.

Assume that a project represents the construction of ten homes valued at $100,000 per home. The construction cost engineers will have prepared a detailed bottom-up estimate for each of the planned homes, subdividing each home into individual cost elements. Assume that the costs covering the site excavation for each unit is estimated to be 10 percent of the total value for each house, set at $10,000 per home.

At the end of the first month, the project manager may want to quantify the earned value position for the full project. The first month's effort may have consisted of the completion of the excavation of sites for all ten homes. Thus the earned value for the first month would be calculated at $10,000 (for each completed excavation) times ten homes, or $100,000 in total. The measured earned value for the full project will be the equivalent of one full home ($100,000), although not one home will have been completed.

The construction industry often uses this approach in making progress payments to suppliers, using a simple but effective form of earned value. However, individuals in the construction industry often refer to this method of calculating physical performance as a "schedule of values" and rarely do they use the term earned value. But conceptually it is the earned value method: calculating actual physical progress against actual costs.

6) Earned standards

The use of planned standards to initially set a budget and then to subsequently measure the earned performance of repetitive work is perhaps the most sophisticated of all the methods, and requires the most discipline on the part of the participants. It requires the prior establishment of equivalent unit standards for the performance of the tasks to be worked. Historical cost performance data, time and motion studies, set-up, tear-down, and lost time factors, etc., are all essential to the process of measuring performance against earned work standards.

This type of work measurement is typically performed by the industrial engineers who originated the earned value concept in the first place. Interestingly, the industrial engineers typically refer to this method as equivalent work measurement rather than earned value. But it is the same concept, earned value pure and simple.

There is no single method of setting earned value that works best for all types of activity. Probably the best approach for any firm to take is to allow for multiple measurement methods to be used, with the one employed for individual work packages based on the collective judgments of the CAP managers working closely with industrial engineers. The use of measuring earned standards is typically limited to repetitive or production work.

7) *Apportioned relationships to other discrete work packages (Items 1 thru 6 above)*

Apportioned performance measurement is an acceptable technique with earned value. But it requires a mature organization which has kept historical performance records and understands the relationships of related functions working on common deliverables.

An apportioned task is one which has a direct intrinsic performance relationship to another discrete work package, called a "measurement base" task. Measurement bases for apportioned tasks could be represented by any of the six discrete methods described as Items 1 to 6 in Figure 9.2.

One such example of an apportioned measurement relationship might be that of "factory inspection," which typically would have a direct performance relationship to the "factory fabrication" labor it would be inspecting. However, the inspection budgets would likely be set at a different value (perhaps only five or six percent) of the factory fabrication labor base. When the (apportioned) labor for factory inspection would be planned, it would be set with a direct alignment to its base work package, the factory fabrication labor. Later, when the earned value for factory fabrication labor might be measured at, say, a cumulative 48 percent, the factory inspection work would also declare an identical performance value of a cumulative 48 percent.

When measuring the earned value "schedule" position for apportioned tasks, the values used will always reflect the same percentage (earned value) as that of its related discrete base. Since the time phasing of the planned value for the inspection will always approximately match that of the fabrication labor, any schedule variances reflected by the fabrication labor, positive or negative, would be similarly reflected in the apportioned factory inspection work. Sometimes apportioned tasks may trail their discrete base tasks by perhaps a single reporting period, and that is acceptable. The apportioned tasks may start and finish one period later than their direct base task.

However, "cost" relationships for apportioned tasks can be substantially different from their base tasks. A cost variance for the apportioned work package will reflect the difference between the earned value achieved for the base work package and the actual costs incurred for the apportioned work. The cost variance position of the (apportioned) inspection effort may be substantially different from that of the fabrication labor, because the inspection work package will relate the same earned value percentage with relation to whatever actual costs the inspection work may have incurred. Thus, if the manager of the inspection work package were to double the number of inspectors from those set in their approved budget, the inspection (apportioned) work package could reflect a negative cost variance, even though the base effort for fabrication labor might be reflecting a different cost variance position.

An apportioned work package will always reflect an identical schedule position from that of its base work package, because the planned value and earned value will be the same for both tasks. However, cost variances may be substantially different for the apportioned work package, because cost variances will reflect the apportioned actual costs, which may be higher or lower than their initial budgeted amounts. As used in software projects, an apportioned relationship might be "code testing" apportioned to a base called "code design."

8) Level of Effort (LOE) recommendation: Always "Quantify" and Quarantine."

Level of Effort (LOE) activities are those tasks which may be necessary to support a project, but which are more "time" sensitive than "performance" related. Examples of such tasks might be those performed by the project manager and immediate project management staff, like scheduling, budgeting, procurement, contract administration, field engineering, security, cooking, bottle washing, working the help-desk, etc. In other words, LOE tasks involve indirect work on projects.

Whenever these functions are charged directly to a project, they normally start at the beginning of the effort and continue for the full term of a project. However, they will generally have no measurable or deliverable outputs. One could almost make the case that these tasks should be charged to an overhead pool, but that is a different issue.

The problem with LOE work packages is that whatever budget is authorized in the baseline plan, the planned value automatically becomes the earned value for the project with the passage of time, and this happens regardless of what physical work does or doesn't take place! LOE tasks "automatically" earn whatever was approved in the plan, up to the full limits of the planned value budget. For example, if the planned value was approved for ten field engineers, but only two engineers actually worked, the earned value would be shown as ten, or precisely what was approved in the plan. There would always be a zero schedule variance, because, again, earned value always matches the planned value with LOE work packages.

However, since the performance measurement was set at ten, but actual costs incurred were for only two, the cost variance for the period would be a positive 500 percent cost variance! Stated another way, the cost performance efficiency factor for field engineering in this period would be a plus five times perfect performance. This may seem like an absurd example, but with LOE tasks the absurd will happen. Is this true performance measurement? We think not. The problem is that LOE work packages tend to distort the discrete measurement in the project, and often mask bad performance that needs management's attention. The only issue is how much LOE distortion is acceptable.

Perhaps a real-life example may help. On a given project to develop a new high-technology vehicle, engineering was behind schedule in the release of their design. The engineering earned value performance was not keeping up with the planned schedule. However, the factory tooling function was reflecting a positive schedule position and was actually under-running its costs. How could this miracle happen? Engineering was running behind schedule with its design release, but manufacturing was making the tools. Incredible.

A quick review indicated that the engineering tasks were being measured discretely, as was appropriate. However, the tooling function had unilaterally changed its earned value measurement methodology from discrete to LOE. They were showing earned value performed, although the delivery of actual tools was running seriously behind schedule. Fortunately, the project's scheduling system independently reflected a disconnect between the positive LOE earned value performance and the non-availability of factory tooling.

How might one solve the disparity of distortions caused by LOE work? One approach would be to always "quantify" and then to isolate or "quarantine" the LOE work. Let us discuss both approaches.

In every instance where LOE tasks are allowed in the baseline, the extent of the LOE contamination in the baseline needs to be understood. Always "quantify" the value of the LOE in the project's baseline. This is accomplished by dividing the value of the LOE work by the total value of the project baseline (formula: LOE value divided by budget at completion [BAC] value).

Project managers are often shocked by the unexpected total of the LOE in their baselines. Excessive LOE is sometimes an indication that the project organization does not accept the earned value concept, and will go along with it only as long as no one measures "my performance." Authors' point: If the value of LOE tasks exceeds 5 to 10 percent of the total baseline, true performance is not being measured. Rather, the passage of time in the project is being measured, and the excessive LOE contamination needs to be done away with.

How might one live with this condition? In fact, there are often legitimate LOE tasks on a project, like the project management. But excessive LOE tasks can distort accurate performance measurement. One approach would be to carefully convert all LOE tasks to subjectively measured percent complete estimates. Subjective performance measurement estimates are preferable to allowing LOE distortions.

A second approach to managing LOE is to "quarantine" all LOE tasks outside of the project baseline being measured, rather than measuring the LOE tasks, and instead of allowing LOE actuals to offset discretely measured work. See Figure 9.4 for an illustration of this discussion.

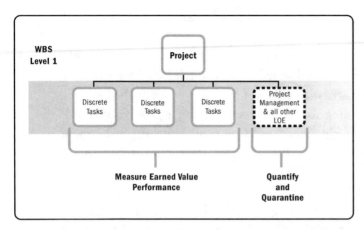

Figure 9.4 *LOE Effort: Always Quantify and Quarantine*

A Work Breakdown Structure (WBS) should be used to completely define all project scopes. And discrete earned value measurement methods should be used on all effort which has project deliverables, that is, discrete tasks. But any work which has no deliverables should simply be quarantined as "Project Management and all other LOE" and placed into an isolated element like that shown to the extreme right in Figure 9.4. LOE should not be measured, since it reflects nothing but the passage of time.

If you allow for LOE tasks in your baseline, and most projects do, a good approach to manage it is first to understand how much LOE you have. Then, either convert it to percent complete discrete measurements, or exclude it altogether from your measurable project baseline.

CONTROL ACCOUNT PLANS (CAP): THE MANAGEABLE SUBPROJECTS OF EVPM

With projects employing earned value, the point at which performance will be created, monitored, and measured is within a generic type of management control cell referred to as a Control Account Plan, or simply the CAP. Since the rewrite of the earned value criteria by industry in 1996, the same abbreviation "CAP" has continued, but the term was changed from Cost Account Plan to Control Account Plan. Both terms are identical in concept, although the title "control account plan" is likely more representative of the intended purpose of these cells.

CAPs are created by the project manager and team at selected points within the project's WBS. This concept was covered earlier and illustrated within Figure 5.1, with the earned value CAP shown on the right side of the display. CAPs are placed at selected levels in a WBS, at Levels 2, 3, and 4, down to the lowest point where management will want to control a homogenous grouping of work.

The CAP is essentially a subproject, a point of control where the project manager focuses during the performance of an earned value project. It is that point where the project's authorized work, resources, and time requirements will all be integrated. Within the CAPs, the cost and schedule performance indices will emerge, telling management where they must take action. The CAP in earned value is the fundamental building block which forms the project's measurement baseline. Each CAP will be a self-contained management control cell. And, in order to be viable, each one should contain the eight basic elements listed in Figure 9.5.

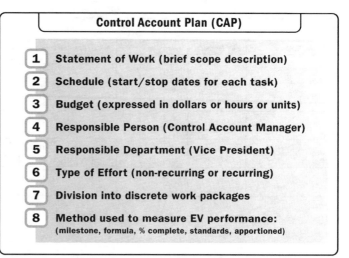

Figure 9.5 *Elements of a Control Account Plan (CAP)*

Items 1, 2, and 3 as listed represent the integration of scope with schedule and costs. Earned value requires an integrated baseline. Item 4 requires the designation of someone to be held responsible for the performance of each CAP, typically carrying the unofficial title of Control Account Manager, or CAM. While there are no absolute rules for what is to be contained in the CAPs, the eight elements listed in Figure 9.5 are fairly typical. At a minimum, each CAP must define the scope, schedule, costs, and also a responsible person, as indicated by Items 1 through 4.

Budgets for CAPs may take any measurable form: dollars, hours, units, standards, etc., or any value that can be quantified and subsequently measured. Indirect costs may or may not be included within the individual CAP budgets. Some firms hold their project managers responsible for total costs, including indirect, while others hold the project manager accountable only for direct costs, or possibly only direct labor hours.

Indirect costs may or may not be included within each CAP or simply added to the top project value, perhaps conveniently housed in a separate CAP containing all indirect burdens. The only absolute rule for budgeting is that all project dollars must be accounted for by the project, and that whatever items were budgeted to a project to form the planned value must also be consistently measured to reflect the actual earned value. Some organizations hold their project managers responsible for management of direct costs, or direct hours, only and have a financial person convert the project metrics into budgeted dollars. The determination of precise project costs will vary from company to company.

Displayed in Figure 9.6 is a sample CAP which lists four discrete work packages. For each of the four work packages shown, the planned value, the resulting earned value, and the actual costs for each work package is displayed on a separate line. This

Control Account Plan (CAP)									
Work Packages	EV Method	Item	Jan	Feb	Mar	Apr	May	Jun	BAC
1) Work Package #1	Weighted Milestones	Plan Earn Actual	△50	△75	△75	△50	△50		300
2) Work Package #2	Fixed Formula (25/75)	Plan Earn Actual	△25	△75	△25	△75	△25	△75	300
3) Work Package #3	Percentage Complete Estimates	Plan Earn Actual	100	100	100	100	100	100	600
4) Work Package #4	Percent Complete with M/S gates	Plan Earn Actual	100	100 33%△	100	100 67%△	100	100 100%△	600
5) Total CAP	n/a	Plan Earn Actual	275	350	300	325	275	275	1800

Figure 9.6 *A sample Control Account Plan (CAP)*

is a simple six-month CAP, but it may serve to illustrate certain important points. Different earned value methods are used to plan and subsequently measure performance in each work package.

Work package number 1 uses a "weighted value milestone" method. Five milestones are listed, and each carries a discrete value, with the total budget set at 300. The 300 can be represented in dollars, units, or anything which can be measured. The milestone shown in January must be completed in total before the value of 50 can be earned. Discrete milestones are like "on/off" switches: Each milestone must be 100 percent complete before its value can be claimed.

Work package number 2 has three tasks, each with a value of 100, and the sum of which has a budget at completion of 300. This work package uses the "fixed formula" of 25/75 to plan and then measure the performance of each of the one month long tasks. When a given task is opened, the earned value is set at 25 percent, and only on total completion of this task can the other 75 percent be claimed. The fixed formula method works well for short-term tasks, and should not exceed one or two reporting periods.

Work package number 3 employs a manager's subjective "percentage complete" estimate to measure earned value performance. This method is the most simple to calculate, but it is also the technique that is most potentially subject to inaccuracies. Percentage complete estimates work well because they are easy to administer, but they also must be watched closely by management, because pressures to perform can result in overly optimistic calculations of earned value by work package managers, which may temporarily distort the measurement of performance.

Work package number 4 uses the combination of (subjective) "percent complete" estimates combined with (objective) "milestone gates" to keep the performance estimates honest. Here the responsible work package manager may subjectively estimate the value of work earned up to 200, at which point certain predefined performance criteria must be met before the 200 value can be exceeded. The percent complete estimates with milestone gates incorporate the best of both techniques: ease of administration combined with accurate objective measurement.

One important point needs to be stressed about the relationship of the planned value (budget) to the earned value. The planned value (budget) effectively sets the "ceiling" for the earned value that may be claimed for each work package. For example, work package number 1 sets the total planned value budget (called the Budget at Completion, or BAC) at 300 for the completion of all five milestones. The earned value of 300 is the maximum that can be claimed for the completion of these five milestones. Should their completion require the expenditure of 500 or even 1,000 in order to finish, all that can be earned is the total of the planned value budget of 300, nothing more.

CONTROL ACCOUNT PLANS (CAPS) IN THE PRIVATE SECTOR

Some positive trends are occurring within private industry in the use of earned value to manage its projects. These trends are the result of private industry experimenting and innovating with the technique, and using it in ways that make sense to their primary customers, and to themselves as project managers. Many project managers have discovered an exciting new tool to help them better manage their work.

As we continue to attend various international conferences, and in particular the annual PMI® Global Congress, we find more and more professional papers being delivered on the use of earned value to manage projects. But an interesting observation is that most of these professional papers are describing earned value applications in ways that never previously existed with the more formal, U.S. Government-mandated applications. Industry has taken hold of earned value and is using it to better manage projects, and not simply sending off status reports that are likely never read.

One of the more interesting trends is in the size of the CAP, the point where earned value is initially planned and then subsequently measured. The size of earned value CAPs has been on the increase, and this alone will make the concept more viable as a project management tool. The increased size of the control point is the result of two changes in the definition of what constitutes an earned value CAP, which is simply a subproject to be managed.

In the first place, project managers are focusing their attention on larger segments of homogenous work, and on higher levels of the WBS, thus incorporating greater segments of project scope within each CAP. Additionally, they are including all of the functions performing this work. Thus, with the use of larger CAPs set at higher levels of the WBS, and the inclusion of all functions supporting the CAP, project management is focusing its attention on fewer, but more critical, management control points for projects.

In addition, both industry and government are starting to employ a combination of measurement methods to plan the baseline and then to measure earned value performance. The use of a combination of (subjective) percent complete estimates, in conjunction with discrete (hard) milestones as measurement gates, provides ease of use with objective measurement.

Three specific examples of earned value applications are worth reviewing here, because they may well represent the future trend, as the concept shifts from a government-imposed reporting requirement to the private sector, because the project managers have found utility with earned value.

Case #1: A CAP used on a high-technology vehicle development project

Shown in Figure 9.7 is an example of a large multi-functional CAP used to develop a high-technology project. The period of performance spanned several years. This CAP employed two discrete methods to measure its earned value performance. For the first two phases covering the layout design work, the CAP manager's (subjective) percent complete estimate was employed, but used in conjunction with tangible (hard) milestones each with pre-defined advancement criteria as gates. In the latter phase, fixed formula tasks (25% to start each task, and 75% when completed) were used for the final effort. The approach worked well! Performance was accurately measured over a multi-year period.

Figure 9.7 *Control Account Plan (CAP) for hi-technology vehicle*

The detailed initial planning was the key to making it work. It took the cooperation of various functions. First, the technical management had to accept earned value as its management tool. The project manager and the chief engineer (sponsors) gave the concept their full endorsement, and the other technical managers, including the multi-functional team leaders, followed senior management's example. This major or "super CAP," as illustrated in Figure 9.7, was effectively an amalgamation of several subordinate CAPs, each defined within the framework of the project WBS. The estimating, budgeting, and scheduling functions each met with the various technical team leaders to establish their performance plans.

The CAP was separated into three distinct parts, which collectively constituted 100 percent of total effort. Part one represented the conceptual layout work, which was estimated to be 30 percent of the total design effort. Part two was designated assembly layouts, and represented another 45 percent of the total job. The final phase consisted of a series of small manufacturing build and procurement-buy packages, and represented the final 25 percent of the job.

Parts one and two used the same earned value measurement approach. They both used the CAP manager's subjective estimated percent complete value to set the cumulative earnings each month. However, because each phase constituted a large-dollar-value segment of work, the conceptual phase alone represented 30 percent of the total job, and phases one and two would be further subdivided into four performance segments, each measured by specific completion milestone criteria. Milestones would be set up for the four sub-phases, representing the 25 percent, 50 percent, 75 percent, and 100 percent points of completion for the work.

The four specified milestones would act as "sanity-check gates." The CAP manager would (subjectively) estimate the earned value position to be anywhere from zero to 25 percent for the initial work in the conceptual phase. However, to get past the 25 percent milestone gate, the CAP had to meet certain pre-specified (very specific) advancement criteria. Such criteria were previously established and approved by management. Once these selected advancement criteria were satisfied and verified, the estimated performance values could then go beyond the 25 percent milestone.

Illustrated here is a simple but effective way to measure project performance, and it incorporates the best of (subjective) manager percent complete estimates with specific (tangible) milestones which use pre-defined standards that must be satisfied. This approach still required the oversight of senior management as "checks" on the estimated values in order to challenge excessive percent complete estimates, and to assure the accuracy of the completion of milestone criteria. This approach worked well in the management of a high-tech vehicle, and similar models can work on any project.

Case #2: A CAP used to manage an architectural design project

Shown in Figure 9.8 is a second example of a CAP, this one using "weighted milestones" to manage the performance of an architectural design procurement contract in the construction sector. This CAP was used to monitor the performance of a design seller working on a cost reimbursable

Figure 9.8 *Control Account Plan (CAP) for architectural design work*

type contract which had a fixed fee, and then to authorize the release of fee payments to the supplier based on their performance against specific-value milestones.

However, this same approach can work effectively on a fixed-price procurement to authorize payments to sellers based on their completed work. Those working on government contracts making progress payments often call these Performance-Based Payments, but it is earned value, pure and simple.[52]

Prior to the award of the contract, the project buyer and the contracting seller jointly agreed on the total design effort, and then subdivided the 100 percent contract value into a series of discrete measurable pieces, each represented by specific completion requirements. Each milestone will have pre-defined criteria to be achieved in order to be considered complete, and each will be given a fixed performance value, as is displayed in Figure 9.8. For simplicity of administration, each milestone is often rounded to the closest 10 percent value.

This approach is conceptually simple, and yet it works well. Earned value does not have to be a complicated process.

Case #3: A CAP used on a software project.

We now approach an area which is perhaps the new frontier for project management: the effective management of software projects. How can one measure the performance of something that cannot be precisely defined, or even quantified, in total? That is a reasonable question. One possible answer is to define in detail that portion of a new project which it is possible to quantify, and leave the remaining undefined work in gross planning packages. In these cases, management will make a preliminary commitment to a new project, until the project can be reasonably quantified.

Figure 9.9 shows a third example of a project employing earned value, this one containing six CAPs to manage the performance of a software project. This is the same software project that was previously defined earlier with the WBS in Figure 6.7. While the total project will be budgeted within the six CAPs as listed, only the first two CAPs will be planned in detail and authorized to begin

Figure 9.9 *Control Account Plans (CAPs) for a software project*

52 See Federal Acquisition Regulation (FAR), subpart 32.10.

work. The last four remaining CAPs will be subsequently planned in greater detail, but only after the project's requirements have been defined, analyzed, and approved by management.

For both of the two initial defined CAPs, a combination of subjective percent completion estimates will be employed, but with use of specific milestones as gates. In order to be completed, each milestone must meet specific criteria in advance of starting the work. The subjective estimates of percent complete cannot go past any milestone until that milestone is completed.

Note that the first CAP, covering "Requirements definition," used four milestone gates at the 25, 50, 75, and 100 percent points. Compare this with the second CAP, covering "Analysis of requirements," which used only three milestones at 35, 70, and 100 percent. It is up to the CAP manager, working closely with the cost estimators, to set reasonable values for each milestone gate. Obviously, the project manager will want to review and approve each CAP prior to authorizing work to commence.

This is an example of a software project employing a simple, but effective form of earned value, measuring that effort which can be defined up to the point where the total project can be quantified.

THE PERFORMANCE MEASUREMENT BASELINE (PMB)

Establishing a Performance Measurement Baseline (PMB), a baseline against which performance may be measured, is an essential requirement of earned value project management. The PMB is the reference point against which a project will measure its actual accomplished work. It will tell whether the project team is keeping up with the planned schedule, and how much work is being accomplished in relation to the monies being spent. While the PMB is critical to the measurement of earned value performance, they are not all alike. We need to understand the anatomy of the PMB.

The primary question: What is the makeup of the PMB as authorized by management? The answer: It all depends on the particular company. What does (senior) company management hold its project managers responsible for in the area of cost performance? Our unofficial findings are that the responsibilities of project managers for cost management vary considerably from one company to another company, and even from one project to another project within the same company. There are no absolute procedures which apply universally to all companies. Project managers are often held accountable for differing levels of cost performance on their projects. Thus, what constitutes a PMB for one project may well be different from the PMB on another project—yes, even within the same company.

To illustrate this point, we have attempted to define a spectrum of cost responsibilities for project managers, as shown in Figure 9.10. This figure begins with the

Figure 9.10 *Composition of Performance Measurement Baseline*

more limited responsibilities, as with Item 1, where the project manager is charged with controlling only direct labor hours, period. In many organizations, the project manager will be charged with managing direct labor hours only thus their project PMB will be composed of purely direct labor hours. While someone in the organization (likely finance) will need to convert the direct labor hours into dollars for management reviews, in this situation that is not the responsibility of the project manager.

With each additional item from 1 through 8, the responsibilities of the project managers for cost control are broadened, and they are held accountable for managing additional categories of costs, as with overheads (indirect costs), procured materials, other direct costs, and yes, even profits. Total accountability for all profit and loss of a given project is shown in Item 8.

Many project managers will have limited responsibility for managing all categories of project costs, thus their performance baselines will be represented by the lower numbers, as illustrated in Figure 9.10. Other project managers will be charged with greater roles. However, in order to track earned value performance, they must understand precisely what management expects them to control.

Perhaps a couple of specific examples will help illustrate the point we are making. We display two examples of a Performance Measurement Baseline (PMB)—one for a simple project, as in Figure 9.11, and another on a complex project, as shown in Figure 9.12.

It is likely that the majority of projects in existence today employ the kind of simple baseline illustrated in Figure 9.11. Here the project manager has divided the project into five points of management control, five subprojects, represented by the five CAPs listed in the figure.

Each CAP will contain a specific content of work to be accomplished, an authorized budget to accomplish the work, and a timeframe for completing the work. Each CAP may be comprised of direct labor hours, as in Item 1 in Figure 9.10, or of hours within labor categories, per Item 2, and so forth. The PMB for this simple project will be composed of whatever categories of costs management expects the project manager to control. These CAPs may also include other direct cost (ODC) items, like materials, subcontracts, travel, and even indirect costs. It is always a good practice to isolate direct labor items from procured materials and ODC.

What about a category of costs called Management Reserves (MR)? Again, there are no universal rules to follow. In some cases, senior management will allow the project manager to have and control MR. In other cases, senior management will want to control the MR. Our preference is that, if the project manager owns MR, it be placed in a separate CAP strictly controlled by the project manager. MR should never be left in the various functional CAPs, where it will likely be consumed.

For an illustration of the PMB for a more complex project, quite often representing an external company contract performed for a profit, refer to Figure 9.12. Here the project is progressively subdivided into

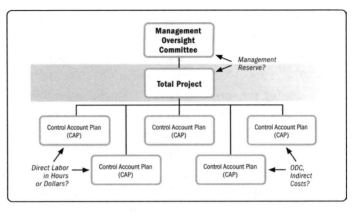

Figure 9.11 *Performance Measurement Baseline: simple project*

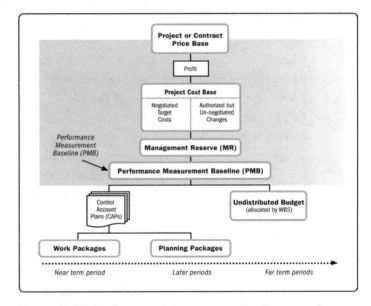

Figure 9.12 *Performance Measurement Baseline: complex project*

various categories of costs, beginning with the total project or contract price base. After dedication of the anticipated profits by the chief financial officer, the project manager is left with the project cost base.

The project cost base is that value the project manager has to manage. It will include all categories of both direct and indirect project costs, even though the indirect costs will be beyond the immediate control of the project manager. Nevertheless, the project cost base must be provided for all project costs, except for any forecasted profits.

One important issue for project managers is the necessary division of the authorized project cost base into two distinct parts: (1) those firm project costs that have been negotiated, and (2) any soft changes that have been authorized but not yet negotiated. In order to keep the project cost baseline consistent with a changing environment, the performance measurement baseline (PMB) must include both the negotiated scope and also that effort which is recognized as a legitimate change, but the exact value of which has not been settled. Deciding precisely what value to budget for the authorized but un-negotiated work is always a challenge for the project manager. However, all authorized changes must be included in the project's performance baseline in order to maintain the integrity of the work being measured.

The PMB is displayed at the center of Figure 9.12, and it is indeed central to the earned value management process. Within the PMB will be housed two categories of budgets: the allocated budgets taking the form of CAPs and the undistributed budgets for the far-term periods, often representing authorized but un-negotiated changes.

While far-term undistributed budgets will reside at a higher summary planning level, such budgets need to be allocated to a specific element of the project WBS. Until undistributed budgets move into definitive CAPs, they may or may not be assigned to specific organizations for performance. However, all budgets within the PMB must be identifiable to a specific WBS element and properly time-phased in order to maintain the integrity of the PMB.

The CAPs comprising the PMB will be represented by two distinct categories: detailed work packages for the near-term effort, and gross planning packages for the distant work. There are no absolute rules for making the distinction between what constitutes a work package and what constitutes a planning package, or even undistributed budgets. These somewhat general categories will vary by project and by company.

However, employing the "rolling wave" planning concept, managers of projects with durations of up to three years may well plan all of their CAPs down to the work package level. In other projects exceeding three years in duration, near-term effort may be defined in definitive work packages, but out-year tasks in higher-level planning packages may be left out until they approach the period of performance. Projects with a less than five-year duration may have no use for undistributed budgets, except to temporarily house any authorized but not yet negotiated changes in scope.

Once the performance measurement baseline has been established based on individual CAPs, the next appropriate action is to time phase the baseline to form a total project performance curve, as is dis-

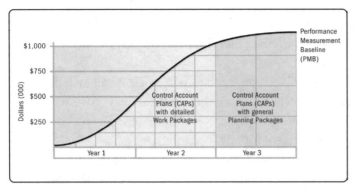

Figure 9.13 *Sum of Control Account Plans (CAPs) = PMB*

played in Figure 9.13. Here we have illustrated a project baseline of sufficient duration to warrant the use of both definitive work packages for the near term (Years 1 and 2), and planning packages for the far-term effort (Year 3).

MAINTAINING THE PROJECT BASELINE: MANAGING CHANGES IN SCOPE

A wise person is alleged to have once said: "There are three certainties in life: taxes, death, and changes to project scope." That wise individual must have worked on projects similar to ones we have all enjoyed.

It is always frustrating to work hard to establish a project baseline, to have all parties agree on the baseline, and then to watch the changes begin. It would likely not be possible to eliminate all changes. Changes to project scope often result from a desire to make improvements in the final product deliverables. But if we cannot eliminate changes altogether, then we must at least strive to control the changes. Changes should represent what we intend to do, and not simply what we were unable to avoid.

Setting a firm baseline in place based on an agreed-to scope of work is a key initial action required by all project teams. Closely aligned to this task is the need for the project manager to have in place some type of change control procedure that will allow the approval or rejection of proposed changes based on a deliberate determination by the team. Changes in work scope should not inadvertently happen because someone failed to prevent them. Rather, scope changes should only result when specifically approved by the person authorized to make them—the project manager. The bottom line is, project managers need to have enough clout to say "no" to proposed changes.

In order to manage changes effectively, project managers need to keep track of all deliberate or inadvertent pressures they encounter to change direction. Controlling a baseline requires both information and an information retrieval system. Each action that alters or potentially alters the approved baseline needs to be carefully tracked so that the project manager may make a conscious decision to approve or to reject each change.

Shown in Figure 9.14 is a simple baseline change control log. The first line item on such a log would be the initial approved project baseline

Figure 9.14 *EVM requires baseline control*

value. The next lines are reserved for the change traffic, listed in chronological order as they occur. Each change or potential change should be listed as it surfaces, as a line item on the log.

As each potential change develops, the information will need to be systematically added to the log. For example, the rough order of magnitude (ROM) dollars need to be estimated and logged and the authorized not-to-exceed (NTE) dollars need to be shown, leading ultimately to a negotiated amount and resulting in a change order (CO) issued.

Effective project management requires that records and logs be kept and that some type of information retrieval system be put in place and maintained. Any of the automated spreadsheets or simple databases can facilitate this critical task for the project.

In Conclusion

Creating a detailed, bottom-up project plan is necessary in order to employ the earned value concept. Such plans need to be built upon detailed and individually measurable CAPs, the sum of which will form a project's time-phased PMB. The measurement of project performance takes place not at the top project level, but rather within each of the detailed subordinate CAPs. Each CAP (or subproject) must be measurable at all times: the amount of work planned (the planned value), the amount of authorized work accomplished with its authorized budget (the earned value), and the resources consumed (actual costs) and converting the planned value into the earned value.

It is likely that most PMBs are set on a monthly incremental basis. However, it is becoming increasingly popular to measure the performance of direct labor hours on a weekly incremental basis. If management desires weekly performance measurement, such metrics must be incorporated at the time the PMB is initially set, not as an afterthought. Tangible weekly measurement metrics must be specified to allow for weekly oversight.

Managing all changes to the project scope as they occur is essential to maintaining the approved project baseline, and necessary for successfully employing the earned value concept.

10

Employ Earned Value Measurement on Project Procurements

Project Procurements Are Unique.

How important is the management of procurements to the success or failure of a particular project? Answer: It all depends on what is being purchased by the project. Projects are unique, and sometimes their required procurements can also be unique.

Realistically, there are often extremes. Some projects may have zero things to buy. Everything that is done on these projects may be done using company resources: their own people, their own facilities, capital equipment, etc. Other projects may well procure a few items, but such buys are limited to commercial commodities which are readily available from retail stores or on the Internet. Procurements on these projects are routine, low risk. The only risk is one of timing. All procured articles must be available to the project in time to support the master schedule.

However, at the other extreme are projects which may buy as much as 75% to 95% of their project scope from other firms. Often these procurements require the development of something new, something which does not presently exist. Projects in this category which buy most of their scope from external sources would include the development of new systems, and items acquired for the U.S. Government, whether they be new weapons systems, environmental clean-up, information systems, etc. Construction projects buy most of their work from other firms. Information technology projects to create a new management system, ERP, MRP, etc., are normally done by outside firms under some type of a procurement arrangement.

Information technology (IT) work has become increasingly important to organizations, and sometimes most of this work is done with in-house staff. However, increasingly the IT effort today is done as a result of corporate "outsourcing" strategies, which is a deliberate policy of procurement. At times, the IT outsourcing companies later elect to "offshore" much of the work, which is also a deliberate procurement decision. And when the offshoring results in the creation of "virtual teams" to produce something new, the accurate measurement of project performance becomes quite challenging. Earned value in these cases may well have an important role in the management of IT projects, outsourcing, offshoring and virtual teaming.

The point we are making is that each project must be assessed on a case-by-case basis by the project manager. If the procurement of scope carries with it significant risks in terms of dollars, complexities, and long durations, it may well be beneficial to the project to employ earned value on these buy items. Each project must decide this for itself.

However, there is an important difference between the measurement of performance of the external buy items and the monitoring of internal direct labor. We need to fully understand this distinction.

LABOR VERSUS PROCUREMENTS: THE FUNDAMENTAL DIFFERENCES

Measuring the earned value performance of internal direct labor is typically quite easy. Most companies have in place some type of a labor reporting system which is generally good, particularly when compared against how most firms track the status of their procurements. Direct labor reporting is usually done on a weekly basis. It doesn't matter whether day one is a Saturday or a Sunday or a Monday; seven calendar days later, the actual books will close and the results will be known. They will know how many labor hours have been expended, how much money has been spent, and they can determine the actual hourly rates. Everything about direct labor is normally done on a weekly basis. Thus earned value measurement of labor is fairly easy.

Remember the rule: In order to employ earned value on any project the organization must have the ability to accurately measure three independent dimensions: (1) the planned value (the authorized work plus authorized budget), (2) the earned value (authorized work completed plus the authorized budget), and (3) the actual costs to accomplish the earned value. These three dimensions are displayed in Figure 10.1. The primary focus is on the earned value. The formula of earned value less the planned value gives us the schedule variance. And the earned value less

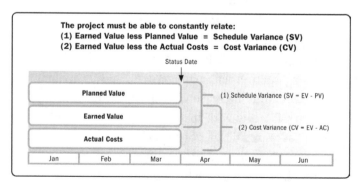

Figure 10.1 *The challenge of EVPM: Determining the CV and SV*

the actual costs provides the cost variance. It is relatively easy to measure these three dimensions in direct labor.

However, this is not the case with the purchased items. The tangible performance milestones needed to plan and then to measure earned value often span several accounting periods, and are frequently performed by different functions. With procurements it is difficult to synchronize the three dimensions of earned value.

Let us trace through some key events that accompany procurements on projects, and note the various functions which perform the work.

1. The project manager must define the items to be procured. This is usually done by conducting a make or buy analysis, typically under the direction of the project manager, or staff.

2. They must define the technical requirements of the purchases. This is done by the engineering or design organizations and results in a procurement specification.

3. They must request that a procurement be made by issuing a formal Purchase Requisition, which is normally done by the Project Manager, or staff.

4. A formal order to buy must be given by the Buyer, who issues a Contract or Purchase Order.

5. The purchased items must be received, inspected, accepted, or the purchased services verified. This consists of taking physical possession of the commodities and/or of verifying their satisfactory completion. Various functions perform this work.

6. Payment must be made for the purchased goods. The Accounts Payable organization must issue a check to the seller, and the costs recorded on the accounting ledger.

Each of these events represents a necessary task in the procurement process. In particular, the actual costs must be determined and related to the measured earned value. A measurement of earned value versus the resulting actual costs is needed in order to determine the cost efficiency. Without knowing the actual costs, one cannot determine the cost efficiency and thus employ the earned value concept.

However, these necessary procurement milestones may take place weeks or even months apart, and they often are performed by different functions. How do you measure a planned value, earned value, and then determine actual costs for these procured items? Answer: You must separate the work into distinct physical tasks, then plan, schedule, add a budget for each task, and then measure the actual performance for each task. And to further complicate the process, often the actual costs on the books may not truly represent the earned value being measured. In these cases you may need to "estimate" the relatable actual procurement costs because the sellers may not have been fully paid, or sometimes they have been overpaid for their services. Managing procurement costs is not as easy as managing direct labor costs.

The question for each project to answer: Is it worth the extra effort to employ earned value on the procured work? The answer is yes, if the procured items carry high risks, challenging complexities, new technologies, and are vital to the success of the project. The answer is probably no, if the project is simply buying routine materials or services. Each project must carefully assess its needs. Earned value measurement may not be warranted in all cases.

Issue: Often Procurement "Cost Actuals" Need to be "Estimated."

The third critical dimension in the measurement of earned value is the actual costs. But with the purchased items, as contrasted with direct labor, the actual costs on the accounting books may or may not accurately reflect the work being measured.

What is so difficult about tracking the actual costs of the purchased items? We suggest you refer to Figure 10.2 for an illustration of this discussion. Shown at the top of the figure are the three dimensions of earned value. As of any point in time in the life cycle of a project, the three dimensions of earned value must be measured.

The relationship between the planned value and earned value provides the schedule variance (SV). Even with the procured work, these two relationships are fairly easy to determine. Both planned value and earned value can be readily measured using the project's scheduling system. The six key functions of procurement as listed above can be planned and then earned by updates to the project's master schedule.

But by contrast, the project's earned value cost variance (CV) consists of the relation-

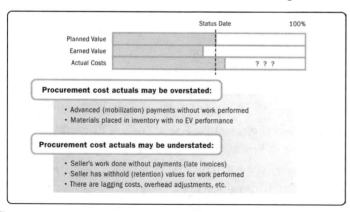

Figure 10.2 *Sometimes you must "estimate" the cost actuals*

ship between the earned value achieved, less the actual costs consumed to accomplish the work. The CV is particularly important, because poor cost performance is normally non-recoverable by the project. If one overruns the costs for completed work, these represent sunk costs. They are not likely to be offset and recovered by performance on later tasks. Thus negative cost variances are most critical to track. However, in order to determine the cost variance one must know how much money was spent to accomplish the earned value. One must have accurate cost actuals.

Let us discuss the issue of actual costs for procurements from two extremes: Actual costs can sometimes be "overstated" on the accounting books, while at other times costs can be "understated." In these instances, selected procurement costs may need to be "estimated" by the project in order to match the earned value being measured.

A word of caution: We are not suggesting that the procurement cost actuals on the accounting books be adjusted or manipulated. Rather, they should be temporarily "estimated" to allow for an accurate presentation of procurement cost status to management.

Sometimes procurement cost actuals may be overstated (must estimate downward).

In the construction industry, it is not unusual for the owner to authorize some type of an "advance" or "mobilization payment" to assist the performing contractor of a new project. The purpose and payback timing of such payments must be determined in order to synchronize the physical earned value performance with the actual recorded costs. If such advance payments were to be used strictly for the mobilization of construction forces, and such work might take place within a short time period being measured, then a separate task labeled "mobilization" effort may be sufficient. This task may be planned, performed, and the actual costs incurred during a single timeframe. The three relationships of the earned value method (planned value, earned value, and actual costs) would thus be synchronized as of the reporting period.

If, however, the advanced payment is to be used partially for site mobilization and partly to aid the constructor with its initial cash flow, then the two activities must be divided into two separate work tasks in order to relate the payments to the physical work being measured. This would be particularly true if the cash-flow credits were to extend over several months before repayment of funds back to the owner. Two work packages must be established and measured separately: (1) contractor mobilization, perhaps a one month task; and (2) cash-flow advance, perhaps allocated and recovered over a longer duration, say six months.

Another condition of (temporary) overpayment may occur whenever the project purchases common materials, some of which may be immediately consumed by the project, and some of which may be put into the project inventory for later use. Sometimes these stored materials will be transferred to other projects, in which case a borrow and payback accounting control process must take place.

It is not uncommon to buy materials for multiple projects, but for administrative convenience, and to charge the costs and store the materials on a single (the largest) project. However, such practices can distort the measurement of cost performance on a given project. Solution: The surplus or inventoried materials must be placed into separate work packages so that both the performance and actual costs may be accurately reported against the proper project.

Sometimes procurement cost actuals may be understated (must estimate upward).

Sometimes the very opposite condition may occur with the procured items. Earned value performance for procurements may be accurately monitored and properly claimed, but the actual costs for accomplishing the work may not yet be fully recorded on the project's accounting ledger. Performance results will be distorted. How can this happen?

Many projects are initiated with a significant amount of the workforce comprised of both company and non-company personnel, often called "purchased labor." These purchased professionals go from project to project to help work the peak labor loads. They are treated like regular company employees, and their work is most often directed by internal company supervision. A planned value performance baseline is set for all direct, company, and purchased labor, and their work is earned in a normal fashion.

However, sometimes missing in the equation are the actual costs for the purchased labor to compare against the earned value being credited. The result can be a distorted cost efficiency rate which can mask problems which need to be addressed by management. How does this happen? Often it is a combination of factors, including the late submittal of invoices by the purchased labor firm, the slow processing of invoices, and late payment of invoices by accounting. In these cases, the actual costs for the purchased labor must be estimated in order to accurately match the earned value credited.

Let's now discuss another example of distortions that can happen with seller progress payments. Again we will use the construction industry as an example, because it seems to monitor its suppliers' performance about as well as any industry. Whether the job is fixed-price or cost-reimbursable, in order for a supplier to be given progress payments for construction work, the supplier must demonstrate that it has physically performed the work. Sounds a little like earned value, and it is, but the cost engineers in the construction industry typically do not refer to it as such.

In construction the performing seller must define the job in the form of detailed sub-tasks, with a budget value assigned to each task, the sum of which must total the costs of the contract. They typically call this a "schedule of values." In order to be paid for the work, the supplier must carefully estimate the value of the work accomplished for each task. They determine the percentage complete, and give the earned value for each task.

Assume that the total construction job has a contract value of $1,000,000. After the first month the supplier may estimate by individual task that they are ten percent complete with the total job, or $100,000 complete. If the project manager agrees with this estimate, a check for $100,000 will be requested, less what is called a "retention" or "withhold." Retentions or withholds will vary by contract but are typically in the range of 5 to 20 percent of the requested progress payment. Such withholds are held and not released until the job is fully completed. In this example, a check for $100,000 less, say, 10 percent may be issued, so the accounting ledger will reflect a net value of only $90,000.

If the project were measuring its earned value performance, it might claim $100,000 in earned value, but will have only $90,000 in actual costs on the accounting ledger. Cost performance would thus incorrectly reflect a positive 1.1 cost performance index (CPI), when in fact performance should only be 1.0. Eventually, when the retention is subsequently paid to the supplier the inflated cost performance will return to its correct position. In the meantime, however, the overvalued performance of the contracted work at a CPI of 1.1 may well serve to hide poor performance of other critical areas that need the attention of the project manager.

It may be a cumbersome process to have to "estimate" the actual costs of procurements. But if earned value credit is claimed, it is important to make sure that the related cost actuals being reported match the work claimed. To do otherwise is to present to management a positive cost position which may be distorted.

SIX STEPS TO EMPLOYING EARNED VALUE ON PROJECT PROCUREMENTS

The decision on whether and how to employ earned value management on the procured items can be an important one for any project. In some cases the procured work will be absolutely critical to the very success of the project, in which case earned value may be warranted. But in other cases what the project buys may simply be routine commodities, in which case the detailed planning and oversight required for earned value measurement might not be warranted. This must be decided for each project individually.

If a project elects to employ earned value on its procurements, it must be understood that it will require more effort to employ the concept on buy items than on

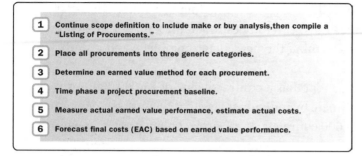

1 Continue scope definition to include make or buy analysis, then compile a "Listing of Procurements."

2 Place all procurements into three generic categories.

3 Determine an earned value method for each procurement.

4 Time phase a project procurement baseline.

5 Measure actual earned value performance, estimate actual costs.

6 Forecast final costs (EAC) based on earned value performance.

Figure 10.3 *Six Steps to Employing Earned Value on Procurements*

the in-house direct labor. More detailed planning and oversight will be required. And to compound the difficulty, "turf-wars" will sometimes break out between the procurement organization (the buyers who will have exclusive procurement authority) and the other line organizations (like technical and the project office) who will not. "I am in charge" conflicts sometimes arise between functions who should be working in concert.

Assuming that the project has elected to employ earned value on all or some of the procurement work, it must be determined how best to accommodate this with the least amount of effort. The authors suggest that projects employ a simple six-step process like the one displayed in Figure 10.3. We will next explain each of these necessary six steps.

Step 1—Continue the scope definition process to include a "make or buy analysis," and then compile a listing of all the work to be procured from the outside.

All projects will need to define what work will be done. This is called the scope definition process. But in addition to defining what will be done, it is often a good practice to go one step further and specify who will be doing the work. This is particularly important when some of the most critical project work will be done by an outside organization under a legally enforceable contract.

Procurement relationships are typically non-forgiving, in that you must correctly specify what you want to buy, or pay for costly changes. The project needs to compile a complete listing of the anticipated buy work. This is typically done by conducting a make or buy analysis. The end product will be a listing of all the procured items for the project.

Step 2—Place all defined procurements into three generic categories.

Although all procurements share a common factor, in that they all represent scope which will be procured from outside organizations, not all procurements are the same. Most of the items bought by the project will be routine and commercially available from suppliers. These articles are typically called COTS, for commercial off-the-shelf items. But other buys may require the creation of something new, which does not presently exist. These few procurements may well carry the same or even higher risks than the performance of the entire project. Certain procurements can be key to the success or failure of a project.

In such cases it may be advisable to follow the practice some firms have followed by placing the items to be purchased into distinct generic groupings. Why? Because the project must manage each procured item differently, depending on its complexity and the risks associated with each unique procurement.

Some organizations have found it advisable to place the listing of procured items into the three distinct categories described below, going from the highest-risk procurements down to the routine purchases:

1. **Major (potential high risk) complexity procurements,** or the purchase of something which does not exist, tailored to the project's unique specification. These would be considered critical sub-projects.

2. **Minor (low risk) complexity procurements,** will often represent large monetary values, but the commodities exist and will conform to the seller's existing product specification.

   (Note: Minor product tailoring such as unique name tags or special color schemes would not add risks to the procurement, and thus would not change their classification. However, major alterations to a seller's existing product, perhaps requiring a product re-design and perhaps new product testing, would likely place them into a Category 1 procurement.)

3. **Routine buys of COTS (Commercial Off-the-Shelf) commodities** or purchased services.[53]

The Category 1 items will typically represent only a few procurements on any project. But the very success of the overall project may be dependent on the performance of these few critical sub-projects. Thus they must be managed well if the project is to succeed. Typically these items will represent the creation of something new to the project's specification. They may represent a new component requiring a new design and testing, a major new information technology system, new subsystems, major sub-portions of the project, etc. Earned value will likely be warranted on all of the Category 1 procurements. These items will be few in number, but high in both risks and costs.

---

53 Quentin W. Fleming. (2003). *Project Procurement Management: Contracting, Subcontracting, Teaming.* Tustin, California: FMC Press, p. 14.

Category 2 buys can also represent big-budget items and long-term commitments by the project. But the risks of failure are relatively minimal since the deliverable products exist. These are items which have been developed by the sellers to the seller's own product specifications. Some examples could be electrical generators, radar systems, transportation vehicles, crane rentals, etc. Since these items are typically high-value and are consumed by the project upon delivery, earned value measurement is likely also warranted. Meeting schedule performance of these items is very important.

The Category 3 buys are often a nuisance to manage, because there are so many detailed items to order, track, receive and inspect. The risks: These articles must also be available to support the project schedule. However, earned value management may or may not add to the control of such items. Most companies have in place a type of material requirements planning system (MRP) which may be adequate to control these articles. It may not be beneficial to employ earned value measurement on this category of buy items.

What we are suggesting is that projects follow Vilfredo Pareto's 80/20 rule when employing earned value on the procurement work. Category 1 buys represent high risks and big budgets, and Category 2 items will be large, discrete, and easy to track. Together, Categories 1 and 2 might represent only 10 to 20 percent of the items to be bought, but perhaps 80 to 90 percent or more of the pro-

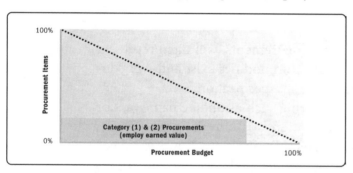

Figure 10.4 *Applying Vilfredo Pareto's Rule to Procurements*

curement budget. By contrast, Category 3 buys would likely constitute perhaps 80 percent or more of the procured units, but only 20 percent or less of the budget dollars. Pareto's 80/20 principle should be employed and earned value should be applied to only the big budget, high risk items. Let the company's existing MRP or material control system manage the Category 3 buys. Timing is all important. Our suggested approach is illustrated in Figure 10.4.

Step 3—Determine the appropriate earned value metric for each type of procurement.

Once the buy items have been listed and categorized, a management decision can then be made as to how best to plan and subsequently measure the physical performance of each category, that is, how to covert the planned values into earned value. There are numerous possibilities available which were discussed in the last chapter.

Displayed in Figure 10.5 are the three broad generic procurement categories, followed by a listing of the possible methods available to measure performance.

With Category 1 or 2 procurements, either weighted milestones or percent complete estimates with milestone gates will work well. With Category 1 procurements, the construction industry will often require a resource loaded critical path method (CPM) network which can be quickly summarized to display a time-phased "schedule of values." An example of a seller schedule of values is shown in Figure 10.6.[54] The seller's planned values would be represented by items 1, 2, and 3. Performance updates (earned value) to support progress payments would be reflected by items 4 and 5.

On major U.S. government-sponsored projects and selected critical procurements which would warrant the full and formal earned value measurement, the project buyer may require EVM in accordance with the ANSI/EIA 748 Standard.[55] The

Figure 10.5 *Place Procurements into Three Generic Categories*

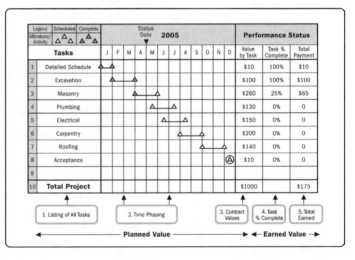

Figure 10.6 *Seller's Schedule of Values provides a simple form of EVM*

Federal Acquisition Regulation (FAR) provides the appropriate solicitation and contract clauses for requiring the full employment of the ANSI/EIA 748 Standard.

Category 2 procurements are listed in the center of Figure 10.5. Since this category is often represented by high-value discrete line items, they are easily tracked

54 Ibid, p. 212.
55 American National Standards Institute-Electronic Industries Association.

individually. Many companies use the fixed-formula method on these articles. Often they will plan for 25 percent of the budget to be earned when an order is placed, and the other 75 percent earned when the components are delivered and accepted. Actual costs must be estimated.

On fixed-price orders with multiple deliveries, the FAR has created what is called "Performance Based Payments" under FAR subpart 32.10. Here the buyer and seller must agree on performance measurement metrics which when completed will trigger a payment to the seller. The sum of the payments must add up to the value of the purchase order. Interestingly, FAR subpart 32.10 represents earned value measurement in its finest form. However, no place in the solicitation or contract clauses does the term earned value appear. We find that interesting also.

Category 3 procurements are listed at the bottom of Figure 10.5. Should the project elect to employ earned value on this category, three methods as shown are recommended. A manager in charge of production can estimate the percentage completion value of these bulk parts each month. Or the use of milestone gates can be employed to give objectivity to the estimates. Finally, some firms with good historical performance records may elect to determine an apportioned relationship of these purchased materials to a base account to measure the earned value performance. Fabrication or manufacturing labor against bulk purchased parts is sometimes used as the measurement base.

Step 4—Time phase a project procurement baseline.

Once all procurements are placed into three generic categories and a decision is made on what items and what methods will be used to measure performance, the procurements must then be time phased to form a procurement baseline. Performance of the buy items will typically be measured on a monthly basis. Weekly earned value measurement may be available to measure direct labor, but not for procurements.

The one exception to monthly measurement of performance may happen with "purchased labor" employees. If a given firm has a direct labor management system which will allow for purchased labor to be incorporated, this category of purchases may be planned and earned on a weekly basis. However, the cost actuals will need to be "estimated" as was mentioned above. Invoices and payments are slow to be processed.

Step 5—Measure the actual earned value performance, and estimate the actual costs.

On a monthly basis, earned value will need to be measured on the procured items. As with direct labor, the focus will be on the earned value achieved. Variances from both the schedule and costs will need to be highlighted.

One of the (legitimate) criticisms of earned value over the years has been that the contractor and subcontractor data being presented is often one or two months older than the comparable internal project data. This is often the case when actual cost data from the suppliers is required to present status. The availability of actual cost data from major suppliers (Category 1 and 2 procurements) will often pace the presentation of key supplier performance. This does not need to be the case.

The near real time measurement of seller performance can be achieved rather easily by a focus on the high-risk, high dollar value procurements, represented by Category 1 and 2 procurements. Their planned value and earned value can be monitored with the use of any of the methods listed in Figure 10.5. And if the project "estimates" the related cost actuals, near real time cost performance can be presented.

Step 6—Forecast the final expected costs (EAC) based on earned value performance.

It is likely that the primary purpose of employing earned value on a project is to get an early warning alert when the costs exceed the authorized budget, and to get that alert early enough to deal with the problem. Executive management and project management are entitled to know how much money it will take to complete a given project. This is called the Estimate at Completion (EAC).

Project procurements can sometimes have a major impact on final EAC costs. It all depends on the magnitude of the procurements, and the inherent risks. Let's discuss the procurement EAC process by generic category starting with the easy category, the COTS or routine buys.

Category 3 COTS procurements may represent most of the procurements, but there is nothing complicated about them. Either a company material requirements planning (MRP) system or a manager's estimate should accurately quantify the final costs for this category of buys. Budgets are established for these items based on two variables: an assumed quantity (usage), and an assumed cost (price). At the point where orders are placed for these items, it is usually known whether or not the budget is adequate to do the job. Thus if the costs being paid for the articles increase over budget, or more units are being consumed, it is known and an accurate forecast of final costs can be made.

Forecasting an EAC is perhaps easiest for Category 2 buys, because they will be few in number, and typically large in value. These items can be tracked individually by the project's buyers who can set the planned value and earned value, and accurately estimate the actual costs.

Now let us discuss the real challenge: Category 1 major complexity procurements. These buys usually carry the highest risks, because the seller is creating a new product to the buyer's unique specification. Sometimes the final deliverable product may not work for a variety of reasons. The seller may not have performed well, in which case they must keep trying until they get it right. Depending on the contract type, cost-reimbursable or fixed-price, seller performance can have a big impact on project costs. Defective products from one seller can sometimes impact the performance of other sellers. With Category 1 procurements, a simple form of earned value may be warranted, as illustrated in Figure 10.6.

Major complexity Category 1 procurements can experience cost growth for a number of reasons. Each of these procurements, and they will be few in number, must be individually monitored and a forecast made of final EAC costs. Assuming that the earned value has been properly measured, and actual costs accurately estimated, a cost performance index may be available for each of these buys. The most accurate assessment of EAC costs would likely be to take the total budget for each Category 1 buy and divide it by the seller's cumulative CPI. This approach would provide a reasonably accurate EAC to use to forecast the final required costs for the procured items.

Procurement cost projections must be incorporated into the total project EAC.

LESSONS LEARNED: PERFORM A "PRICE" AND "USAGE" VARIANCE ANALYSIS.

After the project is over it is often a good practice to stand back and ask yourself: "What happened? Did we perform according to our plan, or were we off?" With regard to the purchased items, and sometimes direct labor also, it is a good practice to conduct what is called a price and usage variance analysis.

Background: When the earned value criteria were rewritten by private industry in 1996, later becoming the ANSI-EIA 748 Standard, an important process was dropped from the compliance requirements. No longer were contractors required to perform a price and usage variance analysis on the items which were bought. The reasoning behind this change escapes us. How can one get progressively smarter in the future if one does not take the time to fully understand how well or poorly he or she performed in the past? We call this lessons learned.

A price and usage variance analysis is most often applied against materials that are purchased for the project. But this same analysis technique can also apply to direct labor budget results. Any time a budget is established based on an assumed price (the costs per unit or the per hour labor rate) times the assumed usage (the number of planned units or estimated labor hours), this type of analysis will work.

The price/usage analysis compares the original "basis of estimate," which set the budget, with the actual performance results. Let's take a specific example. Assume a budget is issued for $120. Actual results come in at $192. What happened?

If the budget was set at $120 for procured material items, the basis for setting the $120 budget may have been an assumed quantity of 10 units at $12 per unit. Later, when the item was bought and the work was done, the actual results came in at $192, an overrun of -$72. What happened? Did we consume more than the budget for 10 units allowed, or did the actual purchase unit price go up? Or, as is most often the case, were there changes to both the units consumed and the prices we paid? Unless we understand precisely what happened, how can we improve our performance the next time we bid on similar work? We need to conduct a price/usage variance analysis.

The formula for a price/usage variance analysis is illustrated in Figure 10.7. You must first determine if you spent more money per unit than was planned, then determine if you used more units than were provided for in the budget. Most often it is a combination of both factors, but one factor may be the primary cause. In this illustration, the -$72 overrun was primarily caused by an increase in the unit purchase price. But the increased quantity also contributed to the overrun.

As a result of the price/usage analysis we now know that two-thirds of the overrun was caused by an increase in purchase price, and one-third was caused by increased usage. With this knowledge, we can hopefully establish a better budget the next time we propose the costs of similar work.

Also, as was mentioned earlier, this same type of analysis can be useful when reviewing what happened on direct labor budgets. Sometimes the basis for setting the budget estimate assumes junior labor rates, but then senior people are put on the job. A price/usage variance analysis may help set a better labor budget the next time around.

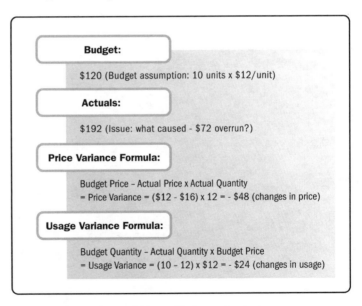

Figure 10.7 *Price and Usage Variance Analysis*

11

MONITOR PERFORMANCE AGAINST
THE EARNED VALUE BASELINE

A BASELINE WHICH ALLOWS for the measurement of earned value performance must be established by the project. Such baselines will be formed from detailed sub-projects, which are typically called Control Account Plans, or CAPs. Earned value CAPs are the points chosen by the project for management control. The sum of these sub-projects, or CAPs, will add to the total project baseline. Management reserves and profits, if any, are left outside of the performance measurement baseline (PMB).

In Figure 11.1 we have illustrated a project with only five CAPs listed across the bottom. As projects increase in size more CAPs will be added, allowing for adequate control. What's the proper number of CAPs for a given project? The answer is, it all depends on a given project's size, duration, complexity, and associated risks. There are no absolute guidelines as to the proper size of CAPs. Each project must determine its own proper span of management control. However, a fewer number of CAPs seems to work best.

Complex projects requiring a large number of CAPs may elect to group them into logical project teams, sometimes called integrated product development teams, or IPDTs, typically relatable to the project's Work Breakdown Structure (WBS). Performance measurement will still take place within each CAP, but categorized for management oversight into higher level teams. A typical project manager employing earned value

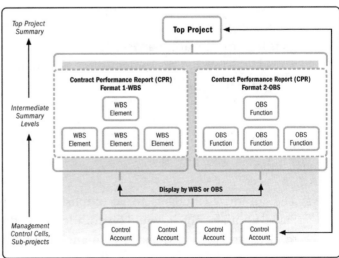

Figure 11.1 *An Earned Value Baseline equals the sum of all CAPs*

125

will first look at the top project summary, then drill down to look at results by WBS, then down to the individual CAPs which may be experiencing problems.

Sometimes it will be desirable to summarize the CAP performance by either the WBS, or the functional organizational breakdown structure (OBS), or both, as is illustrated in Figure 11.1. Four of the formal earned value criteria require a summary of performance by both the WBS and OBS.[56] However, that is more detail than the authors recommend for most projects. One summary of CAPs, by WBS, is generally sufficient for most projects.

To be viable, each earned value CAP must integrate three elements: (1) a defined scope of work typically expressed in the form of work tasks; (2) a timeframe to start and finish each task, i.e., the schedule; and (3) an authorized budget. Each control account plan will be performed and measured separately, and the sum of all CAPs will constitute the total project baseline. Earned value performance measurement focuses on exceptions to the baseline. The earned value concept exemplifies "management by exception."

Management will want to assess the long-term trends in project performance and take the necessary actions to maintain their planned course. Earned value is a sort of strategic trend indicator providing answers to a number of questions. For example, if the project were to continue at the present rate of performance, where would it end up? Based on the detailed plans and performance results, how much money will be needed to complete the total project? How long will it take to complete all of the work for the total project?

The purpose of earned value measurement is to discern the long-term performance direction of the project, and to be able to forecast as early as 20 percent complete what the ultimate cost and schedule requirements will be, based on actual physical performance. It provides a kind of *50,000-foot observation platform* for busy executives to monitor the long-term direction of their projects. Somewhat analogous to "critical path management" and the "float" positions, earned value metrics provide reliable indices to determine how much money and how much time it will likely take to finish the total job.

BEFORE GIVING APPROVAL: VERIFY THE VIABILITY OF THE PROJECT BASELINE.

The authorized budgets to accomplish the authorized work must be achievable. Stated another way, it would be pointless to authorize budgets which are impossible to meet, and then to track performance against the impossible targets.

---

56 See earned value criteria numbers 5, 17, 18, and 25 as summarized in the Appendix to this book.

Prior to giving official approval of the baseline, one important issue for any project manager to determine is the viability of the proposed baseline Some proposed project baselines may be flawed: accidentally, unintentionally, or sometimes deliberately. If the proposed project baseline is not realistic or achievable for whatever reason, it would be pointless to authorize it and then attempt to measure per-

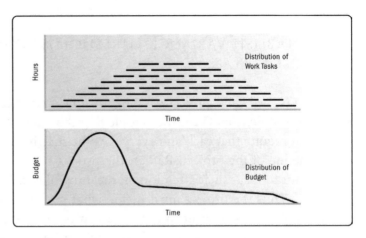

Figure 11.2 *Danger: "Front-Loaded" Baselines*

formance against it. Suggestion: First verify that the proposed baseline is doable.

One fundamental problem with project baselines can be that the authorized budget is simply too small to accomplish the authorized work. Severe competition for new business will sometimes result in inadequate budgets to accomplish the required work. Whenever this condition occurs, there is the temptation to create what is called a "front-loaded" project baseline to hide the problem. Management at all levels should take care to avoid giving approval to a front-loaded baseline. The following explains this issue further.

Illustrated in Figure 11.2 is an example of a front-loaded baseline. Displayed in the top section is a listing of all the work to be done, task by task. Shown across the bottom is a distribution of the authorized budget to accomplish this work. It would appear at first glance that there is a serious mismatch between the time phasing of the authorized work and the time phasing of the authorized budget. The distribution of budget is skewed to the left of the physical work. Accidentally or intentionally, the budget is loaded on the front part of the project.

Performing organizations, when short of adequate budget, will sometimes place adequate budget in the near-term, and then set inadequate budgets in the far-term, hoping that changes in scope will bring them fresh additional budgets. This condition needs to be watched out for.

This type of assessment can be made at the total level on a small project, or on larger projects by examining the individual CAPs, project teams, or WBS elements. The message here for project managers is to always take care to verify that there is a proper phasing of the required work versus the authorized budgets. Performance should not be tracked against unrealistic targets. Executive management, and the paying customers, have a right to know the full truth, and project managers have an obligation to report it.

ESTABLISH VARIANCE THRESHOLDS TO FOCUS ON "EXCEPTIONS" TO THE PLAN.

An earned value project baseline must be created from the bottom up based on the sum of detailed CAPs. But employing the management by exception concept does not require that each and every CAP be strictly monitored by someone throughout the life of the project. Rather, the project manager and the project team will only want to focus their attention on meaningful exceptions to baseline plans.

Thus the project must define what constitutes "meaningful" deviations from its plans. It will want to rely on a computer buzzer to go off whenever acceptable tolerances have been breached. Each project must therefore define what constitutes acceptable performance levels in order to avoid being inundated with data. These tolerances are called variance thresholds. A performance variance threshold is simply the point of unacceptable deviation from the authorized plan, i.e., management by exception.

Figure 11.3 *Thresholds for Variance Analysis (plus or minus values)*

Such variances will usually focus on at least three segments of project performance, as illustrated in Figure 11.3. For example, items 1 and 2 will be used to monitor *incremental near-term* performance as set by the project manager. Such increments will certainly represent monthly performance, but sometimes also weekly and, in extreme cases, daily performance. The frequency of project status reviews will normally determine what constitutes the proper increment to track. Incremental variances are reflective of immediate past performance and will typically incur wide deviations, a "good week," a "bad week," etc.

Items 3)and 4 reflect the *cumulative* cost or schedule performance position and will be more stable indicators of the long-term direction of the project. The cumulative positions are needed in order to forecast the final cost results on the project.

Lastly, item 5)represents the *end-position*. These critical deviations will reflect the differences between what management has authorized in the form of a total project budget and what it might require to complete all of the project work. These variances are most significant and demonstrate why we employ earned value on projects. As early as possible, at the 20 percent completion point, we want a projection of how much the project is likely to cost so that management can take immediate actions on the remaining effort.

There are no absolute guidelines for setting variance thresholds. Each project must experiment and determine its own variance levels. Thresholds can be expressed in percentage values, e.g., a 5 percent variance level, or in absolute numerical values, e.g., $10,000 increments. Sometimes projects will set positive variance thresholds at twice the value as a negative variance simply because they want to focus their attention on what is going wrong with the project.

It is not uncommon for the initial variance settings to be too tight, thus inundating the project team with too much data, much of it of little significance. No problem. Variance levels can easily be relaxed for the next measured period. Experimenting will lead to finding the right tolerance to track.

VARIANCE ANALYSIS OF INDIRECT (OVERHEAD) COSTS

There are two categories of costs a project must deal with: direct and indirect. Direct costs are relatively easy to identify and control because they are typically initiated by people working directly on the project. These costs generally represent direct labor, travel, purchased materials, computer, etc.

The second category of costs is not so easy or obvious. These are called indirect, or sometimes overhead or burden costs. These are also legitimate, but ones which cannot be identified against any given project or contract. These costs are accumulated in organizational pools (engineering, manufacturing, offsite, etc.) then allocated back to projects based on some established methodology, typically distributed as a percentage of direct charging labor. Some organizations with significant procurement effort will accumulate the costs of buying items and allocate such costs over the procured items. The indirect allocation processes will vary depending on the industry involved, but must be defined and consistently applied.

How significant are these indirect costs? Such costs will vary by industry from as little as perhaps 15 percent allocated over direct labor, to as much as 300 percent in certain industries where huge investments in capital equipment and machinery are required. The aerospace and defense industry is an example, where indirect burdens can be in the 200 to 300 percent range.

The significance of these costs is profound in the management of project costs: Direct costs can be controlled by the project manager, whereas indirect costs cannot. In fact, while the project manager may be held responsible for controlling all project costs, indirect costs are beyond the capability of any project manager to control.

Indirect costs can only be controlled by executive management, several pay grades above most project managers. What can project managers do to protect their best interests and not be blamed for conditions beyond their control? Answer: Keep good records of the relationship of "controllable" direct labor to the "uncontrollable" indirect costs. If indirect costs become excessive, exceed the budget, or overrun, the project manager must delicately remind senior management that it was their job to keep indirect costs under control. Easy for us to say!

There are two approaches to budgeting indirect costs on projects, and the choice will vary by company. For a helpful illustration of this discussion, we suggest you go back and review Figures 9.11 and 9.12. Both are examples of projects made up of the sum of CAPs. The issue: Where should indirect cost budgets be placed? Some firms follow the practice of allocating indirect cost burdens into each CAP, thus holding each CAP manager responsible for the results of indirect cost performance.

Another approach, and one practiced by many other firms, is to place indirect costs into a separate CAP, perhaps entitled "indirect costs." This approach makes the analysis of cost results a little less complicated. The budget is established based on the approved relationship of direct labor to indirect burdens, perhaps set at a rate of 100 percent. If costs go up, it results in an overrun of project costs. Should indirect costs go down, as they sometimes do, the project has a budget windfall.

What happens in real life? If indirect costs underrun, such funds are taken back by the project manager or senior management. If indirect costs go up over the budget, executive management has been known to suggest: "Can't you help us with OUR problem; perhaps use a little less direct labor on this job?"

The management of indirect costs is a necessary part of project management. That's why project managers are paid such outrageously high salaries! (Just kidding.)

There are project management software packages on the market to analyze and help control costs by category, including indirect costs. If the project manager is responsible for all project costs, including the impossible (indirect costs), they must keep track of the variances between the original budgeted baseline and the actual results being experienced.

DISPLAYS FOR MANAGEMENT OVERSIGHT

Management needs to be continuously aware of how well or how poorly each project is performing. Because earned value requires a detailed bottom-up baseline, actual performance can be tracked at various levels of a project. At a minimum, an earned value project will be monitored at the top summary level, and within each of the detailed CAPs which will sum to the top project level. As projects increase in size and complexity, management will often find it advisable to monitor and manage summary levels (project teams, for example) which will typically relate to the project's WBS.

While earned value pro-
vides a wealth of reliable data
to track, there are likely no better indicators of the health of a
project than the two common
efficiency indices called the
Schedule Performance Index
(SPI) and the Cost Performance
Index (CPI). These two indices
can represent either incremental project performance, or a
cumulative position reflecting
a more stable long-term direction for a project.

Figure 11.4 *Tracking the cumulative CPI & SPI Performance*

Cumulative SPI and CPI curves are displayed in Figure 11.4. Also shown across
the top of the chart are three major project milestones which can be compared
against the earned value curves. This chart can represent any level of interest to
management: the top project, individual CAPs, project development teams, WBS or
functional OBS displays.

The interesting aspect of tracking the cumulative SPI and cumulative CPI is the
ultimate direction each curve will take. At some point in time all SPI curves will
level off, then make their way back up to ultimately touch the 1.0 line when all the
authorized work has been completed. Although the project may be late to the original baseline plan, at the completion of the project there will be no schedule variance.
The formula for the SPI: earned value divided by the planned value.[57]

By contrast, the CPI curve is much more important and permanent. The CPI
typically does not fully recover back to the 1.0 line after performance reaches about 20
percent complete. The reason: If the project spends more than the budgeted amount for
a given segment of work, such variances represent an overrun of costs. Rarely, if ever,
are overruns recovered by subsequent performance. Cost overruns usually represent
permanent losses. The formula for the CPI: earned value divided by actual costs.[58]

Now let us review a different earned value display, perhaps one of the more
popular, illustrated in Figure 11.5. These charts are often referred to as side by side
displays and actually represent two separate data charts.

Both charts display data over a common time scale across the bottom. Both track
the same major milestones across the top. However, the vertical scales and data displayed are different on both charts. The left chart reflects cumulative performance
data for the total project, while the right chart focuses on the resulting variances
from performance.

57 *PMBOK® Guide* — Fourth Edition, 2008, p. 183.
58 Ibid, p. 183.

Figure 11.5 *Side by side displays to monitor performance*

Also of interest to management is the level of management reserve still available to the project. In this case management reserve is shown in the right chart, and there is still sufficient management reserve to cover the negative cost position.

Variance thresholds as discussed above come into play here. Once these variances have been refined to the point where they reflect only critical issues facing the project, management can focus its valuable time on only the critical issues. Each project manager must decide what type of management displays work best for the team. Displays can be easily modified to reflect whatever is deemed important to the project, which may change from the start to the finish of a particular project.

SPECIAL ISSUE: THE MEANING OF AN EARNED VALUE SCHEDULE VARIANCE (SV)

One more item needs to be understood when discussing the monitoring of performance. It may come as a surprise to many that an earned value negative "schedule variance" may not necessarily constitute a serious scheduling issue for a project. Rather, the earned value schedule variance simply reflects a variance from the approved baseline. Such deviations may or may not be critical to the project. You do not want to allocate valuable resources in the form of overtime and added people, if the negative schedule variances are not critical to completing the project on time.

As was pointed out earlier in Chapter 7 and illustrated in Figure 7.3, being ahead or behind the schedule often depends on where each task was placed in the baseline. Most earned value baselines reflect a best guess, perhaps the most likely position for each task. The time placement of a task may have little or no relationship to the project's critical path. Unfortunately, with some projects, perhaps many projects, there is little understanding of their true critical path positions.

A negative schedule variance in earned value simply means that the project has fallen behind in accomplishing its scheduled work, or the planned value. The formula is earned value (EV) less planned value (PV) equals a schedule variance (SV). As a general rule, management at all levels dislikes being behind schedule, no matter how serious the schedule variance may be. It is often an emotional issue resulting in a decree like: "Everyone on overtime," or "Bring in more people for this job!"

It is sometimes misleading to look at an earned value schedule position and rely on it alone to provide the project's schedule position. Other scheduling tools with measurement metrics are needed to discern a project's true schedule position. Earned value metrics alone may not portray an accurate assessment of schedule status.

A little history is in order. In the mid-1980s the Department of Defense (DoD) commissioned the prestigious consulting firm of Arthur D. Little to study the earned value concept and report back to them on their findings. This firm described the meaning of earned value schedule variances about as well as any we have heard. We will thus quote a couple of sentences from their final report to the DoD, inserting the term "earned value" ahead of what was then called "C/SCSC":

> *An earned value (C/SCSC) schedule variance is stated in terms of dollars of work and must be analyzed in conjunction with other schedule information such as provided by networks, Gantt charts, and line-of-balance.*
>
> *By itself, the earned value (C/SCSC) schedule variance reveals no "critical path" information, and may be misleading because unfavorable accomplishments in some areas can be offset by favorable accomplishments in others.*[59]

Whenever a project is employing earned value and it experiences a negative schedule condition, the true meaning of this condition should be understood. All that the earned value negative schedule variance indicates is that the project has fallen behind in accomplishing its planned work—that is, it is running a schedule position of less than 1.0, as is depicted in Figure 11.6. Recommendation: Tasks that are late to the original baseline plan should be carefully assessed to determine the status of two issues.

Issue One: Are any of the late tasks on the project's critical path, or on the near-critical paths, so as to potentially delay the final completion of the project? If so, overtime and/or additional resources may be warranted.

Issue Two: Are the late tasks considered to be high risks to the project? That is, do they

Figure 11.6 *Earned value schedule variances must be analyzed*

---

59 Arthur D. Little. (1986, July 10) White paper prepared for the Office of the Assistant Secretary of Defense, Comptroller.

constitute a risk of not meeting project objectives? If so, overtime and/or additional resources may be warranted.

If, however, these late to the baseline plan tasks are determined to have a positive schedule float position (slack) and are not felt to represent high risks to the project, then added resources should not be authorized. The reason is that any added resources will have a permanent negative impact on the cost efficiency rate and will produce no positive critical path schedule results. The critical path will determine the earliest time the project can be completed. Unless there are compelling reasons, additional resources should not be automatically spent merely because the project is experiencing a negative schedule variance.

A "WAR STORY"

Whenever management elects to employ earned value on a project, the project manager, the team, and executive management will receive actual performance results not available from any other technique. They will receive cost performance results which are permanent and—as in the case of early overruns of cost, which are rarely if ever recoverable—potentially very serious in nature. Earned value also provides what is called "schedule variances," and this term is often not fully understood by many project practitioners. Important point: A negative schedule variance may or may not be a serious issue to the project. It all depends on the placement of tasks in the performance measurement baseline and the project's critical path(s). Perhaps a real life story will best illustrate this issue.

Going back some thirty years, the U.S. Air Force initiated a new project to build a new aircraft costing billions of dollars and running over a decade in planned duration. It was truly a major project. Formal earned value measurement in the form of C/SCSC compliance was required.

When the performing contractor was ready to submit its first Contract Performance Report (CPR),[60] the finance manager presented the document to the Program Manager for approval. After looking over the document, the Program Manager looked up and stated, "According to this CPR, our project is about one month behind schedule. Am I reading this correctly?" The finance manager responded, "Yes, Sir. That is exactly what it is saying."

The Program Manager shook his head and said, "That is not right. We missed a critical test. Until we pass that test, we are closer to three months behind schedule. Our critical path schedule shows us three months late to schedule." Then the Program Manager gave this direction: "This CPR looks fine, so go ahead and submit

---

60 Then called a Cost Performance Report (CPR).

it. But please put a note somewhere to the effect that although the CPR shows the project to be one month behind schedule, the Program Manager's assessment based on critical path analysis is that the project is closer to three months behind schedule." The CPR was submitted with that notation.

Moral to this story: Earned value cost performance is always critical, but negative EVM schedule performance may or may not be. The importance of the schedule variance is that it is one of the first indicators to management that performance is falling behind the baseline plan. Earned value schedule results and final time forecasting should be used in conjunction with critical path analysis.

12

FORECASTING THE FINAL COST
AND SCHEDULE RESULTS

THERE ARE NUMEROUS REASONS why organizations are beginning to employ at least a simple form of earned value to help them better manage their projects. Earned value requires that projects work to a fully defined and "integrated" baseline, meaning that the defined scope of work must relate to the authorized resources, which are then locked into a timeframe for performance. We know of no other technique which fully integrates the project's scope with costs and schedules, thus providing an accurate measurement of project performance.

But perhaps the single most compelling justification for employing earned value is that it enables the project manager to be able to quickly "statistically" forecast the (probable) final cost and schedule results on the project from as early as the 20 percent completion point. With earned value, the project does not have to be 70 or 80 percent spent before it is known that it has a cost problem. The 70 percent point is too late to alter the project's final course. Earned value gives a project manager an "early warning" signal in time to take corrective action, in time to influence the final results by taking aggressive actions . . . now!

Displayed in Figure 12.1 is an example of what we are describing. This project has been defined and a total budget (BAC) authorized for the work. The project has completed only 20 percent of its work, but it is off to a bad start. Performance has not kept up with its scheduled plan, and it is spending more money to perform the completed work than management has budgeted. It is both behind schedule and experiencing an overrun. With an earned value baseline in place, a forecast of

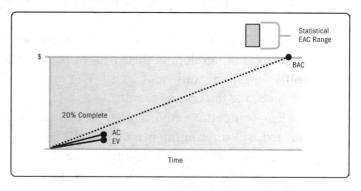

Figure 12.1 *Cost risks can be managed . . . with an "early warning"*

137

how much will be needed in added resources and time to complete the total project can be made quickly. Earned value predicts the final performance results by providing a statistical range of values, in time to take aggressive management actions should the forecasts be unacceptable.

Using earned value data, such early forecasts have been proven extremely reliable. They are based on a combination of two factors: (1) the implementation of a detailed bottom-up performance plan, and then (2) the subsequent measurement of actual performance against the project plan. These two factors have been shown to provide accurate statistical forecasts.

Two performance indices resulting from earned value are needed to forecast the project's final cost and schedule results. The first and most valuable is called the Cost Performance Index (CPI), which represents that delicate relationship between the value of the work physically completed and/or in-process and the actual costs incurred for doing such work. Spending more money than one physically performs results in an "overrun."

The second index needed to forecast final results is the Schedule Performance Index (SPI), which measures the work accomplished to the baseline plan. These two indices can be used independently or in conjunction to statistically predict the final results quickly and accurately.

Three Factors Determine the Final Project Results.

While the earned value performance indices can be most useful in predicting the final results on any project, the benefits from these indices are dependent on three critical factors. Each of these factors deserves some discussion, because they can influence the utility of the performance indices in predicting the final cost and schedule results.

Factor #1: The quality of the project's baseline plan

Not all project plans are created equal. Some individuals and companies are quite good at developing their project plans. Others are not. Some people consistently "fire first" and "aim later." The quality of project plans will vary and will influence the final project results.

The competitive environment under which a given project plan may be implemented will often influence or bias the project manager's strategy. Competition sometimes results in risk-taking by the creators of the plans, and will also incorporate varying degrees of uncertainty into the final baseline plans. Project plans are often different depending upon the amount of competition present when management gives its final approval. Earned value simply measures performance against the baseline plan, whether the plan is realistic, ambitious, or even impossible to meet.

The quickest way to experience "scope creep" is to not adequately define the initial project scope. The surest way to "overrun" project costs is to under-budget the project. The quickest way to assure a schedule slip is to mandate a completion date which is impossible to achieve. Earned value accurately measures project performance, but must assume that scope definition is adequate, and that the project has been given an achievable budget and a realistic schedule.

Factor #2: Actual performance against the approved baseline plan

Once the project plan has been approved and implemented, another important variable comes into play. This variable is the actual performance results measured against the authorized plan. Is the project's performance meeting, exceeding, or falling behind the approved project plan? Such performance factors can be quantified and monitored for the duration of the project.

Both the cost performance index (CPI) and the schedule performance index (SPI) efficiency factors can be watched for trends, and also used to statistically forecast the final results for any project employing earned value.

Factor #3: Management's determination to influence the final results

A third factor is the most critical and can often influence the project's final results. If project management closely tracks the earned value performance trends and does not like, or cannot accept, the final forecasted results, to what extent will management take aggressive actions on the remaining work to alter the final outcome?

Final forecasted results are not necessarily preordained. Final project results can often be altered, but only when aggressive management actions are taken early. There are several critical variables. To what extent will project performance data be monitored and the data believed by management? What actions will be authorized to alter the management approach on the remaining project tasks? And finally, if the project's final forecasts are unacceptable, to what extent will all discretionary (non-critical) work be eliminated, budgets reduced, risks taken, and so forth, in order to bring the final projected results down to acceptable levels?

Aggressive project management actions, if taken quickly, can often alter the final projected outcome for the project.

THE PROJECT MANAGERS "OFFICIAL" ESTIMATE AT COMPLETION (EAC)

(Formula: EAC = AC + Bottom-up ETC)

When individuals accept the responsibility for all aspects of project performance, including the technical quality, costs and schedule performance, they in effect put their careers on the line. If things go well, management knows precisely who to credit. If things go poorly, management also knows precisely who to hold accountable. Thus when it comes to forecasting the final cost results on any project, the person holding the job title of "project manager" should have a major say as to the value of the final forecast, called the estimate at completion (EAC).

How do projects typically estimate their final costs? The *PMBOK® Guide* describes this process about as well as any book we have read, so we will paraphrase their suggested approach.[61] Most projects, when it becomes apparent that they are going to exceed management's authorized budget, will take their total costs for the work performed and prepare a new detailed estimate to complete (ETC) all of the remaining work. The formula is thus: Cumulative Actual Costs plus a new ETC. This forecast is likely the most reliable, because it builds on the actual experience of the project for the work performed to date.

However, what's wrong with this approach? Answer: Preparing the ETC is a royal pain in the neck! Preparing a new ETC is *non-project work.* The same people who are performing on the project, who are often frustrated because they are running behind their initial schedule, must now stop doing real project work and prepare a new baseline plan called the ETC. Rightfully, most project professionals resent (perhaps hate) doing an ETC. And to add insult to injury, there is never a budget to cover the "ETC preparation." Management is often unsympathetic and says: *"What's the big deal? You've got all night and this weekend to prepare a new ETC."*

Whenever a project commits to employing even a simple form of earned value, the project team will want to focus on the actual results against their baseline plan. They will look for

Figure 12.2 *Monitoring earned value performance*

61 PMBOK® Guide — Fourth Edition, 2008, pp. 184-185.

exceptions to the plan and monitor the schedule variances and cost variances, as displayed in Figure 12.2. Perfect schedule performance can be quantified as 1.0. For every dollar of work planned they achieve a dollar of earned value. For every dollar spent they get a dollar of earned value, thus also achieving a perfect cost performance of 1.0. The focus is on the earned value achieved versus the schedule plan and the cost actuals. These same baseline variances can be converted into efficiency factors taking the form of the CPI and SPI, which can be used to forecast the final project results.

By employing earned value, any project can develop an independent range of statistical EACs in a matter of seconds. The range of statistical EACs can then be compared against the project manager's latest official EAC, or even used in lieu of the project manager's EAC should management have sufficient confidence in the earned value process in place. In the latter case the project can then avoid the undesirable necessity of stopping real project work to prepare a new detailed ETC.

And if the forecasted value is undesirable or unacceptable to management, actions can be taken immediately to bring the projected final costs down to acceptable levels.

EARNED VALUE METHODS TO INDEPENDENTLY FORECAST A "RANGE" OF FINAL EACS

Earned value management allows any project to continuously monitor its cost (CPI) and schedule (SPI) efficiency rates, reflecting their actual performance trends. These efficiency indices can also be used to statistically forecast the expected final position on a continuous basis. Projects which elect not to employ earned value miss this opportunity to precisely quantify their actual performance.

Over the years numerous formulas have evolved to statistically forecast the final estimated EACs on any project employing earned value. By last count, there were close to twenty distinct formulas available to predict the final cost position. However, in this discussion we will limit ourselves to suggesting just three of the more accepted formulas, as portrayed in Figure 12.3. These three formulas will provide the project with a "best case," a "most likely case," and

Figure 12.3 *Forecasting a Range of Estimates at Completion*

a "worst case" scenario. These three independent EACs can be quickly compared against the project manager's "official EAC" to assess whether or not the project might be experiencing a cost problem.

One important point to understand: by preparing a range of EACs we are not trying to pick a final forecasted number for the project. That task rightfully belongs to the project manager and is typically done with a bottom-up ETC as described above, not with a statistical forecast. Rather, we are simply attempting to assess whether or not the project may have a cost problem which needs management's immediate attention.

The processes of statistically forecasting a range of final cost estimates will center on setting three variables for a project as of any given point in time:

First: Determine the total of actual costs incurred to date, *which is always a challenge, but it is critical to relate to the earned value credited.*

Second: Determine the value of the Work Remaining (WR), *which by definition is considered to be the budgeted value for the uncompleted work. This is typically expressed as the total Budget at Completion (BAC), less the Earned Value already accomplished, which equals the WR.*

Third: Divide the Work Remaining (WR) by some performance factor (PF), *like 1.0, the cumulative CPI, or the CPI times SPI, for example.*

With use of these three variables, the estimated final costs to complete a project can be statistically forecast within a few seconds.

Special Issue: Management Reserve (MR) or Contingency Reserve (CR)

One important issue needs to be mentioned for any project which may have management reserves (MR) or contingency reserves (CR): What do you do with MR and or CR when making a statistical EAC forecast? For many projects this may be a non-issue, because management may not allow MR or CR. However, if there are MR or CR funds available to the project manager, they must be considered while making a final statistical cost projection, and instructions must be given to the spreadsheet. One of three scenarios can impact MR or CR funds when projecting a statistical EAC:

1. The final EAC forecast can *exclude* the full value of the remaining MR or CR funds, which assumes that these funds will not be consumed by the project;

2. The remaining MR or CR can be *divided* by some negative performance efficiency factor (the CPI, or the CPI times SPI), which will increase the final projected costs; or

3. The MR or CR can simply be *added* to the calculated EAC at its full 1.0 value, which assumes that these funds will be consumed, but at their full budgeted value.

Since the allocation of MR or CR typically goes for specific, well defined tasks at the time the budget is released, we would tend to support option number three. We would add the full value of MR or CR to the EAC and expect a 1.0 efficiency rate.

The assumed use of MR or CR funds is a judgment call by the project manager.

Special Issue: Level of Effort (LOE) Tasks

If you haven't gotten the message yet, the authors do not like Level of Effort (LOE) measurement. Our reason: LOE tasks measure the passage of time, period. They do not measure performance of work. Since the measurement of LOE tasks is set on "autopilot," with planned value automatically becoming earned value with the passage of time, irrespective of whether any work was ever done, LOE can seriously distort project performance measurement.

In Chapter 9 we suggested that all LOE work be "quantified" and "quarantined." This approach was displayed in Figure 9.4. With respect to forecasting the final costs for LOE, we do have a suggestion.

Take the quarantined LOE tasks off autopilot. Do not measure LOE work by assuming that planned value becomes earned value with the passage of time. Rather, our recommendation is to convert all LOE tasks to subjective percent complete estimates, as displayed in Item 3 of Figure 9.3. While subjective percent complete estimates are not the best measurement possible, they are far better than the distortions resulting when PV becomes EV automatically.

FORECASTING A "RANGE" OF ESTIMATES AT COMPLETION[62]

The "Mathematical" or "Overrun to Date" Estimate at Completion

(Formula: EAC = AC + BAC – EV)

---

62 This approach is aligned with the *PMBOK® Guide* — Fourth Edition, 2008, pp. 184-185.

Figure 12.4 *The "Mathematical" or "Overrun to Date" EAC*

The first of the three forecasting techniques to be discussed goes by several terms in industry: the "Mathematical EAC," "Overrun to date EAC," or "ETC at budgeted rate." It doesn't matter which. This EAC method is depicted in Figure 12.4, with two formulas which are also displayed in the two boxes across the bottom. The easiest formula to use is simply: Mathematical EAC = Actual Costs, plus the BAC, less the Earned Value. However, in order to compare the three statistical EAC methods using a similar format, we have also provided the formula on the left: Actual Costs plus the Work Remaining (BAC – EV) divided by a 1.0 performance factor (PF). Both formulas will provide the same results.

In this scenario the performance factor for the remaining work is 1.0, which means it assumes that all future work, starting immediately, will be done precisely at the full budgeted rate. Sometimes this is an ambitious goal. This EAC formula is not widely accepted in U.S. Government quarters and has actually been referred to as "useless." However, we like it and it is frequently used within private industry for a couple of valid reasons.

The first reason to use this formula: The Mathematical or Overrun to date EAC is often the first indication to the project manager and executive management that they may have a cost problem on their project. As we discussed earlier, in Chapter 1, if a project spends $300,000 to accomplish only $200,000 of budgeted work, the project has experienced a "cost overrun" for the initial work it has performed. Management deserves to know this fact.

The second reason to use this formula: The Mathematical EAC is important because an early overrun does not typically go away with the passage of time. We have rarely ever witnessed a front-end overrun magically disappearing through exemplary (under-running) performance of the remaining work.

Think about it. In a project baseline, is the best scope definition, the best planning, the best budget, and the best scheduled dates placed in the first half or the last half of the baseline? Answer: It is likely that the best of everything will be incorporated into the first half of the baseline plan. Thus, if a project incurs an overrun in the first half, what are the chances of making a later recovery of the overrun? Answer: little to none. This EAC formula provides a sort of minimum overrun floor that typically does not go away.

Short of a project dropping scope features, or the outright elimination of authorized tasks, an overrun in the early phases of the project is very serious and likely constitutes a permanent loss of funds to any project. The Mathematical or Overrun to date EAC formula adds utility, in that it constitutes the lowest or "best case" scenario in the range of possible final costs for any project.

The "Cumulative CPI" Estimate at Completion

(Formula: EAC = BAC / Cumulative CPI)

The likely most common and most respected of all the earned value statistical forecasting methods, called the *Cumulative CPI Estimate at Completion,* is displayed in Figure 12.5. Two formulas can be used for this method and both are displayed at the bottom of the chart. A long method is shown on the left and the short formula on the right. Considerable scientific data has been accumulated and studied to support this method's reliability as a forecasting method.

Figure 12.5 *The Low-End "Cumulative CPI" EAC*

Take note of the requirement for use of only *cumulative performance data*, not periodic or incremental data. While any project team will certainly want to monitor their periodic position to assess recent performance results, periodic data are too subject to anomalies, sometimes caused by placing good data into the wrong timeframe. Cumulative performance data tends to smooth out variations, but nevertheless retaining its value as a long-term forecasting tool.

The cumulative (not periodic) CPI provides a particularly reliable index to watch, because it has been demonstrated to be an accurate and reliable forecasting metric. The cumulative CPI has been shown to stabilize from as early as the 20 percent point in the project's percent completion point. One particularly important scientific study described the value of using the cumulative CPI to forecast the final cost results on projects:

> **Researchers found that the cumulative CPI does not change by more than ten percent once a contract is twenty percent complete; in most cases, the cumulative CPI only worsens as a contract proceeds to completion.**[63]

---

63 Dr. David S. Christensen. (1994, Spring). Using performance indices to evaluate the estimate at completion. *The Journal of Cost Analysis, of the Society of Cost Estimating and Analysis*, 19.

Let us pause to reflect on these important empirical findings about all projects employing earned value: One, project performance results at the 20 percent completion point will stabilize, and Two, the remaining performance will not likely change by more than plus or minus 10 percent at the point of project completion. What an empirical finding! No other project management technique provides such performance insight.

Some people consider the cumulative CPI EAC formula to represent the "most likely" case to predict final costs to complete all work. Others consider it to be simply the "minimum" final estimate of project costs. Either way, the cumulative CPI EAC has been demonstrated to be most accurate in providing a quick statistical forecast of the final required project costs. Such statistical forecasts, when compared against the project manager's "official" estimate, should never be ignored by executive management.

Just how important is this particular method to the Department of Defense (DoD), who has been using earned value data to forecast final cost results for almost four decades? In 1991, when the DoD transferred the requirement for earned value management directly into their DoD acquisition policy, they also added language specifically requiring that the "cumulative CPI" be employed whenever forecasting the final costs:

> *Provide the estimate at completion reflecting the best professional judgement of the servicing cost analysis organization. If the contract is at least 15 percent complete and the estimate is lower than that calculated using the cumulative cost performance index, provide an explanation.*[64]

There may be valid justification supporting an estimate at completion value lower than that calculated using the cumulative CPI. However, since 1991, all DoD project managers must describe how this (unlikely) event will be accomplished. The cumulative CPI EAC forecast is a vital technique for use on all earned value projects.

The "Cumulative CPI times SPI" Estimate at Completion

(Formula: EAC = AC + ((BAC − EV)/(CPI x SPI))

The last statistical formula with wide professional acceptance in forecasting the final project costs is one that combines both the cost efficiency (CPI) factor and the schedule efficiency (SPI) factor. This method is displayed in Figure 12.6, and its

---

64 U.S. Department of Defense. (1991, February 23). Policy Instruction 5000.2, Part 11, Section B, Attachment 1. Washington, D.C.

formula is shown in the box at the bottom of the chart. Note: There is no short formula to calculate this EAC forecast.

There is a solid rational basis to support the use of a forecasting formula which incorporates both the cost and the schedule efficiency dimensions. The reason: No project team ever likes to be in a position of creating a performance

Figure 12.6 *The High-End "Cumulative CPI times SPI" EAC*

plan, getting management's approval, and then falling behind with their authorized plan. There is a natural human tendency to want to get back on schedule, even if it means consuming more resources to accomplish the same amount of authorized work. The use of paid overtime and additional resources (more people) are often employed, which simply results in permanent, non-recoverable cost damage to their most important efficiency factor, the CPI.

Some people consider this formula to be a "worst case" or high-end EAC scenario. The authors are in this camp. Others, particularly within the DoD, consider it to represent the "most likely" forecast. In either case, the CPI times the SPI EAC is one of the more widely used and accepted formulas to statistically forecast the high-end cost requirements for any project. It should be used any time the project is driven by a specific completion date, which would include most projects.

✳ ✳ ✳

Question: What is the utility of providing a statistical range (low/most-likely/ high) of final cost results for a given project? Simply put, it is to test the reasonableness of the project manager's "official" cost position against a statistical range of possible earned value forecasts. Earned value forecasts can quickly provide management with an understanding of the cost risks facing any project.

If the project manager predicts a final cost performance of the project outside of the statistical range, either above or below it, then the rationale for this position should be explained to all parties who have a vested interest in the project. Those parties with a vested interest in project cost performance would be the project's owner, senior executive management, corporate shareholders, and so forth.

Under the Sarbanes-Oxley Act of 2002, covered in Chapter 15, the Chief Financial Officer (CFO) and the Chief Executive Officer (CEO) will also have an interest in the reasonableness of these final estimated values.

TIME MANAGEMENT: PREDICTING THE PROJECT'S FINAL COMPLETION DATE

How long will it take to complete the project? This is another matter of great interest to any project manager, to executive management, and especially to the owner or paying customer. By definition, a project can only be completed within the outer limits of its critical path, which is defined as:

> **the longest path through a project, and so [it] determines the earliest completion for the work.**[65]

The management of the project's critical path and the near-critical paths are thus vital to the successful completion of any project at the earliest possible date. An important point to understand is that the earned value schedule performance data alone will *not* be sufficient to manage or predict the project's time dimension. Projects need to have a solid scheduling process in place which allows them to manage their critical paths.

As was discussed in the last chapter, earned value schedule variances represent the difference between what was actually physically accomplished (the earned value) minus what was planned to be accomplished (the planned value). The formula is SV = EV – PV.

Negative earned value schedule variances are important, because they are often one of the first indicators of problems. Negative schedule variances indicate that the project is falling behind its baseline plan, period Also, earned value schedule variances may be used in conjunction with the critical path method (CPM) as a way of reinforcing the forecasted date for project completion. However, a word of caution: Do not rely on earned value schedule variances *alone* to help predict the final completion date for a project.

Displayed in Figure 12.7 is a chart that depicts the earned value schedule status. As of the status date, halfway through a

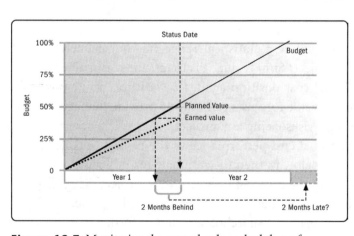

Figure 12.7 *Monitoring the earned value schedule performance*

65 Dr. James P. Lewis. (1995). *Project Planning Scheduling and Control.* (Revised Edition). Chicago: Irwin Professional Publishing, p. 120.

two-year project, the baseline plan calls for completion of so much work, but the project has only accomplished a portion of that work. They are experiencing a negative earned value schedule position.

If we trace the intersection of the earned value line with the status date, then trace backwards to the planned value line, and then move downward to the bottom time scale, we can see that the project is running roughly two months behind its planned value or baseline schedule. Does this late condition automatically translate into a two-month slip of the project's completion date? Not necessarily. It all depends on whether the late tasks are on the critical path, or are high risk activities.

All that can be concluded from earned value schedule performance data is that the project is currently behind its planned schedule. Nothing more. However, there are some professionals in the field who feel that the earned value schedule position can be used to predict the final completion date for the project. The authors do not endorse this theory. Nor have they ever read any scientific studies which support this position.

The most reliable basis for predicting the final completion date of a project is the use of the project's critical path. Earned value schedule data can be useful for reinforcing the projections of the critical path. But, by itself, earned value data are not adequate to manage the project's time dimension, in the opinion of the authors.

The utility of a project's SV and SPI is that they can be used in conjunction with the CV and CPI to predict the final cost requirements on any project. Also, a negative earned value schedule variance is one of the first indicators that a project is not performing to its plan.

In Summary

The bottom-line issue for any project is typically how much it will cost to complete the job, and how much time is there until the project is over. Two reliable techniques for determining these factors are currently available to any project manager: the use of earned value cost performance data, and the CPM.

While many projects today will employ the CPM to manage the time dimension for their projects, the use of earned value measurement data has been somewhat limited. It is our belief that the two techniques work well together and are in fact complementary. When these two proven techniques are used by people working with a single integrated database, they can provide accurate and reliable forecasts to answer the age-old questions: How long will my project take to complete, and how much money will it cost? Earned value data can be used to predict the project's cost dimension, and CPM can be used to predict the project's time dimension.

$$\left(\ 13\ \right)$$

USING EARNED VALUE METRICS TO
MANAGE A PORTFOLIO OF PROJECTS

A portfolio refers to a collection of projects or programs and other work that are grouped together to facilitate effective management of that work to meet strategic business objectives.
— *PMBOK® GUIDE*—FOURTH EDITION[66]

Portfolio management is the coordinated management of portfolio components to achieve specific organizational objectives.
—*THE STANDARD FOR PORTFOLIO MANAGEMENT* —
SECOND EDITION [67]

. . . . effective new product development is emerging as the major corporate strategic initiative of the decades ahead.

. . . . those companies that fail to excel at developing new products will invariably disappear or be gobbled up by the winners.

A vital question in this new product battleground is: How should corporations most effectively invest their R & D and new product resources? That's what portfolio management is all about: resource allocation to achieve corporate new product objectives.
—*PORTFOLIO MANAGEMENT FOR NEW PRODUCTS* [68]

THE DEVELOPMENT and infusion of new products is vital to the continuous success of any organization. The decisions executives must make as to which new products to develop are essentially subjective calls dealing with a combination

---

66 PMBOK® Guide —Fourth Edition, 2008: ANSI/PMI 99-001-2008, Project Management Institute, p. 8.
67 The Standard for Portfolio Management —Second Edition, 2008: ANSI/PMI 08-003-2008, Project Management Institute, p. 4.
68 Robert G. Cooper, Scott J. Edgett, and Elko J. Kleinschmidt. (1998). *Portfolio Management for New Products.* Reading, Massachusetts: Addison-Wesley, p. 1.

of factors: the marketplace, technical issues, the risks, how much to invest, when payback can be expected, etc. Will the new product, once available, satisfy the perceived needs in the marketplace? And will our particular new product be the one embraced by that market?

The employment of earned value metrics in the management of a portfolio of projects will not by itself assure that executives will make the right new product choices. That is an intrinsic executive skill. But earned value and the unique metrics it can provide will help executive management make better choices by providing accurate, reliable and timely data to reinforce their decisions. How are our projects doing? What is the real total cost and status of our ongoing projects? How much will it actually cost to complete these projects? Is there enough money to fund all of the desired projects, or must some projects be terminated early? If the organization lacks the resources to complete all projects, which ones should be continued, and which ones cancelled? If there is a shortfall of funding, the earlier that fact is addressed, the better it will be for the organization.

Earned value management and the data it provides can help management make these difficult choices. EVM metrics provide a common language so that true comparisons can be made, one project against all other projects. But an interesting observation: With all the material written on the subject of portfolio management, not once have the authors ever read about the use of earned value metrics in the process of making portfolio decisions. How unfortunate.

While a number of metrics become available with earned value, two in particular would seem to be most critical: the Cost Performance Index (CPI) and the To Complete Performance Index (TCPI). Both can be compared to all projects within an organizational portfolio.

The CPI represents work physically accomplished and the budget for such work, compared to the actual costs spent to accomplish the work. The CPI thus represents the cost efficiency factor for a given project. If a project spends more than its budget, that is an overrun which can be used to predict the final costs of a project with a high degree of confidence.

The second EVM metric of particular use in portfolio management is the TCPI. It represents the standard of work which must be accomplished in the future, the performance bar, in order to meet the financial goals set by management. The TCPI is a most powerful metric resulting from employing earned value. However, the TCPI hasn't been discussed yet, and we need to fully understand its utility. It can be a most valuable aid in the management of a portfolio of projects.

The To Complete (the remaining work) Performance Index (TCPI)[69]

Unfortunately, one of the most valuable metrics resulting from earned value employment has been kept almost a secret among a few gurus working in the earned value community. This stealth metric is called the "To Complete Performance Index" (TCPI). It should be used in conjunction with tracking the cumulative CPI. The TCPI can be one of the most insightful tracking indices, if only the project manager, the project team, and in particular executive management know what it is and how to interpret the performance data. A typical TCPI display is illustrated in Figure 13.1. The cumulative CPI as shown represents the past work which has been completed, or the sunk costs, and the TCPI constitutes future work, or opportunity costs.

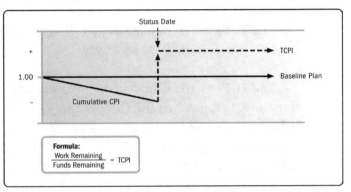

Figure 13.1 *The To Complete (the work) Performance Index (TCPI)*

The TCPI addresses the question: What performance factor (CPI) must the project achieve in order to meet some tangible final financial goal? It takes the "work remaining" (defined as the BAC, less EV) and divides it by the "funds remaining."

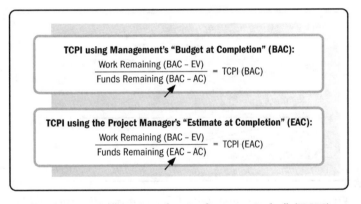

Figure 13.2 *Two "To Complete Performance Index" (TCPI) Formulas*

The funds remaining can be represented by two distinct financial goals, as are displayed in Figure 13.2. The first is management's authorized Budget at Completion (BAC), less the funds used (AC). The second is the project manager's latest Estimate at Completion (EAC), less the funds already used (AC).

The first financial goal for any project is to stay within the original budget (BAC) authorized by management. This is a paramount financial objective, until such time as it becomes obvious that this goal is no longer achievable. At that time the project manager will typically provide a new estimate of the necessary funds required to

---

[69] The PMBOK® *Guide* — Fourth Edition, 2008, contains a new section on the TCPI; see pages 185-186.

complete the project, called the EAC, and request that management authorize the increased funding. Once management authorizes the new EAC, all parties will track performance to the EAC using the formula as displayed at the bottom in Figure 13.2.

Both financial goals (the BAC or EAC) are critical to the success of any project, so both will need to be discussed and understood separately.

The TCPI using Management's *Budget* at Completion (BAC)
(The issue: Is the BAC achievable?)

The TCPI metric is important any time a project experiences negative cost performance, that is, when the CPI is running below 1.0 performance. A negative CPI indicates the project is spending more than it has budgeted for the work completed. It is overrunning its costs. The issue then becomes: Will the current overrun cause the project to need more funds than management has authorized in its budget (BAC)? Figure 13.3 is a project performance chart representing the baseline plan, the cumulative CPI, and the TCPI necessary to stay within management's authorized funds (the BAC).

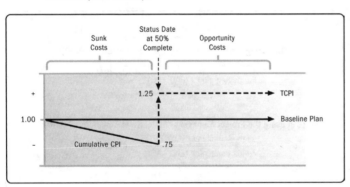

Figure 13.3 *The relationship of Cumulative CPI versus TCPI*

The cumulative CPI can best be thought of as actual "sunk costs." If a project spends more money than it has budgeted for the completed work, those costs are likely gone forever. Early overruns of costs are rarely (if ever) fully recovered by subsequent performance. The remaining work ahead can thus be considered to be "opportunity costs." That is, if any cost improvements are to be made, they must come from the future work.

When managing a portfolio of projects, executives will want to begin the continuous comparison of earned value performance data as early as possible, 10 percent, 20 percent, 30 percent, etc. To illustrate the utility of the TCPI, we will focus on the 50 percent completion point to best describe the concept.

When monitoring the TCPI, the juncture at the 50 percent completion point is critical to any project. It represents the point at which the sunk costs will precisely equal the opportunity costs. At the point of 50 percent complete, a cost performance factor (CPI) of .75 can only be offset by completing all future work at the inverse value of 1.25. How likely is this to happen? Probably not likely, but it is theoretically possible. However, once the project goes past the 50 percent completion point, the sunk costs will exceed the opportunity costs, and the required performance factor to meet the financial goal will increase exponentially.

At some point the project manager and executive management will recognize that "more funds are needed" in order to complete this project. Management then has some hard choices to make: fund the project to completion, or terminate the project.

The TCPI using the Project Manager's *Estimate* at Completion (EAC)
(The issue: Is the current EAC realistic and achievable?)

Once it becomes obvious that a project can no longer be completed within management's authorized funds (the BAC), the next question then becomes: What is the real number needed to complete the project, or the EAC? Please note, here we are not talking about the statistically calculated EACs as discussed in the last chapter—the Mathematical, CPI, or CPI times SPI calculated EACs. Rather we are referring to the project manager's official position on what it will take to complete the project. This is typically created by taking the actual costs to date and then preparing a new detailed task by task estimate to complete the job.

Project managers by their very nature are optimistic individuals. This optimism can sometimes have an influence on what the project manager is willing to accept as a final challenge. One's personal pride often comes into play. Sometimes, the real number of required costs to complete the project is withheld, at least temporarily. The project manager's official EAC may increase each month, a piece at a time. This condition is unfortunate, but too often real.

However, senior management and/or the buying customer deserve to know the full truth, because it is their monies. They may elect to cancel the project and invest their funds in other endeavors. That is where the TCPI based on available EAC funds becomes a critical issue. A TCPI based on the EAC funds can be used to validate the reasonableness of the project manager's official EAC.

We suggest you refer to Figure 13.4 for an illustration of this discussion. In this display we have portrayed the baseline plan, and the cumulative CPI curve which is in negative territory. Also shown are the three statistically calculated EVM formulas: (1) the Mathematical

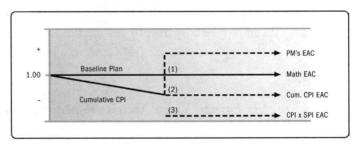

Figure 13.4 *Using the TCPI to validate the Project Manager's EAC*

EAC, (2) the cumulative CPI EAC, and (3) the CPI times SPI EAC. Note that the Mathematical EAC is merely an extension of the baseline plan for all the future work. Also, the CPI EAC is simply an extension of the cumulative CPI.

Assume for a moment that the project manager provides an Official EAC as displayed at the top right line entitled "PM's EAC." The project manager is thus suggesting final costs at a value less than that calculated with the Mathematical EAC. Is this likely to happen? Hardly. This EAC assumes a complete absorption of all overrun work to date. Short of a miracle or dropping scope features, it will not happen. And yet, a project manager will sometimes forecast such estimates to get management "off my back." The PM's Official EAC will not happen. But without the TCPI display, an unrealistic EAC may go unchallenged for several months and the non-recoverable or sunk costs will continue to rise.

It is likely that the best performance the project will do is the Mathematical EAC. It accepts performance to-date, good or bad, and assumes that all future performance will be at the budgeted rate. This is an optimistic forecast but one that is possible, particularly if the risks are minimal on future work.

Now let us assess the second scenario as displayed with the EAC, at the Cumulative CPI line. It assumes that all future work will be at the same performance rate as the past rate. There is considerable empirical evidence to support this formula, particularly with Department of Defense studies. We would classify this as the most likely formula.

Lastly, let us examine the high-end EAC at line 3. This EAC assumes a further deterioration of cost performance at less than the cumulative CPI. Is this a reasonable EAC? Perhaps yes, if the project is running behind its schedule and management wants the project completed by a certain firm date. In this case it will likely allocate more resources to perform the same planned work. Senior management and the buying customer should inquire as to the basis for the forecast in the range of the third level.

The utility of the TCPI based on either the BAC or EAC is that it allows management at all levels to assess the future requirements of a project based on the past earned value performance. It portrays in graphical form the past performance (the sunk costs) in the form of the CPI, versus the future requirements (opportunity costs) in the form of the TCPI, so that management at all levels can feel comfortable that their financial goals can in fact be met. The TCPI can be a valuable aid in the cost management process. It can reduce cost risks by testing the reasonableness of financial goals. The TCPI metric can apply to a single project or to a portfolio of projects.

Using Six Earned Value Metrics to Manage a Portfolio of Projects

Once an organization commits to applying earned value management to the projects in a portfolio, a wealth of unique data becomes available to management. But without getting inundated in more data than can be assimilated, we will focus on only six EVM metrics which seem to add insight to the status and future direction of these portfolio projects. These six metrics are displayed in Figure 13.5 in three categories: schedule and cost performance to date, a range of final cost requirements, and the risks of not achieving management's financial goals.

Project Title: _____ Budget at Completion: _____

Use: Assessing Performance To Date:

    1. Schedule Performance Index (SPI)
    2. Cost Performance Index (CPI)

Use: Forecasting a Range of Cost Estimates At Completion:

    3. EVM Mathematical EAC
    4. EVM Cum CPI EAC
    5. EVM Cum CPI x Cum SPI EAC

Use: Assessing Future Performance Risks:

    6. TCPI (BAC or EAC)

Figure 13.5 *Portfolio Management: Tracking 6 Key Earned Value Metrics*

The first broad issue to address is: How has each project performed thus far? Two EVM metrics focus on performance to date. The Schedule Performance Index (SPI) quantifies the accomplishment of physical work against the baseline plan. The formula: SPI = Earned Value/Planned Value. For example: If 90 percent of the planned work was accomplished, the SPI would be reflecting an SPI of .9. Or, stated another way, they are 10 percent behind their baseline plan. The SPI metric can be compared to any project in the portfolio to determine whether or not each project is keeping up with its planned work. The SPI is one of the first indicators that the project is falling behind its baseline plan.

A related metric is project cost performance, or a question of what we are getting for the funds we are spending. The CPI reflects cost performance, with a formula of CPI = Earned Value/Actual Costs. The CPI is likely the most important EVM metric, for negative cost performance is seldom if ever fully recovered by a project. If a project reflects a CPI of .75, it indicates the project is accomplishing 75 cents of value for every dollar it spends. The project is overrunning its costs by about 25 percent! The .75 CPI can be compared against all other projects in the portfolio to assess the cost performance of each project.

The next issue to be assessed with use of earned value metrics is: What are the final projected cost requirements (called Estimate at Completion, or EAC) for each project, based on actual performance? While a multitude of EAC formulas are available, we will use the three EAC formulas as described in the current *PMBOK® Guide.*[70] The three formulas provide for a range of EACs representing the best case, most likely case, and worst case scenarios.

70 PMBOK® Guide — Fourth Edition, 2008, section 7.3.2.2.

The best case EAC is likely that any overrun experienced thus far is absorbed, and that all future work will be accomplished at the budgeted rate. This approach is presented in Figure 13.4, projection number 1. It assumes that for every future dollar spent a dollar worth of value will be achieved. This is a highly optimistic but achievable forecast.

The most likely forecast is represented by Figure 13.4, item number 2. It assumes that all future work will be performed at the cumulative value of the CPI.

The last forecast, and likely a worst case scenario, is displayed in Figure 13.4, number 3. The future projection is made up of the cumulative CPI times the cumulative SPI, which significantly raises the costs for work remaining. This forecast incorporates a late schedule condition and attempts to recover the late schedule.

The last use of the six EVM metrics attempts to determine whether or not the BAC or the EAC are adequate to do the job. It uses the TCPI to assess the adequacy of funds to finish the total job. It would serve no purpose to measure project performance against an unrealistic budget, or a final estimate that cannot be achieved.

These six EVM formulas will not automatically help executive management make the right choices in the issue: Which projects do we fund, and which projects do we terminate? But it will help in the assessment of the projects making up a portfolio.

14

Implement "Simple"
Earned Value on All Projects

EMPLOYING EARNED VALUE on a project can be easy and yet challenging. The easy part is that there is nothing inherently difficult about the earned value concept. By simply following fundamental project management practices, anyone can employ the concept on any project.

However, the challenging part is that it takes some discipline to consistently employ fundamental project management practices within any organization. And earned value, in order to be measured, requires that fundamental project management practices be strictly followed. If corners are cut, certain basic requirements are bypassed, and then earned value cannot be effectively implemented.

At a minimum, project goals must be set. The project's scope of work must be defined, a measurable baseline plan must be put in place, tightly controlled, and the measurement of actual performance must take place routinely. These are fundamental practices which are often circumvented by organizations not yet ready to move from their "functional fiefdoms" over to "management by projects."

Earned value management as a concept is most often defined by professionals as being fully compliant with all of the 32 criteria described in the Appendix to this book. This is fine for large megaprojects. But most of the projects we work with are not in the megaproject, multi-billion dollar class.

The authors have studied the concept and have summarized just ten fundamental steps which are necessary to implement a "simple" (low-end) form of earned value management on projects. This is "Earned Value for the Masses." These are the minimum requirements necessary to employ simple earned value. With each of these ten steps as described below, we will also make reference to a specific earned value criterion described in the Appendix to this book.

Step 1: To the extent possible, you must define the full scope of the project.
(EVM Criterion #1)

This is perhaps the most important requirement for implementing earned value, and perhaps the most difficult to achieve. Management of certain types of projects, notably software, often give up at this point and refuse to go further. They often relinquish.

On any project, you must define the work to be done, if for no better reason than to know where you are and when you are done. To the extent that you can, you must define 100 percent of the scope of the project. This is true for any project, but it is particularly critical on any project in which you intend to measure earned value.

With earned value we constantly focus on the authorized work which has been completed, plus management's official authorized budget for the completed work. We express the project's status as being "15 percent complete," "25 percent complete," "50 percent complete," and so forth. Point: If we have not defined what constitutes 100 percent of the project, how can we ever assess our percentage completion point? We can't.

Realistically, no new project will ever be defined with absolute precision. But one must make some educated assumptions about a new project in order to quantify and then decompose the work with sufficient confidence that the effort can then be planned, scheduled and budgeted with some degree of certainty. Anything less, and management will be committing to a new project by providing essentially a "blank check." Vague scope definition invites scope creep.

How does one define a new job when specific details are often lacking? There are no absolute answers. But one of the most useful of all tools available to any project manager is the Work Breakdown Structure (WBS). The WBS is to the project manager what the organization chart is to the executive. A WBS allows the project manager to define a new endeavor by laying out all the assumed work within the framework of the WBS, and then decomposing each element into measurable work packages.

Additionally, once the WBS is assumed to constitute a reasonable portrayal of the new project, the WBS framework can then be used to take the next critical steps in the project planning process, including make or buy analysis, risk assessment, scheduling, estimating, and ultimately the authorization of budgets to proceed.

Step 2: You must determine who will perform the defined work, including the identification of all major critical procurements. (EVM Criterion #2)

It does make a difference to the project who will perform the defined work. Experienced workers generally work better and faster than inexperienced people, but they also cost more. Often, using an experienced workforce is a good investment. However, sometimes the project's own organization will have no experience in a particular area, perhaps in developing a critical new component, and the project must send the work to another company for performance. These choices are called "make or buy" decisions, and selecting those items which must be procured for the project is an essential extension of the scope definition process.

Why is it important to identify the work that must be procured? Simply because procurements (versus in-house work) are done under non-forgiving legal arrangements. Formal contracts must be executed. If you commit to buy something which is not what you need, or the requirements must be modified, such changes will be accommodated, but at a price. Sellers love to have changes in scope, because each change gives them an opportunity to "get well" from a competitive bid. Projects will find that it takes time to adequately compile a tight procurement package, which can later be enforced if need be in a court of law. The earlier the procured work is identified and responsibilities assigned, the better such packages can be managed.

By contrast, internal budgets can be executed in a more informal way, and the fact that everyone is on the same payroll allows some margin of slack. But there is no slack with the procured work. Procurements must be done properly at the start, or the project will pay a price.

Lastly, whether the project work is done by the project's own organization, or procured from outside the company, the measurement and reporting of progress must take place. Inside or outside, the project must be able to measure the earned value against the actual costs of the work being performed.

Step 3: You must plan and schedule the defined work. (EVM Criterion #6)

Perhaps the single most critical requirement to implement earned value is to have a formal scheduling process in place. The project's scheduling system will portray the approved work scope, with each task carefully placed into a specific timeframe for performance. In earned value vernacular, the scheduled work (plus its authorized budget) will constitute the project's "planned value." As performance then takes place on the project, that portion of the planned value which is physically completed (plus its budget) constitutes the "earned value." Both the planned value and the resulting earned value emanate from the project's master schedule and must use the same measurement metrics to both plan and then measure the actual performance.

The project's formal scheduling system is thus critical to the employment of earned value, because it is the vehicle which describes the project scope, the planned value, and the resulting earned value. The project schedule is vital to earned value because it reflects the project manager's baseline "planned value" for everyone to follow.

On more complex projects there should be some method to isolate the constraints between one task and other tasks. Typically, to satisfy this requirement some form of critical path methodology (CPM) will need to be employed. The critical path (and near critical paths) on projects must be aggressively managed in conjunction with negative earned value schedule variances. A behind schedule variance (less than 1.0 performance) indicates that the project is falling behind its baseline plan. If the late tasks are on the critical path, or they are high risk tasks, they must be managed to successful completion.

Step 4: You must estimate the required resources and formally authorize budgets. (EVM Criterion #9)

Once the work scope has been fully defined and subsequently planned and scheduled, the next requirement for forming an earned value baseline is to estimate the resource requirements for all defined tasks within each level of the specified WBS. Each defined WBS element must have an estimated resource value to complete all of the specified work. Management will then assess the requested resources and approve a value in the form of an authorized budget. Individual budgets should never contain contingencies or management reserves. Such reserves or contingencies, if they exist, must be isolated and owned by the project manager.

Remember the rule that "planned value" represents two things: the scheduled work, plus the authorized budget. "Earned value" also represents two things: the completed authorized work, plus the same authorized budget. Thus in order to plan and then measure earned value one needs to schedule all defined tasks, along with the authorized budget necessary to complete the tasks.

All authorized budgets must be achievable in order to have a viable project baseline.

Step 5: You must determine the metrics to convert planned value into earned value. (EVM Criterion #7)

How does one measure the conversion of planned value into earned value? Answer: One sets up measurable metrics in the baseline project schedules to quantify the authorized work, and then the completion of the authorized work. Specific milestones, or tasks, with weighted values are measured as they are physically performed. Remember, earned value project management is nothing more than managing a project with a resource-loaded schedule.

Over the years since earned value was first introduced, various methods have been devised to measure project performance. However, the most respected methods use some type of discrete measurement. Specific milestones representing points in time are assigned values, and when they are fully completed the assigned budgeted values are earned. Also, tasks are assigned values which can be measured as they are partially completed, at which time some value is assigned to the completed work through the reporting period.

Step 6: You must form a project baseline, determine the points of management control, and formally authorize Control Account Plans (CAPs). (EVM Criterion #8)

Earned value requires use of an integrated project baseline, meaning that the defined work scope must include both the baseline schedule and the authorized budget. Integration takes place within each of the specified WBS elements.

Project management must next specify its points of management focus, referred to in earned value as Control Account Plans (CAPs). CAPs are placed at selected WBS elements and can best be thought of as subprojects or project teams, subdivisions of the full project. The sum of the CAPs will constitute the total project baseline. The actual earned value performance measurement will take place within each of the specified CAPs. Total project performance is simply the summation of all the detailed CAPs, which can be placed at any level of the WBS.

On commercial type contracts, the total project baseline may sometimes include such things as indirect costs, and even profits or fee, to match the total authorized project commitment. The project baseline must thus include whatever executive management has authorized the project manager to accomplish.

Internal company projects typically do not contain indirect costs, or profits. Many (perhaps most) internal project baselines will simply represent the sum of the defined CAPs, which are exclusively made up of direct labor hours only. The authorized project baseline constitutes whatever management has decided it should be.

Step 7: You must record all direct project costs consistent with the authorized baseline budgets, in accordance with the organization's general books of accounts. (EVM Criterion #16)

A simple requirement: In order to be held accountable for cost management, project managers must be told, by the accounting people, what they have spent on their projects. Pretty basic stuff. But some organizations find this task extremely difficult, even impossible. How can that be? Simply because many organizations have been "functionally" oriented for so long, they cannot see the projects as distinct components. They can tell how much money was spent by their functions, e.g., engineering, test, maintenance, manufacturing, quality, etc., but they cannot tell the project managers what they have spent on their projects. They have not made the transition to management by projects.

In order to employ earned value on any project, the actual costs must be aligned to the authorized project budgets. Remember the rule: Planned value represents the authorized work plus budget, which is then converted to earned work plus the same budget to represent the earned value. Earned value must then be relatable to the actual costs in order to determine the cost efficiency factor, called the Cost Performance Index (CPI). The CPI is the single most important metric for any project employing earned value. Thus cost actuals by total project, and by subproject (CAPs), is an absolute requirement in order to employ earned value.

There is a trend in projects employing earned value, which is to measure performance on a weekly basis. We need to understand what this means, and what it does not mean. Weekly earned value measurement means the measurement of internal direct labor hours. On a weekly basis, the company labor tapes will produce Planned Value, Earned Value, and Actual Hours for internal direct labor hours only. Direct labor dollars, indirect costs, purchased articles, travel, etc., are generally not available on a weekly basis. Weekly performance measurement takes place on the internal direct labor hours only. However, this factor alone can be significant in effective project control.

The requirement for accuracy in the weekly labor reporting is critical. Any error factor in labor reporting will invalidate its usefulness. Errors in labor can occur for a number of reasons. For instance, people charge to the wrong account numbers, they insert the wrong numbers, they continue to charge to completed projects, they charge to projects before authorized, etc.

In order to eliminate errors, some companies have put in place automated direct labor tracking systems for which employees must type in their project codes before starting the reporting cycle. If employees type in an incorrect labor code, the automated system immediately rejects the charge, and the employee must correct the error prior to starting work. Accurate labor reporting is critical to measuring weekly earned value.

Step 8: You must continuously monitor the earned value performance to determine cost and schedule exceptions to the baseline plan: the schedule variances (earned value less the planned value) and cost variances (earned value less the actual costs). (EVM Criterion #22)

Projects employing earned value will need to monitor their cost and schedule results against the authorized baseline for the duration of the project. Management will focus its attention on exceptions to the baseline plan, particularly those greater than acceptable tolerances which were previously defined. Earned value is thus a "management by exception" concept.

A negative earned value schedule variance simply means that the value of the work performed does not match the value of the work scheduled; that is, the project is falling behind in its scheduled work plan. Each behind-schedule task should be assessed as to its criticality. If the late tasks are on the critical path, or if the tasks carry a high risk to the project, then efforts must be taken to get the late tasks back on schedule. However, additional project resources should not typically be spent on low risk tasks or tasks which have positive critical path float.

The single most important aspect of employing earned value is the cost efficiency readings it provides. The difference between the value of work earned and the costs incurred to accomplish the work provides the cost efficiency factor. If the project spends more money than it receives in value, this reflects an overrun condition. Overruns are typically non-recoverable. Overruns expressed as a percentage value have been found to deteriorate, unless the project takes aggressive actions to mitigate the condition.

Perhaps of greatest benefit is the fact that the earned value cost efficiency rate has been found to be stable from the 20 percent point of a project's completion. The cost efficiency factor is thus an important metric for any project manager or enterprise executive to monitor.

Step 9: Using earned value data, you must continuously forecast the final required costs based on actual performance, and keep management apprised so they can take corrective actions if necessary. (EVM Criterion #27)

One of the more beneficial aspects of earned value is that it provides the capability to quickly and independently forecast the total funds required to complete a project, commonly referred to as the estimate at completion (EAC). Based on actual cost and schedule performance against the baseline plan, a project is able to accurately estimate the total funds it will require to finish the job within a finite range of values.

Often management or customers will have a preconceived notion of what final costs should be, or of what they would like them to be. If the earned value statistical forecast of estimated final costs is greater than the "official" project manager's estimate to complete the project, someone needs to reconcile these professional differences of opinion.

Actual performance results on any project, good or bad, are in effect "sunk costs." Such costs represent what the project has actually achieved in performance.

Thus any improvements in performance must come from the future work, the tasks that lie ahead of the project's status date. Earned value allows the project manager to accurately quantify the cost and schedule performance achieved to date. And if the results achieved to date are less than that desired by management, the project can exert a more aggressive posture to influence the future work.

Earned value, because it allows the project to accurately quantify the value of the work it has achieved, also allows the project to quantify the value of the future work in order to stay within the objectives set for the project by management. The single most respected method to forecast the final cost results is to assume that the project will continue at its established cost efficiency rate, or that it will get no better and no worse.

Step 10: You must manage the defined scope baseline by approving or rejecting all changes, and then incorporating the approved changes into the project baseline in a timely manner. (EVM Criterion #28)

The project performance measurement baseline which was initially put into place at the start of the project is only as good as the management of all proposed new changes to the baseline for the duration of the project. Performance baselines quickly become invalid simply through failure to incorporate changes into the approved baseline, with the addition or deletion of added work scope.

All new change requests of the project must be quickly addressed, either by approval or by rejection of such changes. All project managers should have sufficient authority to say "no" to changes.

In order for the initial baseline to remain valid, each and every change must be controlled. Maintaining an approved baseline can be as challenging as the initial definition of the project scope at the start of the project.

In Summary

Earned value project management is not a difficult concept to understand or to employ. It is certainly not as complicated a process as some have made it out to be over the years. The authors have concluded that effective earned value can be achieved by simply applying the ten simple steps listed above. These ten steps can be applied to any project, of any size, in any industry. Earned value is truly for the masses.

We hope that, as you read over the ten suggested steps, you came to the conclusion that employing earned value project management consists of nothing more than simply following fundamental best project management practices. As was nicely stated by a gentleman from the United Kingdom:

> **Whilst you can practice good project management without EVM, you cannot practice EVM effectively without good project management.**[71]

We could not have stated it better.

---

[71] Steve Crowther. (1999, June). Best of British: Earned Value Management. *Magazine of the Association for Project Management*, 13.

15

FULFILL YOUR FIDUCIARY DUTY AND COMPLY WITH SARBANES-OXLEY

BLACK'S LAW DICTIONARY:
Fiduciary: A person having a duty, created by his undertaking, to act primarily for another's benefit in matters connected with such undertaking. The term . . . includes such offices or relations as those of an attorney at law, a guardian, executor, or broker, a director of a corporation, and a public officer.[72]

THE SECURITIES ACT OF 1933:
Any person who – (2) offers or sells a security . . . which includes an untrue statement of a material fact or omits to state a material fact necessary in order to make the statements, in the light of the circumstances under which they were made, not misleading . . . shall be liable to the person purchasing such security from him, who may sue either at law or in equity in any court of competent jurisdiction, to recover the consideration paid for such security with interest thereon.[73]

THE SARBANES-OXLEY ACT OF 2002:
Sec. 906. Corporate Responsibility for Financial Reports
Certification of Periodic Financial Reports—Each periodic report containing financial statements filed by an insurer with the Security Exchange Commission . . . shall be accompanied by a written statement by the chief executive officer and chief financial officer. . . .

Criminal Penalties—Whoever . . . willfully certifies any statement as set forth . . . knowing that the periodic report accompanying the statement does not comport with all the requirements set forth in this section shall be fined not more than $5,000,000, or imprisoned not more than 20 years, or both.[74]

---

72 Garner, B. (2009) *Black's law dictionary.* (9th ed.). Eagan, MN: Thomson West.
73 Securities Act of 1933. (May 27, 1933, ch. 38, title I, Sec. 12, 48 Stat. 84.)
74 Sarbanes-Oxley Act of 2002. (July 30, 2002, ch. 63, title 18, United States Code, Failure of corporate officers to certify financial reports.)

Well, this section of the Sarbanes-Oxley Act of 2002 (commonly called SOX) will certainly get people's attention, particularly if their job title happens to be "chief executive officer." No more lame excuses like: "I know nothing about accounting," or "I was a bad student," or "I hire accountants to do that stuff." There is now too much at stake. Penalties, and even jail time!

The second edition of this book was released in the summer of 2000. A lot has happened to Corporate America since that time, particularly affecting publicly traded companies. As the authors stated in their second edition, which, remember, was at a time period one year before the Enron (et al.) messes hit the headlines, and two years before the Sarbanes-Oxley Act of 2002 came into effect:

> It has been the contention of the authors that there is often a duty created on the part of selected corporate officers and government officials, based on the offices they hold. That duty would require them to employ all proven management tools in the performance of their jobs, including, and in particular, EVM . . . . This duty would extend to project managers, the chief financial officers, chief information officers, and certainly chief executive officers of most corporations.
>
> These individuals can in part meet this fiduciary duty by employing a simple but effective form of earned value in the management of their projects.[75]

With the revelations coming from Enron, WorldCom, Tyco, and others, it is obvious that certain executives in the corporate world did not take seriously their fiduciary duties to the investing public. Whether the passage of the Sarbanes-Oxley Act of 2002 will make a difference remains to be seen. We remain convinced that if performance on projects can have a "material" impact on the profit or loss of any company, that at least a simple form of earned value management must be—repeat, *must* be—employed to accurately forecast the final costs of these projects. To do otherwise is to ignore the impressive empirical work done by the U.S. Department of Defense (DoD) over the past four decades.

Putting a positive spin on financial reports, or, "cooking the books"

There are numerous ways corporate executives can put a "positive spin" on their financial reporting to the public. Some methods are legal, others are blatantly illegal. The illegal ways are now being addressed by a number of dedicated groups, including the United States Congress, the U.S. Securities and Exchange Commission

---

75 Fleming, Q. W. and Koppelman, J. M. (2000). *Earned Value Project Management* (2nd ed.). Newtown Square, PA: Project Management Institute.

(SEC), the U.S. Department of Justice, the states' attorney generals, and others. With the signature of the President of the United States on the Sarbanes-Oxley Act of 2002, the spotlight is now on every CFO *and* CEO to give an accurate portrayal of their true financial condition. To review this mandate, we need to understand what is required by SOX. To quote directly from the Act:

> The Commission shall, by rule, require, for each company filing periodic reports under section 13(a) or 15(d) of the Securities Exchange Act of 1934 . . . that the principal executive officer or officers and the principal financial officer or officers, or persons performing similar functions, certify in each annual or quarterly report filed or submitted under either section of such act that
>
> (1)   The signing officer has reviewed the report;
> (2)   Based on the officer's knowledge, the report does not contain any untrue statements of a material fact or omit to state a material fact necessary in order to make the statements made, in light of the circumstances under which such statements were made, not misleading;
> (3)   Based on such officer's knowledge, the financial statements, and other financial information included in the report, fairly present in all material respects the financial condition and results of operations of the issuer as of, and for, the periods presented in the report;
> (4)   The signing officers
>   (A) are responsible for establishing and maintaining internal controls;
>   (B) have designed such internal controls to ensure that material information relating to the issuer and its consolidated subsidiaries is known to such officers by others within those entities, particularly during the period in which the periodic reports are being prepared.[76]

However, there still may be a legal way for corporate executives to effectively cook their books and put a positive spin on questionable long-term project performance. Perhaps it should not be legal, for at best the practice is highly questionable. This approach is to simply ignore the early performance indicators on major new projects (capital, software, etc.), which often span several fiscal years. Projects could be directed to wait until all actual funds have been expended in order to predict a final overrun of costs. Not a good course of action to take. By then, it could be too late to recover. Is this a material issue for a public company? The authors are of the belief that it could be.

---

76 Sarbanes-Oxley Act of 2002, Sec. 302, Corporate Responsibility for Financial Reports.

Some obvious examples of major capital investment projects that could impact the firm's bottom line would be: the development of a new commercial aircraft, the construction of a new corporate headquarters, an IT outsourcing project, a commitment for a new corporate enterprise resource planning (ERP) system, construction of a new factory, the decommissioning of a nuclear reactor, etc. These are just a few examples of multi-year projects that, if performed poorly, could have a "material" effect on the profitability of any organization, and of course, the resulting annual bonuses of their managing executives.

The prevailing attitude of many firms would seem to be that whenever they make a long-term commitment to fund a major new project that spans multiple fiscal years, there is no legal obligation to ascertain and report on both the current status and final required costs. A recent best-selling book on the Enron affair perhaps typifies this type of corporate attitude:

> *. . . the truth is that there is no entirely satisfactory way to account for complex deals that extend over several years.*[77]

Respectfully, the authors disagree with this assertion. There is a method, a proven and accurate method to measure the current status and estimate final required costs on major capital projects that span multiple fiscal years. That technique is called earned value management (EVM). It is a concept that was originated more than 100 years ago by industrial engineers as they measured cost results in American factories. And further, the DoD has successfully employed this technique for the past 40 years on its major systems acquisitions. Earned value will not prevent an overrun. But it will tell executive management that an overrun of costs is likely, and highly probable. And it will provide a prediction of final required cost estimates within a range of values. These predictions should not be ignored by management.

Private industry has been slow to adopt this proven technique to manage major projects for a variety of reasons, some valid and some frankly self-serving. Perhaps it is sometimes advantageous not to know the true conditions and final costs of major projects, particularly if such public knowledge would have an adverse impact on year-end corporate revenues, the price of company stock, and resulting executive bonuses. But is there a higher fiduciary duty to report the true conditions, and does the Sarbanes-Oxley Act make it mandatory to report such conditions to the public? Perhaps.

---

77 Fusaro, P. C. and Miller, R. M. (2002). *What Went Wrong at Enron*. Hoboken, NJ: Wiley.

Focus on Value of the Work Accomplished (i.e., the Earned Value)

Today, unfortunately, most corporate financial executives likely measure their cost performance on projects by using only two dimensions: the projected costs versus the actual costs. Thus, if the entire allotted budget is spent, they are right on target. If less was spent, then there is an underrun of costs. If more is spent, then an overrun exists. To the authors, this is not *cost* performance, but rather *funding* performance. What is missing is the measurement of the "value of the work" performed for the monies spent. This we call earned value management (EVM).

Let us discuss an example of a project with some assumed numbers. If a given project's budget was set at $100 million, only $90 million was spent, but it had only accomplished $80 million in work value. What should you call this condition? Respectfully, we feel it should be called what it is: a $10 million overrun of costs. The missing third dimension on most corporate scorecards today is a measure of the value of the physical work accomplished for the monies being spent.

The Sarbanes-Oxley Act raises an issue: In this scenario, would a $10 million overrun of total project costs be considered a "material" financial issue to a company? Perhaps. It all depends on the impact a $100 million project might have on a given firm's financial status. This will vary from company to company.

A century ago the industrial engineers, led by the father of scientific management, Frederick W. Taylor, were correct in their assessment of what represented "true" cost performance in their factories. Cost performance represented to them the difference between the accomplished work (represented by earned standards) and the actual costs incurred. It was not the difference between the planned costs and actual costs. Today, many corporate executives still do not grasp this simple concept and are content to focus on projected costs versus actual costs, and call this their "cost performance."

The early industrial engineers created what they called their "planned standards," representing two components: the authorized physical work and the authorized budget for the authorized work. Planned standards represented simply their baseline plan. It was only when such work was completed that they could determine their true cost performance.

Thus, a century ago, Taylor et al., focused on the "earned standards" that represented physically accomplished work, plus its original authorized budget. They then compared the earned standards against the actual hours expended to determine their true "cost performance." It worked then. It can work now.

Earned Value Management (EVM)

The DoD was the first group in modern times to adopt this early industrial engineering factory concept for use in the management of projects.

In 1962, the DoD had a major capital project called the "Minuteman Missile." This project employed hundreds of people, cost millions of taxpayer dollars, and spanned several fiscal years. The U.S. Air Force project staff recognized their duty to the taxpayers to report the accurate financial status of this major project. They adopted this simple industrial engineering concept to their one-time-only major project, and to their surprise, earned value measurement worked for them.

They broke the project into discrete pieces and separate tasks. They then added an authorized budget to each task. When each task was completed, they credited its completion, and they "earned" its original authorized budget. They compared this completed work, which they called the "earned value," against the costs spent to accomplish this work. The result gave them an accurate reflection of their true cost performance, available with no other project management technique.

Since 1977, the DoD's Pentagon has kept track of the performance of hundreds of projects, reflecting actual performance—the good, the bad, and the downright ugly. In total, they have now analyzed more than 800 separate projects. Individual company names are kept private. The results have been spectacular: They have been able to demonstrate the predictability of final project cost requirements based on earned value data. These studies have also supported the belief that early cost overruns are rarely (if ever) offset by subsequent performance. Thus, overseeing early cost performance is vital to successful project cost management.

With EVM, the single most important tracking metric is called the "CPI," or the "Cost Performance Index." The CPI represents that delicate relationship between the earned value accomplished divided by the actual costs spent to accomplish the work. The cumulative CPI has been demonstrated to be a stable predictor of final costs at completion, even as early as the 20 percent completion point of any project.

The CPI can thus be used to accurately predict the final cost position of any project, even those spanning multiple years in performance. If the cumulative CPI registers a .80 performance value, it means that for every dollar that was spent, only 80 cents of value was earned. This can also be called an overrun. Early overruns are very serious indicators, as subsequent performance rarely ever recovers early overruns.

Most importantly, the cumulative CPI can be used (starting at the 20 percent completion point) to accurately forecast the final project cost results with amazing precision. For example, if a five-year $100 million project has experienced a cumulative CPI of only .80 at the 20 percent completion point, one can forecast the final cost results within a finite range.

Simply take the $100 million project budget and divide it by the CPI of .80. Immediately, the final project forecasted costs would be about $125 million, or a cost overrun of approximately $25 million. How good is this forecast? Empirical studies support the position that it will be accurate within plus or minus 10 percent from the $125 million final costs.

Important point: The $100 million authorized budget would not be adequate to finish this project. This raises a Sarbanes-Oxley issue: Would a $25 million projected overrun of final costs constitute a "material" financial issue? Perhaps.

Scientific analytical research done by the DoD supports the use of this doctrine.

FINANCIAL REPORTING TODAY

There is no valid reason today why all companies cannot accurately measure and report on the true cost position of all their capital projects by employing a simple form of earned value management. This technique should also be applied to perhaps the most challenging jobs we face today, the management of software projects. Using earned value to manage long-term capital projects is essential to meeting the corporate executive's fiduciary duty to their shareholders.

The Sarbanes-Oxley Act was signed into law July 30, 2002. It would seem to reinforce the contention that there is a fiduciary duty placed on corporate executives to tell the whole truth when reporting the financial condition of their companies. This duty would include an accurate assessment of the true current status, and the final required costs to finish all multi-year projects.

Employing a simple form of earned value management can help corporate executives meet this fiduciary duty and, in particular, their legal obligations under the Sarbanes-Oxley Act.

Appendix

The (32) Earned Value Management (EVM) System Criteria

FOUR PLUS DECADES AGO, in 1965, the United States Air Force defined what they required from private industry in order to employ earned value in the performance of government funded projects. The result was a document entitled the Cost/Schedule Planning and Control Specification (C/SPCS). It contained 35 specific criteria to be employed on all major projects. Two years later the Department of Defense (DoD) formally accepted these same criteria with a slightly changed title, the Cost/Schedule Control Systems Criteria (C/SCSC). Any firm wanting to perform on new projects for the DoD had to comply with these 35 standards as a precondition to winning a new contract. C/SCSC was to be consistently applied to DoD projects.

A few decades later, in 1995, at a formal meeting of the Management Systems Subcommittee of the National Defense Industrial Association (NDIA) the NDIA subcommittee accepted the task of examining and rewriting the DoD's criteria for earned value management. Their objective was to make the criteria more user-friendly and more compatible with the needs of private industry.

Over the next eighteen months the NDIA subcommittee met, discussed, and established their own re-reworded version of the DoD's Cost/Schedule Control Systems Criteria. When released, the new industry document was entitled the Earned Value Management (EVM) System Criteria and contained just 32 criteria, three less than the original C/SCSC. On December 14, 1996, to the surprise of many, the Under Secretary of Defense for Acquisition and Technology accepted the NDIA industry rewrite of the earned value management criteria, verbatim.

The significance of this change was not in the revised wording of the criteria, or in the minimal reduction in their number from 35 to 32. Rather, the critical difference was in the "attitude" toward the earned value management process. In 1997 there was a shifting of the EVM system ownership from that of a United States Government requirement, to that of ownership by private industry. Private industry would now embrace the earned value management technique not because it was a government mandate, but because it represented a set of "best practice" processes available to project managers in the private sector.

One additional event deserves mention. The NDIA subcommittee continued its effort of converting earned value management into a broad-based international best practice. The subcommittee requested that the revised earned value management criteria be formally issued as an American National Standards Institute-Electronic Industries Association standard. In July 1998, the NSIA/EIA Standard 748 was formally published. Then on August 17, 1999, the DoD accepted the ANSI/EIA 748 Standard for applications to all DoD projects, formally replacing the C/SCSC.

What follows below is a verbatim reproduction of the 32 EVM System criteria, followed by an "unofficial" interpretation of each criterion by the authors. Please understand that the narrative interpretation which follows each criterion represents the authors' views, and only their views. They are provided for your general guidance only.

The 32 EVM criteria are divided into five logical major groups.

✳ ✳ ✳

GROUP 1-ORGANIZATION CRITERIA (FIVE)

Purpose of the Organization Criteria:

- To require that the entire project scope be defined, including make versus buy choices.
- To require an integrated project baseline (scope + schedule + costs) with use of a WBS.
- To establish management control responsibilities with use of Control Account Plans (CAPs).
- To assign performance responsibilities for all CAPS to the functional organizations.

Problems with the Organization Criteria:

- Functional organizations starting work with an inadequate project scope definition.
- Rejection of the project's WBS by functional "fiefdoms."

The first group of criteria deals with the requirement for any new project to be completely defined, and planned, prior to starting performance of the work. Today, we would typically call this effort defining the scope of the project. Think about it: Earned value measurement cannot take place without some definition of what constitutes 100 percent of the project.

This effort starts with a requirement to specify all of the assumed project deliverables to be accomplished. Such definitions are best accomplished with use of a work breakdown structure (WBS) in order to completely capture all of the proposed work. The WBS provides for the integration of all project tasks, together with their estimated resources, with each task planned within a specific timeframe for performance. Once defined, some one individual or specific organization must be held accountable for the performance of each of the defined project tasks.

Any comprehensive definition of project scope must also include the make versus buy choices for all segments of work, isolating in particular that effort which must be procured from other (outside) organizations. Management responsible for the authorization and control of indirect costs must also be identified.

The major problems in meeting these initial criteria have been an inadequate definition of the total project scope, a poor definition of make versus buy, and the rejection of the project manager's WBS by selected functional organizations.

EVM Criterion # 1:

Define the authorized work elements for the program. A work breakdown structure (WBS), tailored for effective internal management control, is commonly used in this process.

The first criterion requires that any new project be defined, to the extent possible, before starting the work. A WBS is typically recommended (required) for use in this process. The WBS is a product-oriented, hierarchical family tree which describes the major segments of a project and is used to specify all deliverables: hardware, software, services, and data. The WBS is used to specify all of the assumed work, and is perhaps the single most important requirement for the successful employment of earned value. Each level of the WBS provides a progressively more detailed description of the work to be accomplished.

All major line items and project deliverables must be identified somewhere within the WBS. All functional organizations must then work within the scope defined by the project's WBS. Any effort that is requested of the project that cannot be identified within the WBS is potentially out-of-scope effort, and authorization is needed in order to accommodate such work.

The project WBS allows management to concentrate on logical groupings of project work, the subprojects, for measurement of performance. At the lowest selected levels of specified WBS, elements will be placed in control account plans, or CAPs, which are the points where earned value performance and management control will take place for the project. A CAP can best be thought of as a subproject, a project team, an integrated product team, or perhaps simply as a point of project management responsibility and control.

All project management CAPs must contain four elements in order to be viable: the authorized scope of work for the CAP, a specified timeframe for performance, an authorized budget, and a specific individual or organization to be held accountable for performance of each CAP. The summation of all specified CAPs, plus management or contingency reserves, if any, will constitute the total project.

EVM Criterion # 2:

Identify the program organizational structure including the major subcontractors responsible for accomplishing the authorized work, and define the organizational elements in which work will be planned and controlled.

This criterion requires that all tasks as defined within the project's WBS be identified and assigned to a specific (internal) functional organization for performance, or designated as an external buy item as a part of the project's make versus buy process. The project's WBS is compared against the company's organizational breakdown structure (OBS) to allow for the assignment of each of the project's tasks to a specific organization for performance. This process will produce what is typically called a project responsibility assignment matrix (RAM).

All tasks identified in the project WBS must be assigned to a specific organization for performance, including that work which will be procured from outside of the company, that is, contracted or subcontracted to another company for performance. This criterion requires that the project make specific organization assignments of all identified work.

EVM Criterion # 3:

Provide for the integration of the company's planning, scheduling, budgeting, work authorization and cost accumulation processes with each other, and as appropriate, the program work breakdown structure and the program organizational structure.

The intent of this criterion is to require the integration of the project's management process both with the way the work is defined with use of the WBS, and with the functional organizations who will be performing the effort. This requirement specifies that projects employ a single management control system with a common information database flowing though the contractor's functional disciplines. The CAPs, which will have tasks allocated to specific functions, provide the basis for organizations to perform with a common database.

Companies, particularly those with large and well-established functional organizations, often have had difficulty satisfying this criterion. Each of the various functional organizations often have their own performance agendas, and each wants to manage their own affairs in their own particular manner. Sometimes functional goals can be at odds with project goals. Master scheduling, cost estimating, work authorizations, budgeting, cost accumulation, each of the various functions, etc., must all work within a single database as specified by the project WBS.

The CAP provides the fundamental building block for earned value performance management and makes it possible for the various functional units to work from a common database. The defined CAPs (subprojects) allow projects to monitor performance from two perspectives: by WBS, to determine the project results; or by OBS, to focus on functional results.

EVM Criterion # 4:

Identify the company organization or function responsible for controlling overhead (indirect costs).

The United States Government acquisition personnel are acutely aware that costs associated with any given project contain both direct and indirect costs. While there is generally minimal controversy over the application of direct project costs, there is much concern over both the content and the proportionate application of indirect costs applied to a given project. Thus four (numbers 4, 13, 19, and 24) of the 32 criteria deal specifically with the management of contractor indirect costs . . . even though any given project manager will have minimal (likely zero) influence over such indirect costs. That is why they are called indirect costs, because they are non-specific to any given project. Only the very senior corporate executive management can influence indirect costs, not any given project manager.

This criterion requires that all indirect costs as a category be clearly defined, and responsibilities formally documented. Those individual managers who are responsible for authorizing and controlling overheads must be identified, generally with some type of delegation of authority which stipulates the limits of such authority. Such activities may be centralized or de-centralized, as long as there is consistency in application, and a clear assignment of responsibility.

The allocation of indirect costs to specific projects must be consistent for *all* projects in the organization, and defined somewhere in procedural documentation.

Such costs may not be arbitrarily applied to a given project inconsistent with such procedures. The government is particularly sensitive to the consistency of application of such costs as they are allotted to different types of contracts within a firm's cost reimbursable versus fixed price contract base. Their concern is that contractors could be tempted to try and maximize profits on their fixed price work, at the expense of cost (open-ended) reimbursable contracts.

EVM CRITERION # 5:

Provide for integration of the program work breakdown structure and the program organizational structure in a manner that permits cost and schedule performance measurement by elements of either or both structures as needed.

Four (numbers 5, 17, 18, and 25) of the 32 criteria deal with the same issue of forming a project baseline which can be measured from two perspectives: by the project's WBS, and by the functional organization's OBS. This is the first of the four criteria dealing with this single issue.

This requirement is met by forming CAPs, which can be summarized by either the project WBS or by the functional OBS. With the use of multi-functional project team CAPs, the individual Work Package tasks within each CAP must be identified to a specific function in order to satisfy the requirement for an OBS roll-up.

✳ ✳ ✳

GROUP 2-PLANNING, SCHEDULING AND BUDGETING CRITERIA (TEN)

Purpose of the Planning, Scheduling, and Budgeting Criteria:

- To require the employment of a formal planning, scheduling and budgeting system.
- To require the formation of a project baseline, which allows performance to be measured.

Problems with the Planning, Scheduling and Budgeting Criteria:

- Lack of discipline in the functional organizations.
- Project baselines which are either "front-loaded" or "rubber."

In the second major grouping of the criteria, there are 10 requirements which must be satisfied, making this the single largest group. Here it must be demonstrated that the project employs a single, integrated management control system within which it can implement a formal project performance baseline for all of the defined project scope. Each project must be authorized by management, planned, scheduled, the resources must be estimated and then formally budgeted, and all work performed within the project's formal baseline.

Should the project have set aside any management (or contingency) reserves, such values must be strictly controlled by the project manager (or other senior management) and isolated outside of the project's performance baseline. All such reserves which are subsequently released by the project must be formally transferred into the project's performance baseline. This group requires that a formal management control system be in place for the full life cycle of the project.

There have been several problems experienced with this group of criteria. One of the most common has resulted from a general lack of discipline by the functional organizations supporting the authorized project. It is not possible to measure project performance when the functional departments doing the work can be casual about keeping records of their own performance.

Other problems have been experienced with the control of authorized budget for authorized work in the performance baseline. The inadvertent (sometimes intentional) front-end placement of budget without a corresponding level of work scope, called baseline "front-loading," and or the inadvertent (sometimes intentional) shifting of authorized budget into earlier periods without a corresponding shift of authorized work, called "rubber base-lining," have created opportunities for any company wanting to "game" the earned value management process.

Earned value management requires formality and organizational discipline from those performing the work on a project, or the measurement of actual performance will be questionable.

EVM CRITERION # 6:

Schedule the authorized work in a manner which describes the sequence of work and identifies the significant task interdependencies required to meet the requirements of the program.

This criterion requires that contractors have in place a formal scheduling system to support their projects. In particular, the organizations must issue a comprehensive project master schedule (PMS) for each project which sets forth all critical milestones and key tasks representing the project. The project's planned value will be determined by compliance with this criterion.

On the larger and more complex projects, and in organizations where there are numerous projects being performed simultaneously, the project master schedules (PMS) may be reinforced by subordinate schedules as appropriate, often in the form of detailed functional schedules. However, all schedules within the enterprise must be in concert with the requirements contained in each project's PMS.

The key issue is the traceability and consistency of the key program milestones specified in each PMS. Functions must schedule their work in accordance with the requirements defined in project master schedules. The schedules must portray the logical sequence of all work to be accomplished, and each CAP must contain the baseline start and stop dates, from which project completion dates can be forecasted.

Nowhere in any of the criteria do they specify that a particular scheduling technique must be used. However, the criteria do require that contractor scheduling systems interdependencies and constraints. Since only critical path method (CPM) schedules will show such relationships, a strict interpretation of this criterion might suggest that earned value management requires the use of some type of CPM network schedules.

EVM CRITERION # 7:

Identify physical products, milestones, technical performance goals, or other indicators that will be used to measure progress.

This criterion is related to the one above, and requires that projects must have the ability to measure their physical performance, as defined within the tasks displayed in project schedules. Just what constitutes the physical completion of the work is the central issue.

Projects must specify what physical products, outputs, metrics, milestones, and technical performance indicators will be used to measure actual work accomplished against the schedule plan. Determining how the earned value will actually be measured is the requirement of this criterion. There are numerous methods with which to measure physical work accomplishment, and the projects must specify which of these methods they will employ.

EVM Criterion # 8:

Establish and maintain a time-phased budget baseline, at the control account level, against which program performance can be measured. Initial budgets established for performance measurement will be based on either internal management goals or the external customer negotiated target cost including estimates for authorized but undefinitized work. Budget for far-term efforts may be held in higher level accounts until an appropriate time for allocation at the control account level. On government contracts, if an over target baseline is used for performance measurement reporting purposes, prior notification must be provided to the customer.

When this criterion specifies "a time-phased budget baseline," it is imposing a precise term in earned value management called the "Performance Measurement Baseline" (PMB). It is important that this term be fully understood. We are discussing the project baseline against which performance will be measured.

The PMB is defined nicely in the industry ANSI/EIA 748 Standard for Earned Value Management Systems as:

> PERFORMANCE MEASUREMENT BASELINE—The total time-phased budget plan against which program performance is measured. It is the schedule for expenditure of the resources allocated to accomplish program scope and schedule objectives, and is formed by the budgets assigned to control accounts and applicable indirect budgets. The Performance Measurement Baseline also includes budget for future effort assigned to higher Work Breakdown Structure levels (summary level planning packages) plus any undistributed budget. Management Reserve is not included in the baseline as it is not yet designated for specific work scope.

The project's performance measurement baseline is made up of the sum of the project's subprojects or CAPs. Management reserve (MR) is considered to be outside of the PMB, until specifically authorized and allocated for specific work within the PMB.

The PMB must include all authorized project work. Authorized but not yet definitized project work may exist in various soft forms: authorized but not yet estimated, authorized but not yet proposed, authorized but not yet negotiated, negotiated but not yet covered by a change order, etc. However, in order to accurately measure performance, all work being done by the project must be included in the PMB.

On projects which run for a long duration, it may be inadvisable or even impossible to budget the far-term effort down to the specific CAP level. In such cases, far term budgets may be allocated and kept at the higher level WBS elements, in what are called "planning packages." This is simply the "rolling-wave" budgeting technique. It is critical to the integrity of EVM systems that the far-term budgets be tightly controlled to prevent co-mingling with the near-term fully budgeted CAPs.

Generally, control account plans should be opened consistent with their scheduled start date, not before. If a situation calls for starting work on a CAP prior to the planned start date, such work must be authorized by the project manager on an exception basis. The across the board initiation of work earlier than planned could adversely impact the authorized funding and distort the performance measurement. The concern is that overruns might be disguised if budgets were allowed to be shifted back and forth casually between time periods.

This criterion also requires that indirect project costs be allocated into the PMB, but not necessarily within the individual CAP budgets. There is no requirement that indirect costs be included within each CAP. However, if left outside of individual CAP budgets, indirect costs must be allocated in some way so that the full value of the PMB includes both the direct and indirect costs. Some projects accomplish this by creating a separate CAP covering indirect costs.

The term "over target baseline," or OTB, as used in the criterion is a kind, gentle, and ambiguous term for describing an "overrun." For some reason, EVM practitioners, or more likely their management, have always been shy about calling an overrun what it is: an "overrun." The final sentence of this criterion merely suggests that if the project sets its budgets to an OTB or overrun, they should only do so with the blessing and concurrence of the customer and/or management. We would certainly hope so.

All projects require a well-defined and formally controlled PMB in order to measure earned value performance for the life of the project.

EVM CRITERION # 9:

Establish budgets for authorized work with identification of significant cost elements (labor, material, etc.) as needed for internal management and for control of subcontractors.

The total project must be budgeted, and such budgets must reflect the type of costs associated with the budgets. Costs which must be identified would be direct labor; the indirect burdens; the various types of procured items, including materials, contracts, or subcontracts; and all other direct costs such as travel, computer, etc. Such budgeted costs must be formally controlled according to internal company procedures. The functional organizations receiving the budgets must be identified.

Budgeted values must represent the project costs which have been negotiated. If there have been authorized changes which have not yet been negotiated, the budgets must include an estimated value for all such authorized work. Project budgets must be issued in a formal, documented and controlled manner down to the various CAP levels.

EVM Criterion # 10:

To the extent it is practical to identify the authorized work in discrete work packages, establish budgets for this work in terms of dollars, hours, or other measurable units. Where the entire control account is not subdivided into work packages, identify the far-term effort in larger planning packages for budget and scheduling purposes.

Many of the 32 criteria are related to other criteria, and often will expand on the requirements imposed in other criteria. This one expands on the requirements for a definitive Performance Measurement Baseline (PMB). Here discrete work packages must be created for near-term tasks to the greatest extent possible, followed by larger planning packages in the far-term. All budgets must be time-phased over the full life of the project.

Under this criterion the project must demonstrate that it has established discrete budgets to the greatest extent possible in a way which represents how the work will be performed. All effort which is shown in far-term time-phased planning packages will subsequently become definitive work packages as they approach the near term periods for performance. This criterion had previously specified that discrete work packages must be of relatively short duration, but that wording was dropped in the industry revision to the criteria.

All work packages must contain metrics to allow for the objective measurement of work accomplishment. The project must be able to differentiate between near-term work packages and far-term planning packages so that specified work and budget cannot be indiscriminately co-mingled.

All direct budgets must be expressed in measurable units, as in hours, dollars, standards, or other types of measurable costs. All work package tasks must be assigned to a specific function for performance.

EVM Criterion # 11:

Provide that the sum of all work package budgets, plus planning package budgets within a control account equals the control account budget.

This criterion simply requires that the sum of all work package budgets and planning package budgets within any CAP must equal the authorized budget for that CAP. All authorized budgets must relate to a specific statement of work to be performed, except for management reserve budgets which are held outside of the performance baseline.

EVM Criterion # 12:

Identify and control level of effort activity by time-phased budgets established for this purpose. Only that effort which is unmeasurable or for which measurement is impractical may be classified as level of effort.

This criterion allows for earned value measurement by use of level of effort (LOE), but only for that work which cannot be measured by either discrete or apportioned means. Of the three types of work tasks to be measured with earned value (discrete, apportioned, or LOE), without question, LOE measurement is the least desirable.

LOE tasks must be identified, time phased, and kept to a minimum. With LOE tasks, the earned value accomplished always equals the planned value, irrespective of whether any work was done. LOE in effect measures nothing but the passage of time, not physical work accomplishment.

This criterion requires that LOE budgets when used must be formally maintained and controlled, as with any other effort. Neither budget nor earned value for the LOE tasks may be shifted independently to the left or right, for this would distort the reported status of a project.

Examples of typical LOE effort are the project manager and staff, a field support engineer, guard services, scheduling, information-desk help, etc., each of which performs activities more related to time passage than to physical output. Certain tasks may be justifiable as LOE, but they must be kept to a minimum to prevent the distortion of measured performance.

EVM Criterion # 13:

Establish overhead budgets for each significant organizational component of the company for expenses which will become indirect costs. Reflect in the program

budgets, at the appropriate level, the amounts in overhead pools that are planned to be allocated to the program as indirect costs.

Most firms will have some type of indirect expenses which are allocated over the direct costs. Some of the larger firms may have several categories or pools of indirect costs. Typical categories of such pools might be: engineering burden, manufacturing burden, material burden, general and administrative expenses, and sometimes even a special study or partial field burdens.

Each company must specify the number of indirect pools it will have, and he types of costs and methods for controlling each of their independent burden centers. Such costs must be tightly managed with each of the respective pools to preclude the possible manipulation of such costs by a contractor. Any changes to either the direct bases or burden pools must be accommodated according to formal internal procedures.

Lastly, in the event that burdens are not applied to individual control accounts, and the criteria do not require application of burdens to control account plan budgets, the contractor must indicate at what point in the WBS and organizational summaries such burden costs will be added.

EVM CRITERION # 14:

Identify management reserves and undistributed budget.

This criterion deals with two categories of project costs: Management Reserve and Undistributed Budget.

Management Reserve (MR), sometimes also called contingency funds, represents an amount of the total budget baseline which is withheld by the project manager to cover the unknowns, or the bad things which are sure to happen but cannot be specified with certainty. MR funds are held outside of the project's Performance Measurement Baseline (PMB).

All MR must be tightly controlled, and every transaction which either adds to or takes from the MR must be documented and approved by the project manager. MR is by definition outside of the PMB. Therefore, no management reserve may be included in either control account budgets or organizational budgets. MR is typically expected to be consumed during performance of the project. If unconsumed at the conclusion of the project, it becomes an underrun.

Undistributed Budget (UB) represents funds applicable to project work which has not yet been placed into authorized budgets. Undistributed Budget is by definition a part of the project's PMB, as contrasted with Management Reserve which is outside of the PMB until a management decision is made to transfer some portion of it into the PMB.

Undistributed budget must be allotted against a specific statement of work, and it must be time-phased and tightly controlled so as not to be used for other work which could mask an overrun. Typically, there are three situations in which undistributed budget may be used:

1. For authorized project changes which are not yet negotiated, where interim budgets are kept at a higher WBS level until negotiations are concluded;
2. For negotiated changes which have not yet been budgeted into CAPs; and
3. For far-term tasks where it might be pointless to define budgets down to the detailed control account level at the present time (using the rolling-wave budgeting concept).

EVM Criterion # 15:

Provide that the program target cost goal is reconciled with the sum of all internal program budgets and management reserves.

This criterion has its focus on the ability to account for all project funds. It is likely a carryover from the time when large cost reimbursable type contracts were commonplace and certain unscrupulous contractors would actually over-budget the total funds on a contract, thus assuring a cost overrun of the project. Today, with the electronic spreadsheets available to us, the utility of this criterion is perhaps debatable.

Contractors must demonstrate that they have not exceeded the total project costs with their approved budgets, and have such control processes documented with internal company procedures.

✳ ✳ ✳

Group 3-Accounting Criteria (six)

Purpose of the Accounting Criteria:

- To require that all projects be given accurate and timely cost reports.
- To require that project costs be recorded as consumed or incurred.
- To require accounting systems which can measure planned value, earned value, and actual costs.

Problems with the Accounting Criteria:

- Difficulty of measuring earned value performance on the procured items.
- Difficulty of determining actual "price" and "usage" variances for work accomplished.

In this third grouping of criteria the emphasis is on the recording of costs for the projects. It requires the segregation of all legitimate direct costs for a given project, together with the appropriate application of the indirect costs allocated to the project.

All firms doing business in the public sector will have some type of a formal accounting system in place which will utilize generally acceptable standards of accounting. Such records must be available for subsequent audit, if necessary.

However, earned value performance measurement also demands a somewhat unique accounting requirement. EVM projects must be able to record their direct costs at the point where performance measurement will take place, typically within the control account plans. Such direct costs must be capable of being summarized both through the project's Work Breakdown Structure as well as the company's functional organizations.

Earned value also requires that a "performance measurement baseline" be created which permits the project's three dimensions of earned value to be measured as follows: the planned value versus the earned value, to measure its schedule performance; and its earned value versus the actual costs, to measure its cost performance.

The major difficulty in meeting this group of criteria has been with the synchronization of the planned value, earned value, and the actual or accrued costs for the work performed. Also, accounting for purchased materials and contracted or subcontracted work to other companies has always been a challenge, particularly when progress payments are given. Measuring the planned value against the earned value and actual costs for purchased items has represented the ultimate challenge for many projects.

EVM CRITERION # 16:

Record direct costs in a manner consistent with the budgets in a formal system controlled by the general books of account.

This criterion requires that project managers be told what they have spent (in direct costs) on their project. Not an unreasonable requirement. However, because some organizations have been functionally dominated for so long a time, they sometimes have difficulty isolating their direct costs against specific projects. They may know how much "design time" has been spent in total for the entire organization, but cannot tell you how much by individual project.

To satisfy this criterion, companies must use generally acceptable methods of accounting for all direct project costs. Any conventional method of accounting may be used, but the preferred technique is the "applied direct cost" method, which simply means that direct resources are accounted for as they are used or as consumed.

It is fairly easy to allocate direct labor costs with their corresponding labor burdens, and other direct costs to a specific project. However, costs for the procured items often provide the ultimate challenge to measuring direct costs consumption on any given project, because they are often consumed in different time periods, sometimes purchased for inventory, or may be transferred into or out of an inventory to another project.

The next two criteria are related and will be discussed together.

EVM CRITERION # 17:

When a work breakdown structure is used, summarize direct costs from control accounts into the work breakdown structure without allocation of a single control account to two or more work breakdown structure elements.

EVM CRITERION # 18:

Summarize direct costs from the control accounts into the contractor's organizational elements without allocation of a single control account to two or more organizational elements.

Criteria 17 and 18 are related, the only difference between them being the direction of the summation of the detailed control account data. Number 17 requires the ability to sum control accounts upward into a WBS segregation to reach the total project costs. Criterion number 18 requires the summation of the same control accounts by the functional organization, to higher organizational levels (engineering, manufacturing, quality, purchasing, testing, etc, for example) to also match the total project costs. Both summations will have the same grand total costs.

Both criteria prohibit the allocation of a single control account to more than one WBS element, or more than one functional organizational unit. Problem: With the increased use of multi-functional project team control accounts, how do you satisfy these criteria without an allocation of costs within a single CAP? Answer: You identify specific work packages within the CAPs to specific organizations, thus the allocation of each work package is directly linked to specific organizational units.

EVM CRITERION # 19:

Record all indirect costs which will be allocated to the contract.

Here is another criterion which addresses the issue of organizational control of indirect costs. This one requires that the contractor be in a position to apply indirect costs uniformly from the point where they are incurred, perhaps allocated into specified pools if multiple pools are used, and ultimately charged against a contract or project. To satisfy this criterion, there must be a formal documented relationship between those persons who have responsibility for the control of indirect budgets and those persons who are able to incur such costs against budgets.

Here the contractor must demonstrate that no manipulation of costs can take place with the allocation of indirect costs between projects, or contracts, and that both the commercial work and government contracts are treated consistently with the allotment of burden costs.

Lastly, the contractors must be in a position to show that the methods they use to allocate indirect costs to the final source are reasonable. Whether the indirect application method chosen calls for an annual financial plan with monthly adjustment of indirect actuals, or a constant rate applied monthly with adjustments at year-end for actuals incurred, the procedures governing such activity must be formally documented, followed, and fully auditable.

EVM CRITERION # 20:

Identify unit costs, equivalent unit costs, or lot costs when needed.

The full life cycle for any new product generally consists of two distinct phases: one phase for the product development, and another to manufacture the item over and over again. The developmental phase is considered to be "non-recurring," and the production effort is considered "recurring."

However, even in the development of a new product there will often be initial recurring costs involved, and it is a good practice to isolate the non-recurring from the recurring costs in order to be in a position to later estimate the repetitive costs for producing the new product. Under this criterion, the project must be able to distinguish between nonrecurring (developmental) effort, and the recurring (production) effort.

This criterion also requires that the project be able to establish unit, equivalent unit, or lot costs for articles to be subsequently produced in the recurring phase. Unit costs may be developed by direct labor hours, direct labor dollars, material dollars, or the total unit price.

Unit costs may be established by isolating the individual costs for producing one unit, or by equivalents of several units, or by lot costs. Under lot costs, a block of selected units will be produced in a single batch at one time. The contractor must isolate the actual average costs of one unit in a given block to satisfy this criterion. The average cost of units in block 1 is then equated to the average unit costs in subsequent blocks 10, 100, 1,000, etc., to determine whether the costs per unit are being reduced, and the efficiency increasing, as the articles being manufactured increase.

EVM CRITERION # 21:

For EVMS, the material accounting system will provide for:
(1) *Accurate cost accumulation and assignment of costs to control accounts in a manner consistent with the budgets using recognized, acceptable, costing techniques.*
(2) *Cost performance measurement at the point in time most suitable for the category of material involved, but no earlier than the time of progress payments or actual receipt of material.*
(3) *Full accountability of all material purchased for the program including the residual inventory.*

Without question, this criterion has been the most difficult for most contractors to satisfy. Certain contractors have actually lost the government's "approval" of their management control systems because they failed to satisfy the demands of this criterion.

The requirement is that all purchased materials be measured in the same accounting period, reflecting the planned value versus the earned value (to determine any schedule variance), and the earned value versus the actual costs (to reflect any cost variance). The problem with procurements is that these actions do not normally happen at the same point in time.

In order to buy something from another company, that something must be defined; that is, a technical procurement specification must be prepared. But a strict interpretation of item 2 in this criterion precludes giving credit for work in the preparation of a procurement specification, and yet procurements cannot happen without specifications.

Another problem is that when giving progress payments to suppliers, it is a common practice to have "withholds" or "retention" values withheld from the supplier until the entire job has been completed. Thus, there will sometimes be a discrepancy between the earned value credited as compared to the actual costs recorded, unless an accounting accrual is made for the withheld cost values, which results in an added task on the CAP manager.

Lastly, it is a common practice for one project (the largest project) to buy materials for other projects and place such items into an inventory until used. Item 3 requires a full accountability for all residual inventory; not unreasonable, but nevertheless a difficult task to satisfy.

One recommendation to all projects is to keep the purchased items versus in-house labor costs in separate control account plans, or separate work packages. The two (make work versus buy work) do not mix well. Materials must be monitored, and sometimes the actual costs must be adjusted by the CAP manager in order to reflect an accurate portrayal of the performance of materials.

✳ ✳ ✳

GROUP 4-ANALYSIS CRITERIA (SIX)

Purpose of the Analysis Criteria:

- To require the "measurement" of actual performance against the authorized baseline.
- To require the "analysis" of actual performance against the authorized baseline.
- To require the "forecasting" of final results based on actual project performance.

Problems with the Analysis Criteria:

- Subjective (soft) measurement of physical performance.
- Excessive use of Level of Effort (LOE) measurement in the performance baseline.
- Senior management's influence over the final forecasted numbers.

This fourth grouping of the criteria imposes two distinct requirements on projects employing earned value. Both are critical to the proper employment of earned value management.

First, the actual performance against the project baseline plan must be monitored, objectively measured, and accurately reported for the project. All significant variances from the project baseline plan must be analyzed and understood, and corrective actions must be taken by management.

Second, based on the actual performance of the project against its own plan, the final required costs and time estimates to complete the project must be routinely forecasted. Such forecasts must be timely in order for the project manager to be able to take corrective measures, and thus alter adverse projections.

The difficulties typically experienced with this criteria group often includes too much "subjective" measurement of actual performance, thus allowing individuals to put a "positive spin" on adverse results and artificially improve the progress being reported to senior management.

Also, projects which have an excessive use of "level of effort" tasks incorporated into their baseline will often experience distorted measurements when actual implementation levels fall short of their baseline plans. LOE results will often mask real problems being experienced, problems which need management attention.

Lastly, senior executive management has been known to exert an unduly optimistic influence on both the reported actual project performance and the forecasts of final costs needed to complete given projects. It isn't necessarily that senior management intends to deceive anyone. Rather, it simply often decrees: "Make this overrun go away!" Sometimes it works. Often it does not.

EVM Criterion # 22:

At least on a monthly basis, generate the following information at the control account and other levels as necessary for management control using actual cost data from, or reconcilable with, the accounting system:

(1) Comparison of the amount of planned budget and the amount of budget earned for work accomplished. This comparison provides the schedule variance.

(2) Comparison of the amount of the budget earned and the actual (applied where appropriate) direct costs for the same work. This comparison provides the cost variance.

This criterion is one which clearly separates earned value management from the traditional approach of measuring cost performance by simply relating the planned costs to the actual costs. Here the requirement is for a monthly (at a minimum) comparison of project performance at the control account level with a focus on earned value results:

1. Measure the earned value achieved less the planned value to determine any schedule variance; and
2. Measure the earned value achieved less the actual costs to determine any cost variance.

While this criterion only specifies a monthly analysis of results, recent experience in industry would suggest a trend toward the weekly measurement of direct labor hour performance. The comparison should be sufficiently detailed to allow for performance measurement by category of direct costs, by external supplier performance, and by organization.

Internal procedures must be in place to require such measurements. If other than actual costs from the general ledger are used to report cost performance, there must be a reconciliation with the estimated costs methodology. Potential overruns or underruns of costs should be predictable with compliance of this criterion.

EVM Criterion # 23:

Identify, at least monthly, the significant differences between both planned and actual schedule performance and planned and actual cost performance, and provide the reasons for the variances in the detail needed by program management.

Previously, this criterion only addressed schedule variances, but with the industry rewording of the criteria, variances in cost performance were also added.

Whenever a project exceeds either a schedule variance or a cost variance from a previously set baseline parameter, typically called a variance threshold, the project must automatically perform an analysis to determine why the acceptable tolerances were exceeded. The analysis should assess the types of costs involved (labor, material, and other direct costs, for example) and discuss the causes of such variances. Typically, a plan for recovery should be developed and the future impact on the final project's cost and schedule determined.

When the project has major segments of its effort performed by another outside company, contracted or subcontracted, and when the supplier's performance exceeds acceptable parameters, the same analysis of results must be performed on the procured work.

EVM CRITERION # 24:

Identify budgeted and applied (or actual) indirect costs at the level and frequency needed by management for effective control, along with the reasons for any significant variances.

This criterion requires that a contractor perform an analysis of any variances of indirect expenses against the original budget. The analysis must cover the types of costs involved, and the indirect pool or pools involved, as may be appropriate.

Indirect expenses are applied as a percentage value against a direct cost base. Actual indirect rates experienced may vary from what was originally planned for two principal reasons:

1. Because actual indirect expenses change upward or downward from the original budgeted amounts; or
2. Because the direct business base over which the indirect costs are allocated change upward or downward, resulting in a higher or lower allocation to a given project.

The changes which are of primary concern to project management are *increased* indirect expenses over those originally planned, or a *smaller* direct base over which to absorb such costs. In either case, the result will be increased indirect costs applied against a given project. This criterion also requires that some management action be taken in response to adverse changes in the indirect rates.

EVM CRITERION # 25:

Summarize the data elements and associated variances through the program organization and/or work breakdown structure to support management needs and any customer reporting specified in the contract.

Projects are typically required to analyze all significant variances at the control account level. However, projects may not be required to formally report all variances to the customer. Rather, formal customer reporting usually takes place at a higher level of the WBS and at a higher organizational unit.

This approach gives the project some flexibility in managing its effort. Many variances which occur at the control account level are never actually reported to the customer or senior management, simply because there are offsetting variances at the same levels of the WBS or OBS. Through corrective actions, projects are often able to bring variances back to acceptable levels without the involvement of the customer or senior management. There is nothing inherently wrong with this concept, and it does give project managers the opportunity to manage their work without undue external involvement.

This criterion requires that a project have the ability to summarize variances upward through the WBS, or horizontally by organization unit. Also, there must be consistency in what is being reported to the customer, versus that which is reported internally to senior management. One set of books only on any project.

EVM CRITERION # 26:

Implement managerial actions taken as the result of earned value information.

This criterion addresses the issue of whether earned value performance data is being used by management throughout the organization. It requires that there be a procedure in effect which initiates corrective actions whenever established cost or schedule performance parameters have been penetrated.

Variance thresholds may be set at a number of monitoring points, reflecting either positive or negative values. Some projects will set a combination of variance points which trigger some type of management action. Variances either over or under a given threshold can indicate either a performance problem, or sometimes simply a problem with the authorized baseline plan. Positive variances are often set at a greater value than negative variances, sometimes twice the value, simply because they often represent questionable planning, rather than poor performance.

EVM CRITERION # 27:

Develop revised estimates of cost at completion based on performance to date, commitment values for material, and estimates of future conditions. Compare this information with the performance measurement baseline to identify variances at completion important to company management and any applicable customer reporting requirements including statements of funding requirements.

A key issue for all projects is how much it will cost to complete the total project, typically referred to as the estimate at completion, or EAC. It is likely that this is precisely why many projects elect to employ earned value management, to require a timely and accurate forecast of the total funds needed to complete the project. If it is going to cost more than management has authorized to complete a given job, management deserves to know this fact as early as possible. Management may elect to not complete a given project and use the remaining funds elsewhere.

Some project managers have been known to put a positive spin on their actual performance results, and perhaps mislead management into unrealistic expectations of the final bill. At other times it may be senior management who will insist on ignoring the actual performance results, and direct the project manager to make overruns "go away." Call it being optimistic, unrealistic, misrepresenting the facts, or whatever, some firms have established a reputation for themselves of consistently making poor projections of the total funding requirements. This is often the case when they are working under cost reimbursable contracts. Therefore, an essential ingredient in any management control system must be the ability to make accurate and timely forecasts of the final costs on jobs.

This criterion requires that EACs be performed routinely based on actual performance to date and a reasonable assessment of the work needed to complete all unfinished work. Such estimates to complete must relate to the current authorized statement of work, and are best supported by bottom-up estimates of the remaining tasks.

Because of their magnitude on the total costs, overhead or indirect costs are also an essential part of any accurate EAC, even though indirect costs will be beyond the control of any given project manager. Historical performance of indirect pools should be considered while forecasting the EAC. Many of the overhead cost items are essentially amortized fixed assets (an administration building, for example), and such costs will not change even though there may be a major drop of direct bases.

A number of issues will pertain to the EAC preparations which can be best handled through documented internal procedures. For example, the frequency with which EACs must be prepared is an important issue which is best determined with documented procedures.

✳ ✳ ✳

Group 5-Revisions Criteria (Five)

Purpose of the Revisions Criteria:

- To require the management of all changes to the approved project baseline.
- To require the timely approval or rejection, and the incorporation of approved changes.

Problems with the Revisions Criteria:

- Work done by the functions without approval of the project manager.
- Slow incorporation of changes into the baseline.
- Poor or no estimates for scope changes.

This last of the five groups of criteria deals with the control of revisions to the approved project baseline. All changes to the approved baseline must be aggressively managed and either approved or rejected in a timely fashion. The quickest way to lose the ability to measure project performance is to ignore changes and work to an obsolete baseline. All such changes to the original baseline must be documented and also traceable back to the original approved baseline.

Changes to a baseline often result from two primary sources: external customer direction, or internal management ideas. No project of any magnitude ever runs its full course without encountering some change, and it is incumbent upon a project manager to dispose of all changes in an orderly and documented manner.

Difficulties often arise in the management and incorporation of project changes. Often new out of scope work is performed without proper authorization, and subsequent approval for the changes never comes. Actual costs are sometimes incurred without a commensurate budget. Often the change approval process is slow, never catching up to the performance baseline.

EVM Criterion # 28:

Incorporate authorized changes in a timely manner, recording the effects of such changes in budgets and schedules. In the directed effort prior to negotiation of a change, base such revisions on the amount estimated and budgeted to the program organizations.

All projects encounter changes both from external and internal sources. In order to maintain a relationship between the work authorized and the actual physical work being performed, a project must incorporate approved changes into budgets in a timely manner.

Just what constitutes "timely" is a debatable question. In some cases "timely" could represent minutes, as when stopping work for a safety issue. In other situations "timely" might allow for days or weeks to pass before incorporation. The outer limit of "timely" would likely be dictated by the project's reporting cycle to management. There must be consistency in what is being reported, and what is actually being worked.

Changes to the working budgets and schedules must be accommodated in an expeditious manner and reflected in the project's baseline. Work which has been authorized, but not negotiated with the customer, must be folded into the project baseline based on an estimated value of the new work and, once negotiated, adjusted to reflect the final settlement with the customer. Newly authorized but unpriced work must be planned and controlled, as with all definitized work.

EVM Criterion # 29:

Reconcile current budgets to prior budgets in terms of changes to the authorized work and internal replanning in the detail needed by management for effective control.

This criterion requires the traceability of all changes currently being worked back to the original project baseline. Since earned value baselines are constructed from bottom-up detail, this requirement is satisfied by providing traceability down to the lowest level of the project WBS.

EVM Criterion # 30:

Control retroactive changes to records pertaining to work performed that would change previously reported amounts for actual costs, earned value, or budgets. Adjustments should be made only for correction of errors, routine accounting adjustments, effects of customer or management directed changes, or to improve the baseline integrity and accuracy of performance measurement data.

Earned value management requires discipline from the performing organization. Measurement of project performance must be objective to the greatest extent possible. If "after the fact" changes to the planned value, earned value, or actual costs can be made, the temptation to manipulate the report card will exist. This criterion prevents the indiscriminate altering of past period data, without a documented justification, and includes both direct and indirect costs.

An exception to this rule may be allowed to correct errors in calculations, and for legitimate routine accounting adjustments. In each case such adjustments should be documented by the person making them.

EVM CRITERION # 31:

Prevent revisions to the program budget except for authorized changes.

A project's total baseline will be comprised of that effort which has been authorized in formal budgets, plus any management reserve held by the project manager. Management reserve is typically expected to be consumed during the course of project performance.

Sometimes a project will experience difficulties in staying within the total limits of its authorized funds and after careful analysis of the work remaining may determine that it would make no sense to continue to measure progress against unattainable cost goals. When such conditions occur, this criterion permits the contractor to budget the remaining work greater than the project baseline, but only with strict approval of senior management or the customer on cost reimbursable contracts.

The project must have procedures which prevent proceeding with any altered baseline until approval is received from senior management.

EVM CRITERION # 32:

Document changes to the performance measurement baseline.

Maintenance of the approved project baseline is fundamental to earned value management. This criterion requires that the project have in place the necessary procedures to preclude unauthorized changes to the project baseline, and that all such changes be traceable back to the original baseline.

Glossary of Earned Value
Project Management Terms

Activity
Effort that occurs over time and generally consumes resources, sometimes also called a "task."

Actual Cost
As used in a typical business setting, the actual costs recorded on the books, expended and sometimes incurred, against a given project.

Actual Cost
As used with earned value management, the costs actually expended and or incurred that relate to the project's budgeted costs. Since these costs must relate to the budgeted costs, they must be in the same format as the budget, which will sometimes cover direct labor hours only, direct labor costs, all direct costs, sometimes with burdens, and sometimes include profits. Actual costs employing earned value must relate by category to the budgeted costs.

Actual Cost of Work Performed (ACWP)
The total costs incurred in accomplishing the work performed. See "Actual Cost."

Actual Direct Costs
Those costs specifically identified with a specific contract or a project, based upon the contractor's cost identification and accumulation system. See "Direct Costs."

ACWP
See "Actual Cost of Work Performed."

Advanced Material Release (AMR)
A document sometimes used by organizations to initiate the purchase of long-lead-time or time-critical materials prior to the final release of a design.

American National Standards Institute/Electronic Industries Association 748 (ANSI-EIA 748)
The document representing the industry rewrite of the original thirty-five (35) Cost/

Schedule Control Systems Criteria. ANSI/EIA 748 Standard was issued in July 1998, consisting of 32 criteria.

Applied Direct Costs
The actual direct costs recognized in the time period associated with the consumption of labor, material, and other direct resources, without regard to the date of commitment or the date of payment.

Apportioned Effort
Apportioned is one of the three approved methods to measure earned value performance (discrete, apportioned, level of effort). Apportioned work measures the performance of another specifically related task, called a base task, and assumes that the performance of the base task represents the same performance results as the apportioned task.

Authorized Un-priced Work (AUW)
Any scope change for which authorization to proceed has been given, but the estimated value of the change has not yet been determined or negotiated.

Authorized Work
All effort which has been authorized and negotiated, plus any work for which authorization has been given but a negotiated value has not yet been agreed upon.

BAC
See "Budget at Completion."

Bar Chart
See "Gantt Chart."

Baseline
The approved time phased project plan.
See also, "Performance Measurement Baseline" and also "Contract Budget Base."

Baseline Review (BR)
A customer review conducted to determine with a limited sampling that a contractor is continuing to use the previously approved performance management system and is properly implementing a baseline on the contract or option under review.

Basis of Estimate (BOE)
The justification or rationale supporting an estimate of required costs, or request for time in a schedule.

BCWP
See "Budgeted Cost for Work Performed."

BCWS
See "Budgeted Cost for Work Scheduled."

Bill of Material (BOM)
A complete listing of all parts, raw materials and purchased items that will go into an article showing the quantity required of each item to make the deliverable units.

Booking Rates
The rates used to record estimated actual indirect costs to a project. The overhead booking rates are typically applied to direct labor, materials and other direct costs.

Bottom-Up Cost Estimate
See "Engineering Cost Estimate."

BR
See "Baseline Review."

Budget
A fiscal plan of operations for a given period.

Budget at Completion (BAC)
The sum of all authorized budgets allocated to a project. It is synonymous with the earned value term "Performance Measurement Baseline" (PMB). The term BAC can have different meanings from organization to organization depending on what management has authorized for the project: sometimes direct labor hours only, direct labor dollars, other direct costs, burdens, profit, etc. The precise authorized BAC depends on management's expectations.

Budgeted Cost for Work Performed (BCWP)
The sum of the authorized work which has been completed, and partially completed, plus management's budget for the completed work. BCWP has been replaced with the term "earned value."

Budgeted Cost for Work Scheduled (BCWS)
The sum of the work which has been authorized, plus management's budget for the authorized work. The total of the authorized work equals the Budget at Completion (BAC). The term BCWS has been replaced with the term "planned value."

Budgeting
Time-phased financial requirements.

Burden
Overhead expenses distributed over appropriate direct labor and/or sometimes the material base. See also "Indirect Cost."

CA
See "Control Account."

CAM
See "Control Account Manager."

CAP
See "Control Account Plan."

CBB
See "Contract Budget Base."

CFSR
See Contract Funds Status Report."

Chart of Accounts
Sometimes also called "code of accounts." Any numbering system used to place costs into logical categories, for example, labor, materials, travel, indirect, etc. A project's chart of accounts is typically based on the corporate chart of accounts.

Code of Accounts
A numbering system often used to identify unique elements of the project's work breakdown structure (WBS).

Commitment
A binding financial obligation, often taking the form of a purchase order.

Compliance Evaluation Review (CER)
A term which has replaced an earlier term, "Demonstration Review" (DR). The CER is the initial formal review of a contractor's management control system and the process to determine whether or not it satisfies the requirements of the earned value management system criteria.

Concurrent Engineering
An approach to the development of new products with the use of multi-functional teams, working in unison from the initial concept until completion of the product. This process is sometimes also called multi-functional teams or integrated product development teams.

Contingency funds
See "Management Reserve."

Contract Budget Base (CBB)
The negotiated contract cost value, plus the estimated value of authorized but un-priced work.

Contract Funds Status Report (CFSR)
A U.S. Government financial report that provides forecasted contract funding requirements.

Contract (was Cost) Performance Report (CPR)
A monthly formal contract cost report generated by the performing contractor to reflect earned value cost and schedule status information for management.

Contract Target Cost (CTC)
The negotiated target costs without fee for the original definitized contract and all contractual changes that have been definitized, but excluding the estimated cost of any authorized but un-priced changes.

Contract Target Price (CTP)
The negotiated estimated contract costs, including profit or fee.

Contract Work Breakdown Structure (CWBS)
A customer prepared breakout or subdivision of a project typically down to WBS Level 3, which: (1) subdivides the project into all its major hardware, software, and service elements; (2) integrates the customer and contractor effort; and (3) provides a framework for the planning, control and reporting of the project.

Contractor Cost Data Report (CCDR)
A DoD report developed to provide actual contract cost and related data in a standardized format.

Control Account (CA)
A point representing the intersection of the work breakdown structure (WBS) and organizational breakdown structure (OBS) at which functional responsibility for work is assigned. Control accounts are the point for the integration of scope, cost, and schedule.

Control Account Manager (CAM)
A member of a project, often assigned to the project by a functional organization, who is responsible for performance of a control account and for the management of resources necessary to accomplish such work.

Control Account Plan (CAP)
A management control unit or subproject in which earned value performance measurement will take place. Was formerly called a "Cost Account Plan."

Cost Control
Any process of keeping costs within the bounds of budgets or standards based upon work actually performed.

Cost Element
A unit of costs typically in the form of direct labor, direct materials, other direct costs, and indirect or burden costs.

Cost Estimate
The expected costs to perform a task internally or to acquire an item from an outside source. Cost estimates may be expressed as a single value, or represent a range of values.

Cost Incurred
Costs identified through the use of the accrued method of accounting, or costs actually paid. Such costs will typically include direct labor, direct materials, and all allowable indirect costs.

Cost Overrun
The amount by which a project exceeds or expects to exceed the authorized costs.

Cost Performance Index (CPI)
The cost efficiency factor representing the relationship between the physical work performed plus management's budget for the completed work (the earned value), divided by the actual costs expended and or incurred to complete such work.

The CPI is likely the most critical metric provided by earned value management. Formula: earned value divided by actual costs.

Cost Reimbursement Type Contracts

A category of contracts based on payments to a contractor for all allowable costs, normally requiring only a "best efforts" performance standard from the contractor. Risks for all cost growth over the estimated value rests with the project owner.

Cost/Schedule Control Systems Criteria (C/SCSC)

Thirty-five defined performance standards which had to be met by private contractors in order to ensure the government that cost reimbursable and incentive type contracts were being properly managed. The (35) C/SCSC were issued in 1967, but were superceded in 1996 by the (32) Earned Value Management System Criteria, and later the ANSI/EIA 748 Standard in 1998.

Cost/Schedule Planning and Control Specification (C/SPCS)

The United States Air Force initiative in the mid-1960s which later became the C/SCSC.

Cost/Schedule Status Report (C/SSR)

The low-end cost and schedule earned value report generally imposed on smaller sized contracts not warranting full C/SCSC compliance.

Cost to Complete Forecast

A time-phased forecast for the completion of all project work. It is typically synonymous with "Estimate to Complete."

Cost Variance (CV)

The numerical difference between the earned value less the actual costs.

CPI

See "Cost Performance Index."

Critical Path

A connected series of tasks in a network schedule representing the longest duration for a project. Any slippage of tasks along the critical path increases the duration of a project.

Critical Path Method (CPM)

A project scheduling technique which uses a logic network to predict final project duration by managing those sequences of activities which have the longest duration to accomplish, thus representing the shortest completion date for the project.

Critical Subcontractor
A contractor or supplier performing a decisive portion of a project which generally requires close oversight, control, and reporting. Critical subcontractors are sometimes designated as a result of customer or management direction.

CTC
See "Contract Target Cost."

CTP
See "Contract Target Price."

CV
See "Cost Variance."

CWBS
See "Contract Work Breakdown Structure."

Deliverable
Any measurable, tangible, verifiable effort produced on a project. Project deliverables are often given a weighted value and are used to measure discrete earned value performance.

Demonstration Review (DR)
A former term which has been replaced by a new term "Compliance Evaluation Review" (CER). The DR was the initial formal review of a contractor's management control system and processes to determine whether or not they satisfied the requirements of the earned value management system criteria.

Direct Costs
Those costs, labor, material, and other direct costs (e.g., travel) which can be consistently related to work performed on a particular project. Direct costs are best contrasted with indirect costs which cannot be identified to a specific project.

Discrete Effort
Discrete is one of the three approved methods to measure earned value performance (discrete, apportioned, level of effort). Discrete tasks will have a specific measurable

end product or end result. Discrete tasks are ideal for earned value measurement, and are the preferred method.

Discrete Milestone

A milestone which has a definite scheduled occurrence in time, signaling the start and finish of an activity. Synonymous with the term "objective indicator."

EAC

See "Estimate at Completion."

Earned Hours

The time in standard hours credited to work as a result of the completion of a given task or a group of tasks.

Earned Value (EV)

The authorized work physically accomplished, plus management's budget for the completed work. Earned Value and percent complete are synonymous terms.

Earned Value Management (EVM) System and Earned Value Project Management (EVPM)

A project management technique which focuses on the completion of authorized work and its authorized budget, called the "earned value," for the purpose of monitoring performance and predicting the final required costs and time necessary to finish the project.

Engineering Cost Estimate

A detailed cost estimate of the work and related burdens, usually made by the industrial engineering or the price/cost estimating groups.

Estimate at Completion (EAC)

A forecasted value expressed in either dollars and/or hours, to represent the projected final costs of a project when all work is completed. The EAC equals the actual costs incurred, and liabilities, plus the estimated costs for completing all the remaining project work.

Estimate to Complete (ETC)

Forecasts which are expressed in either dollars or hours, developed to represent the value of the work remaining to complete a task or a project.

ETC
See "Estimate to Complete."

Event
Something that happens at a point or a moment in time. A significant event is often called a "milestone."

Expenditure
A charge against available funds, evidenced by a voucher, claim, or other documents. Expenditures represent the actual payment of funds.

Fast Tracking
An attempt to shorten a project's duration by overlapping separate activities normally done sequentially, for example, design and then manufacturing. Fast tracking typically adds risks to a project, and is not considered to be a "project teams" or "concurrent engineering" approach.

Fixed-Price Contracts
A category of contracts based on the establishment of firm legal commitments to complete the required work. A performing contractor is legally obligated to finish the job, no matter how much it costs to complete. Risks of all cost growth thus rest on the performing sellers.

Formal Reprogramming
See "Reprogramming."

Front Loading
An attempt by a performing contractor to provide adequate budgets for the near-term work, but at the expense of the later period's effort, which is left under-funded. It is an attempt to delay the acknowledgment of a potential cost overrun, in the hope that the contractor may "get well" through changes in the contract statement of work. Front loading often results from severe competition with inadequate or unrealistic negotiated contract target costs.

Funding Profile
A time phased estimate of funding requirements.

Gantt Chart
A schedule display named after Henry Lawrence Gantt. Likely the most common scheduling display, graphically portraying tasks over a time scale, frequently also called a "bar chart."

General and Administrative (G&A) Expenses

A category of indirect expenses incurred for the administration of a company, typically covering senior executive expenses and corporate headquarters. Such expenses are typically spread over the total direct and burden costs for the organization.

A Guide to the Project Management Body of Knowledge (PMBOK® Guide)

An official publication of the Project Management Institute (PMI), a basic reference and the world's de facto standard for the project management profession.

IBR

See "Integrated Baseline Review."

Independent Cost Analysis

An analysis of project cost estimates conducted by an impartial body, not directly associated with the project.

Independent Cost Estimates

An independent estimate of required project costs developed outside the normal channels, to give senior management assurances that they are authorizing reasonable costs for a given project.

Indirect Cost

Resources expended which are not directly identifiable to any specific project, or contract. These costs are thus allocated over projects based on some formula, typically applied to direct labor costs.

Indirect Cost Pools

A categorical grouping of indirect costs, for example, engineering, manufacturing, test, etc.

Integrated Baseline Review (IBR)

A form of earned value process verification in which the technical project management staff leads the effort to verify that the entire project baseline has been budgeted with realistic values to accomplish all the planned work. The IBR is intended to expose the front-loading of baselines.

Integrated Product Development Teams (IPDTs)

The development of new products with use of multi-functional teams who work in unison from the conceptual start until completion of the product. IPDTs are sometimes also called "concurrent engineering," and are best contrasted with the traditional form of sequential functional development.

Internal Re-planning
Re-planning actions performed by the project for any remaining effort within approved project scope.

IPDTs
See "Integrated Product Development Teams."

Labor Rate Variances
Difference between planned labor rates and actual labor rates.

Latest Revised Estimate (LRE)
See "Estimate at Completion."

Level of Effort (LOE)
LOE is one of the three approved methods to measure earned value performance (discrete, apportioned, level of effort). LOE represents work that does not result in a final product. Examples are field engineering, liaison, coordination, follow-up, or other support activities which are not associated with a definable end product. LOE simply measures the passage of time. LOE is the least desirable method of measuring earned value.

LOE
See "Level of Effort."

LRE
Latest Revised Estimate; see "Estimate at Completion."

Make or Buy
The classification of project scope as to whether it will be performed by the project's organization (Make work) or procured from an outside company (Buy work).

Management by Exception
A management technique that focuses on performance that falls outside of a predetermined baseline.

Management Reserve (MR)
A portion of the total project budget that is set-aside and typically controlled by the

project manager to cover the unplanned problems that are likely to occur but cannot be defined or planned for in advance. Sometimes also called contingency funds, MR budget is in addition to the project's Performance Measurement Baseline.

Management Reserve Budget
See "Management Reserve" (MR).

Material
Property which may be incorporated into or attached to an end item to be delivered on a project or which may be consumed or expended in the performance of the effort. It includes, but is not limited to raw and processed materials, parts, components, assemblies, fuels and lubricants, small tools and supplies which may be consumed in normal use in the performance of a project.

Material Requirements Planning (MRP)
An automated procurement system which uses the bill of material to define requirements, less actual inventory records, and the master project schedule to calculate purchasing requirements for materials.

Milestone
An event of particular importance, i.e., a big event.

MPS
See "Master Project Schedule."

MR
See "Management Reserve."

Multi-Functional Project Teams
See either "Concurrent Engineering" or "Integrated Product Development Teams."

Negotiated Contract Cost
The estimated costs negotiated in a cost reimbursable type contract, or the negotiated contract target costs in either a fixed-price incentive contract or a cost plus incentive fee contract. See also "Contract Target Cost."

Network Schedule
A logic flow diagram consisting of the activities and events which must be accomplished in order to reach project objectives, showing their planned sequence, interrelationships, and constraints.

Non-Recurring Costs

Resources expended against tasks that are expected to occur only once on a given project cycle, as contrasted with costs that will occur over and over as the product is subsequently manufactured. Examples are such items as design, qualification testing, initial tooling, etc.

Objective Indicator

Earned value performance measurement by monitoring tangible deliverables, considered to be the most desirable form of measurement. See also "Discrete Milestone."

OBS

See "Organizational Breakdown Structure."

ODC

See "Other Direct Costs."

Organizational Breakdown Structure (OBS)

A functionally oriented organizational hierarchy used as the framework for the assignment of project task performance responsibilities.

Original Budget

The initial budget established at or near the time a project is authorized, based on management's authorization or the negotiated contract costs.

OTB

See "Over Target Baseline."

Other Direct Costs (ODC)

A category of accounting elements which can be isolated to specific tasks, other than labor and material items. Included in ODC are typically such items as travel, computer time, and direct supporting services, etc.

Over Target Baseline (OTB)

A project baseline which results from the acknowledgement of an overrun, and actually incorporates the forecasted overrun into the performance baseline for the remainder of the work. OTBs should only be used with the approval of senior management and the customer.

Overhead

Costs incurred in the operation of a business which cannot be directly related to the individual products, projects or services being produced. See also "Indirect Cost."

Overrun

Costs incurred in excess of the project target costs on a cost or incentive type contract, or the estimated costs value on a fixed price contract. An overrun is that value of costs needed to complete a project, over the value originally authorized by management.

PAR

See "Problem Analysis Report."

Percent Complete

A measured estimate, typically expressed as a percentage, of the amount of work completed on a total project, or on specific tasks within the project. Percent complete estimates are often used to measure discrete earned value performance, but in a subjective manner.

Performance Measurement Baseline (PMB)

On earned value projects, the PMB is a time-phased budget plan against which project performance will be measured. It is formed by the summation of the budgets assigned to control account plans (CAPs), plus their applicable indirect budgets. For future effort, not planned to the control account level, the Performance Measurement Baseline also includes budgets assigned to higher-level WBS elements. The PMB should not include any management or contingency reserves, which are controlled budgets above the PMB.

Performing Organization

The organizational unit responsible for the performance and management of resources to accomplish a task.

Period of Performance

The time interval of project performance that includes the effort required to achieve all significant project deliverables and schedule milestones.

Planned Value for Work Accomplished (PVWA)

An early term used to represent "BCWP" and now "earned value."

Planned Value for Work Scheduled (PVWS)

An early term used to represent "BCWS" and now "planned value."

Planned Value (PV)

The baseline measurement plan for an earned value project. The sum of the budgets for all authorized work, scheduled to be accomplished within a given time period. The Planned Value consists of the authorized work and authorized budget for the work. Previously called the "Budgeted Cost for Work Scheduled." The sum of all PV equals the Budget at Completion (BAC).

Planning Package

A logical aggregation of far-term work within a control account plan that can be identified and budgeted but not yet definable into specific work packages. Planning packages are usually identified during the initial baseline planning to establish the time phasing of the major activities within a control account and the quantity of the resources required for their performance. Planning packages will be subsequently placed into detailed work packages consistent with the rolling wave concept prior to the start of performance of the authorized work.

PMB

See "Performance Measurement Baseline."

Portfolio

Typically, a logical grouping of related projects, sometimes also called a program, to facilitate the management of a business unit. The term "portfolio" often has different meanings in various organizations.

Price Variance (PV)

The numerical difference between the costs budgeted for a purchased item and the costs actually paid or committed for the item.

Problem Analysis Report (PAR)

A narrative report made by the responsible control account manager (CAM) to explain a significant cost or schedule variance, its probable impact on the project, and the corrective actions to be taken to resolve the problem(s).

Program

A logical grouping of related projects, sometimes also called a portfolio.

Progress Payments

Payments made to a seller during the life of a fixed-price type contract on the basis of some agreed-to formula. Such formulas can be: percentage of work completed as typically used in construction, or simply on costs incurred as with most government type contracting. Performance based payments is a form of progress payments.

Project

A one-time only endeavor, to satisfy a specific statement of work, meeting all deliverables, within a specific start to stop timeframe, typically within finite resources.

Project Charter

A formal document prepared by a project, and authorized by senior functional management, that describes the approach to be employed in the management of a particular project. The charter is often used to give organizational authority to a project manager.

Project Cost Management

A subset of project management that covers the processes required to improve the chances of performing a project within the authorized budget of management. It consists of planning, resource estimating, formal budgeting, and cost control. Earned value performance measurement and forecasting the final costs based on such performance should also be a part of cost management.

Project Management Institute (PMI)

The Project Management Institute, with over 300,000 members worldwide, is the leading not-for-profit professional association dealing in the discipline of the management of projects.

Project Master Schedule (PMS)

Typically the highest summary level schedule for a project, depicting the overall phasing and all major interfaces, critical milestones, and key elements.

Project Risk Analysis

An analysis of identified project risks as to their potential impact on cost, schedule, and technical performance.

Project Teams

See either "Concurrent Engineering" or "Integrated Product Development Teams."

Project Manager

An individual who has been assigned responsibility (and hopefully commensurate authority) for accomplishing a specific unit of work. The project manager is typically responsible for the planning, implementing, controlling, and reporting of status on a particular project.

Program

Typically, an organizational unit made up of the grouping of related projects, often a business unit, sometimes also called a portfolio. Whereas projects are one-time only, programs continue over time until the business objectives are met.

PV

See "Price Variance."

PVWA

Planned Value Work Accomplished, an earlier term for "BCWP." Now called "earned value."

PVWS

Planned Value Work Scheduled, an earlier term for "BCWS." Now called "planned value."

Recurring Costs

Expenditures against specific tasks that would occur on a repetitive basis in a production run. Examples of these costs would be production labor, materials and equipment, tool maintenance, etc.

Re-planning

A change in the original project plan for accomplishing authorized requirements. There are two types of re-planning effort: "internal" re-planning, which is any change in the original plan that remains within the scope of the authorized contract, typically caused by a need to adjust for cost, schedule, or technical problems which have made the original plan unrealistic; and "external" re-planning, which is customer-directed change to a contract in the form of a change order that calls for a modification in the original plan to accommodate that change order.

Reprogramming

A comprehensive re-planning of the effort remaining in a project, resulting in a revised total allocated budget, which sometimes may exceed the current contract budget base. Reprogramming is often another term for describing an "overrun" condition.

Responsibility Assignment Matrix (RAM)

A one-page summary display which is used to show the relationship of a project's Work Breakdown Structure (WBS) with the specific functional organization's assigned responsibility for performing the project work, typically with use of an

Organizational Breakdown Structure (OBS). Usually, the WBS will be displayed along the horizontal axis, and the OBS on the vertical axis.

Responsible Organization
A defined unit within a contractor's organization which is assigned responsibility for accomplishing specific tasks, or control account plans.

Rolling Wave Concept
A method to provide a viable long-term project measurement baseline by dividing it into two parts: detail (work package) planning in the near-term, and gross (WBS element) planning in the far-term. As the project performs the near-term work, the far-term gross packages are then planned in specific detail as their period of performance nears. What constitutes near-term versus far-term must be decided by the project manager.

Rubber Baseline
An attempt by a performing organization to take the far-term tasks and move portions of their budgets to the left, into near-term periods, to disguise cost overrun problems. This approach will move budget only, without corresponding work, to mask near-term cost difficulties. It is an indicator of a likely cost overrun condition.

S-Curve
A graphic display of cumulative costs, hours, percentage of work, or other items, plotted over a horizontal time scale, often used to track cost performance for management. Such curves start slowly, accelerate in the middle, then taper off slowly at the end. The S-Curve is considered to be the normal distribution for such work, and represents essentially one-half of a statistical "bell-shaped" curve.

Schedule
A graphic display of planned work.

Schedule Performance Index (SPI)
The baseline schedule efficiency factor representing the relationship between the earned value achieved, versus the planned value. The formula: earned value divided by planned value.

Schedule Variance (SV)
The numerical difference between the earned value less the planned value.

Scheduling
The act of preparing and/or implementing schedules.

Scope
A definition of the work to be accomplished on a project or procurement.

Scope-Creep
The addition of work as a result of poor or incomplete or vague definition of project scope.

SOW
See "Statement of Work."

SPI
See "Schedule Performance Index."

Standard
A term applied in work measurement to any established or accepted rule, model, or criterion against which comparisons are made.

Standard Cost
The normal expected cost of an operation, process, or product, which typically includes labor, material, and sometimes overhead charges, computed on the basis of past performance costs, estimates, or work measurement.

Standard Time
The amount of time allowed for the performance of a specific unit of work.

Statement of Work (SOW)
A description of a product or service to be procured under a project; a statement of requirements.

Subcontract
A contractual document which legally defines the effort of providing services, data, or other hardware from one firm to another firm.

Summary Level Variance Analysis Reporting (SLVAR)
The analysis of performance variances from a plan, done at a summary level by the amalgamation of related control accounts with homogeneous effort, and a description of the common problems causing such variances.

Surveillance
A term used in earned value oversight to mean the monitoring of continued compliance with an approved and validated management control system.

SV
See "Schedule Variance."

Target Cost
See "Contract Target Cost" and/or "Contract Budget Base."

Task
Also called an activity, something that takes place over a period of time which generally consumes resources.

TCPI
See "To Complete Performance Index."

Teams
See either "Concurrent Engineering" or "Integrated Product Development Teams."

Thresholds
Monetary, time, or resource values used as outside parameters, which if breached will cause some type of management action to occur.

To Complete Performance Index (TCPI)
The forecasted future performance levels, expressed as a CPI, which must be achieved on all remaining work in order to meet some financial goal as set by management. The financial goals are typically two: (1) management's current authorized budget, and (2) the project manager's current estimate at completion.

Total Allocated Budget (TAB)
Sometimes also called the Project Cost Base, it is the sum of all budgets allocated to a project. The TAB consists of the performance measurement baseline (PMB) plus any management or contingency reserves. The TAB will relate directly to the Contract Budget Base.

UB
See "Undistributed Budget."

Undistributed Budget (UB)

Temporary budgeted values for authorized work not yet negotiated, or changes in the far-term, which cannot at present be identified to specific control account plans, but which must be time-phased and allocated to specific WBS elements in order to maintain a viable performance measurement baseline.

Unit Cost

Total labor, material, and overhead costs for one unit of production—that is, one component, one part, one gallon, one pound, etc.

Un-priced Changes

Authorized but un-priced, un-negotiated changes to the contract.

Usage

The number of physical units of an inventory item, components, and assemblies, consumed over a period of time.

Usage Variance (UV)

The numerical difference between the budgeted quantity of materials and the quantity actually used.

UV

See "Usage Variance."

VAC

See "Variance at Completion."

Validation

A term used in earned value to mean the "approval" or compliance with the criteria.

Variable Cost

A cost that changes upward or downward with the production quantity or the performance of services. Variable costs are best contrasted with fixed costs that do not change with a production quantity or services performed.

Variance

The difference between the expected or budgeted or planned values and the actual results.

Variance at Completion (VAC)
Any numerical difference between Budget at Completion (BAC) and the latest Estimate at Completion (EAC).

Variance Threshold
The amount of a variance which will require a formal Problem Analysis Report, as agreed to between the performing project and the customer or management. Variance parameters will differ by project depending on the function, level and stage of the project.

WBS
See "Work Breakdown Structure."

What-If Analysis
The process of evaluating the impact of alternative strategies.

Work Breakdown Structure (WBS)
A deliverable-oriented family tree display of the hardware, software, services and project-unique tasks which completely defines, organizes, and graphically portrays the project.

Work Breakdown Structure Dictionary
A narrative document which describes the effort to accomplish all work contained in each WBS element. The WBS Dictionary will often result in the project or contract statement of work (SOW).

Work Breakdown Structure Element
A discrete portion of a WBS at any level. The single WBS element at Level 1 represents the total project. A WBS element may be an identifiable product, a set of data, a service, or any combination.

Work Package Budgets
Resources which are formally assigned by the project to accomplish a work package, which can be expressed in dollars, hours, standards or any other definitive unit.

Work Package (WP)
A detailed short-span task, or purchased item, identified by the project at the lowest level of a Work Breakdown Structure element.

Work Team Control Accounts

See either "Concurrent Engineering" or "Integrated Product Development Teams."

WP

See "Work Package."

Subject Index